PRAISE FOR *SPORT AND PSYCHOANALYSIS*

"Jack Black and Joseph Reynoso have put together the volume that will mark an epochal moment in the understanding of sport in relation to society. No longer will one be able to dismiss the social and existential significance of sport, thanks to this timely collection. Each essay provides a penetrating analysis of sport's varying aspects as well as how they function psychically for participants and spectators. This is, simply put, a masterwork not to be missed."

—Todd McGowan, author of *Enjoying Alienation*

"Fanaticism, fear, defeat, rage, schadenfreude, exhaustion, triumph, to name only a few of our extreme emotions in the face of sport. In a world which preaches the virtue of work, work, work, it is only when we let ourselves play that we can truly glimpse the intricacy of the human psyche. Let this collection of psychoanalysts be your guide to the grace and disgrace of the world of athleticism."

—Jamieson Webster, author of *Disorganisation & Sex*

"Sport, it is commonly held, can drive us mad. Sport has the power to derail the routine of our daily lives; it can upturn the normality of our everyday exchanges; it can make us aliens to ourselves. And it does all this seldom, it must be said, in a good way. In Jack Black and Joseph Reynoso's collection of essays, we may have found the reason—or, the unreason, should you so prefer—for this particular brand of madness. It is a clinical condition. Certifiably so. Such is the nature of "Sport and Psychoanalysis" that I suspect many a sports-mad personage will now claim that their (anti-) social irremediability is less a madness than a condition underwritten by towering figures in clinical psychology. Who ever knew that Sigmund Freud and Jacques Lacan had it in their clinical arsenal to perform such a rescue act?"

—Grant Farred, author of *The Perversion of Gratitude: An Apartheid Education*

"We emphasize—and over emphasize—sports so much in our society, it is bracing when you read about it from a perspective that contains the shock of the new. *Sport and Psychoanalysis* does exactly that. In the hands of Jack Black and Joseph Reynoso, we get a different perspective on sports that I certainly have never read. What is particularly exciting is that this is not only about how psychoanalysis gives us new insight into sports. It is about how the games we play give us new insight into psychoanalysis."

—Dave Zirin, Sports Editor, *The Nation*, and author of *What's My Name, Fool? Sports and Resistance in the United States*

"Few arenas of contemporary life excite such strong emotion in contests of such ostensibly low stakes as sports. Why do we care so much about games—particularly games played by others we will never meet and with whom we may have little in common? *Sport and Psychoanalysis* takes a critical perspective on a corner of human life that is, in many ways, deeply irrational, but which, despite this fact, is nevertheless extraordinarily meaningful and important."

—Erin C. Tarver, author of *The I in Team: Sports Fandom and the Reproduction of Identity*

Sport and Psychoanalysis

PSYCHOANALYTIC STUDIES:CLINICAL, SOCIAL, AND CULTURAL CONTEXTS

Series Editor: Michael O'Loughlin, Adelphi University

Mission Statement

Psychoanalytic Studies seeks psychoanalytically informed works addressing the implications of the location of the individual in clinical, social, cultural, historical, and ideological contexts. Innovative theoretical and clinical works within psychoanalytic theory and in fields such as anthropology, education, and history are welcome. Projects addressing conflict, migrations, difference, ideology, subjectivity, memory, psychiatric suffering, physical and symbolic violence, power, and the future of psychoanalysis itself are welcome, as are works illustrating critical and activist applications of clinical work.

See https://rowman.com/Action/SERIES/LEX/LEXPS for a list of advisory board members.

Recent Titles in the Series

Sport and Psychoanalysis: What Sport Reveals about Our Unconscious Desires, Fantasies, and Fears edited by Jack Black and Joseph S. Reynoso

The Politics and Psychoanalysis of Comedy by Robert Samuels

Psychoanalytic Conversations with States of Spirit Possession: Beauty in Brokenness by Shalini Masih

Psychic Mimesis from Bible and Homer to the Present: Inner Life Over Time by Nathan Moses Szajnberg

The Healing of Trauma during Pregnancy, Birth, and the First Years of Life: From Dreaming to Being by Norma Tracey

The Borderline Culture: Intensity, Jouissance, and Death by Željka Matijašević

In Search of Return: Mourning the Disappearances in Kashmir by Shifa Haq

Trauma and Repair: Confronting Segregation and Violence in America by Annie Stopford

Psychoanalysis as a Subversive Phenomenon: Social Change, Virtue Ethics, and Analytic Theory by Amber M. Trotter

A People's History of Psychoanalysis: From Freud to Liberation Psychology by Daniel José Gaztambide

Rethinking the Relation between Women and Psychoanalysis: Loss, Mourning, and the Feminine edited by Hada Soria Escalante

Lives Interrupted: Psychiatric Narratives of Struggle and Resilience edited by Michael O'Loughlin, Secil Arac-Orhun, and Montana Queler

Women and the Psychosocial Construction of Madness edited by Marie Brown and Marilyn Charles

Revisioning War Trauma in Cinema: Uncoming Communities, by Jessica Datema and Manya Steinkoler
Women & Psychosis: Multidisciplinary Perspectives, edited by Marie Brown and Marilyn Charles

Sport and Psychoanalysis

What Sport Reveals about Our Unconscious Desires, Fantasies, and Fears

Edited by Jack Black and Joseph S. Reynoso

LEXINGTON BOOKS
Lanham • Boulder • New York • London

Published by Lexington Books
An imprint of The Rowman & Littlefield Publishing Group, Inc.
4501 Forbes Boulevard, Suite 200, Lanham, Maryland 20706
www.rowman.com

86-90 Paul Street, London EC2A 4NE

British Library Cataloguing in Publication Information Available

Library of Congress Cataloging-in-Publication Data Available

Names: Black, Jack (Interdisciplinary researcher) editor. | Reynoso, Joseph S., editor.
Title: Sport and psychoanalysis: what sport reveals about our unconscious desires, fantasies, and fears / edited by Jack Black and Joseph S. Reynoso.
Description: Lanham: Lexington Books, [2024] | Series: Psychoanalytic studies: clinical, social, and cultural contexts | Includes bibliographical references and index. | Summary: "Applying psychoanalysis to sport and exploring how sport can raise questions for psychoanalysis, this book provides novel examinations of sport and associated topics, including race/ethnicity, coaching, ethics, gender, and national identity"—Provided by publisher.
Identifiers: LCCN 2024012954 | ISBN 9781666938425 (cloth) | ISBN 9781666938432 (ebook)
Subjects: LCSH: Sports—Psychological aspects. | Psychoanalysis.
Classification: LCC GV706.4.S6547 2024 | DDC 796.01/9—dc23/eng/20240403
LC record available at https://lccn.loc.gov/2024012954

To my mother, for all her sporting encouragement;
to my father, for raising me a red.

—Jack Black

To my father, for Wrestlemania IV, Dr. J's last game against the Knicks, and all the track meets and basketball games you drove me to when you would have rather been anywhere else.

—Joseph S. Reynoso

Contents

Introduction

Sport: A Psychoanalytic Inquiry

Jack Black and Joseph S. Reynoso

GETTING STUCK: WHY SPORT AND PSYCHOANALYSIS?

The underlying contention guiding this collection is that psychoanalysis can provide a novel approach to theorising our investments in sport. When exploring, examining, discussing, and debating the fascination and frustrations that characterizes sport, what this collection will consider are the very ways in which we become "stuck" in sport. For us, getting "stuck" helpfully describes the degree to which one can both be interested in sport, following a particular team or training regularly, while also being frustrated, angered, and undermined by sport (grievances, which, in most cases, in no way discount or prevent one's very love of sport).

What compounds this contradiction is that a psychoanalytic approach to sport does not necessarily provide or outline any answers to the problems of sport. Rather, we double-down on the fact there is no rational explanation as to why millions of people choose to partake in strenuous forms of physical exclusion for years on end, with the only reward being a medal or personal best for the lucky few—not to mention the multitudes who choose to watch these athletic spectacles. Certainly, this is not to say that sport does not have its explanations. We are all too familiar with the cliched responses and tired explanations: "it makes me feel good," "it keeps me busy," "it releases endorphins," "I enjoy the social-side," "my Dad followed this team, so, in a way, I'm continuing the tradition." What goes amiss in such routine responses is *why* this specific activity—sport, in whatever form—is chosen? When so much of sport requires one to partake in choices that fundamentally affect one's life, then we require a theoretical space in which we can begin to ask important questions of both sport and ourselves.

On this basis, sport is not necessarily detached from our lives, a mere weekend past-time, separate from the world of work (although it can be described as such); instead, as this collection will assert, a psychoanalytic account of sport can allow us to question and explore what it is that makes us human and what is it about our inherent sociality that makes sport such an important part of so many lives. To do so, requires an investigation into the desires, fears, and fantasises that underscore the subject—the very phenomena that psychoanalysis seeks to examine.

To be clear, the following collection should not be so easily associated with the far more popular, sport psychology. While we remain open to the importance of psychological investigations of the subject and sport, as well as the various psychological approaches, theories, and methodologies that this discipline encourages, we seek to deliberately move away from overly focusing on the study of athletic behaviour and psychological motivation. Too often, we see the study of psychology as happily succumbing to a discourse that seeks only to make athletes, at whatever level of performance, "better." This cognitive and behavioural approach focuses predominantly on conscious processes of action, promulgating "a form of 'ego psychology' . . . concerned with adapting people to society instead of enabling them to question it" (Parker 2023). Without discounting the important work that goes into measuring and quantifying the conscious psychic and mental processes of athletes, the focus of this collection will be to consider how a psychoanalytic theory can afford a unique insight into the cultural and political significance of sport.

For this reason, the focus of this collection works adjacent to clinical accounts of psychoanalysis.[1] What the following chapters will provide is an application of psychoanalytic concepts that critically reflect upon the importance of sport, while, at the same time, using sport as an important site for psychoanalytic inquiry. Whether it be exploring the dynamic potentialities of the athletic body (Part I), the psychoanalytic significances of "the coach" (Part II), the tensions and frustrations that emerge from the athlete-fan relationship (Part III), the role of sport in defining and comprising one's identity (Part IV), or uncovering the creativity of play and its fundamental connections to sport (Part V), in each case, we draw specific attention to the problems, contradictions, antagonisms, and tensions that underscore our relations to sport. In this regard, we hope that this collection paves the way in providing an academic companionship between sport and psychoanalytic theory; one that will allow us to explore a number of important gaps in both psychoanalytic theory and sport itself.

Importantly, it is by following Freud's original investigations into what makes being human such an uncomfortable experience, that the application of psychoanalysis belies any quick critique. These critiques have coalesced with some rather unhelpful generalizations, often at the behest of a media perception that propagates a number of popular inaccuracies regarding psychoanalysis. Much of this stands opposed to the numerous benefits of psychoanalytic theory, including its various schools and adherents, which, in both their application and confrontation, collectively provide an unexplored insight into the social practices, actions, and behaviours of the sport's fan and participant.

Furthermore, critically addressing and analysing sport through a psychoanalytic lens can allow us to shed light on the antagonisms and contradictions that sport creates for both its proponents and detractors. This can begin to tackle the myths, fantasies, and overly positive appraisals that characterise the organisation and management of sport—most notable when, at the start of major international sporting competitions, such as the FIFA World Cup or Olympic Games, we are suddenly subjected to pontified declarations of sport's inherent importance and its capacity to cure the world of its intractable problems (poverty, cultural/ethnic conflict, racism, etc.). In view of such assessments, debating what sport is and how we define and relate to it remains an important point of contention—one in which a psychoanalytic interpretation of sport must approach.

ON PSYCHOANALYSIS

With its focus on the peculiarity of the subject and society, the practice of psychoanalysis has evolved a clinical practice that seeks to examine and explore these very peculiarities. Beginning with Sigmund Freud in the late nineteenth- and early twentieth-centuries, psychoanalysis marked a significant departure from traditional psychological and psychiatric approaches, while also playing a pivotal role in the development of modern psychology and psychotherapy. Influenced by the work of Josef Breuer, a physician who used "talking cure" methods to treat patients with hysterical symptoms, Freud's studies in neurology and his encounters with works of philosophy, such as, Friedrich Nietzsche and Arthur Schopenhauer, helped to shape his psychoanalytic practice. In a number of important works, including *The Interpretation of Dreams* (1953 [1900]) and *The Psychopathology of Everyday Life* (1960 [1901]), Freud introduced several key concepts, including the unconscious, the Oedipus complex, and libido, while also laying the groundwork for psychoanalysis as a distinct field of study. Following the formation of the Vienna Psychoanalytic Society in 1902, psychoanalysis gained prominence and expanded internationally through the work of Carl Jung, Alfred Adler, Melanie Klein, and Jacques Lacan, all of whom developed their own psychoanalytic theories and concepts.

Fast forward almost 125 years, and psychoanalysis as a body of thought is one that has permeated beyond its origins in the consulting room to represent a "climate of opinion," to quote W.H. Auden's (1940) memorialization of Freud. Perhaps it is more accurate to say psychoanalysis has become a body of *thoughts,* contrary to its depiction by critics through the years as an antiquated model unchanged since Freud's early monograph *Project for a Scientific Psychology* (1950 [1895]). Whether through ego psychology, interpersonal, object relations, self-psychology, or the relational orientation (just to name a few), the various schools of psychoanalytic thought, alongside the quantitative empirical research that has accompanied it, have developed and expanded its investigations in method, practice, and scope. One only needs to peruse the *Textbook of Psychoanalysis* (Gabbard, Litowitz, and Williams 2012) to see the non-clinical sections devoted to psychoanalytic contributions to topic and fields of thought as diverse as anthropology, film, literature, music, and the visual arts. A broader web search would result in psychoanalytic articles, books, conferences, and videos in recent years devoted to architecture, climate change, comedy, race, poverty, the Sopranos, and war.

Consequently, this collection aims to address the limited attention to sport in the expanding breadth of psychoanalytic theory. Indeed, by looking towards the interstices that underlie psychology, the social sciences, and the humanities, there exists a variety of sporting sub-disciplines examining the psychological, physiological, sociological, and political importance of sport. Whereas the study of sport encourages a decidedly multidisciplinary as well as interdisciplinary account of the subject and society, the benefits of a psychoanalytic approach have, unfortunately, been left unexplored.[2] It is in the psychoanalytic study of sport, therefore, that the contradictions inherent to the subject can be avowed; or, to put it another way, what we disavow in our sporting spectatorship or participation affords us the opportunity to see how our unconscious is structured. Consequently, by way of expounding a psychoanalytic account of sport, this collection offers a return to one of Freud's (1923/1961) essential concepts: the unconscious. Indeed, it is in exploring the unconscious and its various ramifications in sport that this collection will provide a critical consideration of sport's psychoanalytic significance. In order to achieve this, however, let us first consider and introduce the unconscious.

SPORT AND THE UNCONSCIOUS

There is, it would seem, no need to do many of things we end-up doing: whether this be consuming excessive amounts of food; deliberately saying something that will hurt a friend or loved one; or returning once again to our team's stadium in hope of a run of bad form to end, or for the recent success to be maintained. While attending the games of your local team may not initially be conceived as a self-destructive activity, the drive to do so nonetheless strikes a formal comparison to those who choose to partake in, for example, a six-day, ultramarathon in the Sahara Desert (such as those who compete in *Marathon des Sables* [Cherrington et al. 2020]).[3] Similarly, whereas repeatedly being punched in the face may require no further explanation for those choosing not to partake in boxing, for the many that do, the activity itself becomes an important part of their very being—something more than the simple suggestion that it keeps one fit, lets off steam, or provides structure to the day. Equally, though no one would ever deny the importance of their family, when a close family birthday clashes with the "big game," then, one's closest familial ties are immediately put to the test (even when you inevitably choose the family occasion, you're always left "checking the score"). While in either case the sporting fan and participant may be conscious of what it is they are doing, the unconscious desires, fantasies, and fears that drive them to do so are not always so readily made sense of, or even understood.

Instead, competing in sport can often belie any rational explanation, speaking instead to an unconscious enjoyment that, in many ways, works against one's well-being. For this reason, in order to make sense of the unconscious processes that permeate the subject we cannot look to the individual. Popular perceptions of clinical psychoanalysis are perhaps too easily associated with images of the couch—an inherently individualistic practice that has unfortunately marginalised psychoanalysis as a "quack" practice. In such cases, the unconscious is perceived as residing deep within the individual and beset by their own internal pathologies.

In contrast, the aim of psychoanalysis is "to provide a rigorous logic of subjectivity which is not 'purely subjective' in the derogatory sense, the one which would make it a mixture of individual whim, insight and ingenuity rather than a method" (Thwaites 2007, 4), but which regards the subject as constituted by the social—and by this we mean the very desires, fantasies, values, and beliefs that constitute the social field, through which the subject is constituted. What is more, these desires, fantasies, values, and beliefs are not simply socially acquired; that is, they do not prescribe a consistent process of social acculturation but emerge as part of a dialectical process that locates the inconsistencies of the subject as interdependent to the contradictions and antagonisms that underwrite the social relations we share. In other words, the "Subject is not simply an autonomous, free agent, but it is also not simply a mere effect of the structure as fully consistent in itself. It is rather an effect of the gap in this structure, of its inherent inconsistency or incompleteness" (Zupančič 2018, 1). Under this light, what the unconscious reveals is the deep interdependence between subjects and their environments. Due to the various social relations that the subject relies upon, there is in psychoanalysis no boundary between the subject and the social; instead, what constitutes the social interdependences that undergird "the human" is the fecundity of the unconscious.

The relevance of the unconscious is revealed at the interstices of the subject and the social. Sitting beyond the confines of the individual, the unconscious resides in those moments of contradiction that relay the very messiness of the subject's relation to the world as well as the other subjects they interact with. Sport is not immune to these dynamics (Black and Reynoso 2024). Whereas, in his account of the unconscious, 'Freud directed his attention towards the border of the outside-inside division of the human and its Other' (Thakur and Dickstein 2018, 4), it is in accordance with this border that the contradictions and distortions that underlie the unconscious are, to a certain extent, actively pursued in the case of sport.[4]

If the unconscious reveals anything it is that what is perceived to be external to the subject is more often than not internally significant to them—indeed, an integral part of the subject, which is also radically Other. This underscores the fact that the unconscious can never be located in the individual. Here, "the unconscious is not a subjective distortion of the objective world, it is first and foremost an indication of a fundamental inconsistency of the objective world itself, which—as such, that is as inconsistent—allows for and generates its own (subjective) distortions" (Zupančič 2008, 16). These inconsistencies can be identified in the various antagonisms that intersect the social field; antagonisms that bear witness to the fact that one's problems are always forged in accordance with one's inherent sociality.

Given this, we can begin to see why for the French psychoanalyst, Jacques Lacan, "the unconscious is politics" (2023). Again, this is not a politicization of the self, but an intent to examine how the very actions and beliefs that one may hold dear—indeed, that one may consider to be fundamental to one's sense of self—are only ever brought to light in one's social activity (Hanlon and Žižek 2001). This positions the unconscious as revealing that which speaks to the ways in which one is both subjected to but also subjectivized by the sociocultural dynamics in which one exists in. In making sense of one's actions, belief, and behaviours one is always and unrelentingly marked by that which the subject may not necessarily be aware of, but which nonetheless intrudes and introduces itself upon one's social relations and thinking.

This proposes that there is always something Other to the subject; that one's beliefs and actions may not be consciously recognised by the subject, but, nevertheless, become reproduced in their social relations. Nowhere is this more apparent that in the slips that permeate one's speech, from where Lacan asserted that "the unconscious is the Other's discourse" (2006, 10, italics removed). For Lacan, "It is this discourse, which is to say, *the signifying field* in all its ambiguities and unintended enunciations, in all its attempted evasions and slippages of meaning, this signifying field *as it is spoken by the subject*, that, in effect, *is* the unconscious" (Hook 2018, 42, italics in original). This is not to suggest that the subject is nothing more than an empty vessel, through which the Other's discourse is mindlessly recited on behalf of the subject. On the contrary, while the subject has agency, such agency is always dependent on a "social bond," or, as Lacan refers to, a discourse (Žižek and Salecl 1996, 32). Accordingly, while any articulation is subjected to a discourse that is not of the subject's choosing, it is through this very discourse that the subject is required to make meaning—a meaning that is just as much predicated on acts of miscommunication as it is in one's capacity to communicate effectively (Black 2021). In fact, where else can we begin to see the effects of the unconscious than in the mistakes, failures, and miscommunications that befall the sporting athlete? Indeed, the missed shot, the unrequired foul, or the sudden slip, all suggest an unconscious manifestation, a parapraxis, in one's conscious actions.

These descriptions endow the unconscious a strange topology, functioning from both within and outside the subject and revealing that which constitutes the subject, but which can never be known. Importantly, "The unconscious does not refer to things inaccessible to consciousness and does not mean the opposite of consciousness; it rather refers to an active and ongoing process: the work of censorship, substitution, and condensation when facing impossibility, conflict, deadlock, and impediment" (Zupančič 2016, 219). Rather than working in opposition to consciousness, what the unconscious prescribes is a remainder: something from "outside" that complicates our consciousness, residing in the gaps that belie one's conscious experiences. Simply put, we can determine that what the unconscious reveals is that there is always more than what meets the eye. It is these unconscious processes that serve to constitute the subject, but which also suggest something about the social relations that one partakes in.

We may function quite happily in ignoring the residing impact of these gaps and disavowing their affects; yet this nonetheless endows the unconscious an important role in psychoanalytic investigations: no matter the treatment, psychoanalysis can never function to eradicate the unconscious. Instead, attempts to identify the unconscious will always end in failure, but it is at this point of failure that the new is forged. Indeed, new perspectives, new social relations, and new problems are established which serve only to emphasise the irreducibility of the unconscious and its affects.

In light of this, we draw a direct line between the intractable unconscious and the inherent antagonisms and contradictions that sport exposes. This is perhaps best seen in the ephemeral nature of the sporting success: a success which, once achieved, is always immediately followed by the proceeding season, the forthcoming qualifiers, the next bout. While this speaks to the relation between sport and desire, it also opens a path through which the political nature of the unconscious is experienced (Lacan 2023). In much the same way that there is no escaping the unconscious and its political affects, there is also no escape through sport. While characterizations of sport may suggest that it provides an escape from the humdrum of our day-to-day lives, an opportunity to let off steam, and ignore the myriad of problems that encroach upon our daily existence, such characterizations belie the fact that "those who consciously seek flight from the reality of the world and its politics betray themselves in the ways supporting a favorite team delivers individuals into the politics of the world just the same" (Reynoso 2021, 598).

For American audiences, the kinds of contradiction that riddle subjectivity come to bear in the sporting example par excellence . . . the Sunday football game. Prefigured as an escape from politics and the ills of the world, one is nonetheless participating in the celebration of militarism that has come to frame the contemporary presentation (especially after 9/11) of professional athletic events, as writers like Dave Zirin (2008) have discussed in depth. From the outcry against Colin Kaepernick's genuflection to protest black death by police, or athletes showing support for the queer community with various rainbowed gear, many spectators decry the visible entry of politics into the field of play, without consciously realizing what their outrage also reveals. As a reminder that the unconscious should be looked for more at the surface than depth, the upset of the fan at a political display on the basketball court can only laughably be claimed as protecting the sanctity of an apolitical space. The distress contrarily reveals the fan's reaction to the possible interruption of the enjoyment that accompanies the disavowal of the knowledge that everything about attending a sporting event reflects the geopolitical imprint of our capitalistic times.

Broadly applied, it is through the unconscious that we can begin to trace what sport is but also how it is used; that is, its role and function within society, including the importance that it carries. Sport provides a context in which the unconscious is crystalized, forged in the social bonds that sport maintains and exacerbates, including the comradery experienced between teammates as well as the division and violence it can evoke between rival fans. There are unconscious satisfactions derived from these experiences, which go beyond the mere activity of sport. In fact, what this speaks to is the inherent insignificance of sport: its rules and regulations are all invented, the time and money spent on it bears no wider importance, and the drama and excitement it establishes is mostly contrived via a global media-sport complex that demands our enthrallment, just as much as our anger and distaste (Maguire 2011; see also Black 2021). Thus, while sport is inherently "nothing," it nonetheless means "something" for a vast majority of the world's population—including its detractors (Black and Reynoso 2024). It is only when conceived through our desires, fantasies, and fears that sport's unique significance can be observed.

One important area where these observations can be made is in the unconscious repetitions that sport evokes. Whether it be consecutive fixtures and seasons, the annual tournaments, or the multiple weekly training sessions, so much of sport relies upon repetition. It was this repetition that troubled Freud, noticing as he did the various repetitions that constituted the lives of his patients. Whether this was apparent in their dreams or mistakes, it was in their speech that Freud identified the importance of repetition for the subject. It would seem that it is this same repetition that underlies our investment in sport. No matter the defeat, no matter the failure, sport, for many, requires one to return, once more, to the gym or the training ground. It is in this sporting repetition that a way to the unconscious in sport and the enjoyment it evokes can be traced.

Furthermore, what we hope to have emphasized in these opening remarks is the underlying concern that psychoanalysis offers no cure. In psychoanalysis, there is no life beyond the antagonisms and contradictions that underlie our unconscious investment in sport. When the approach of ego-psychology is to overcome the resistances that the unconscious prescribes (Miller 1995), it is, on the contrary, in our unconscious repetitions that sport's psychoanalytic importance can be acknowledged. What sport provides is the opportunity to encounter and engage with the unconscious.

For this reason, we locate our psychoanalytic approach to sport in the unconscious desires, fantasies, and fears that underscore our enjoyment—an enjoyment that is paradoxically reflected in both the fleeting sporting success, but also, more importantly, in the enjoyment that is obtained in the very subversion of this success: the inevitable disappointment and defeat which in no way prevents one from returning to the sport they love. It is in this sense that we can begin to uncover why sport's appeal, as well as the inequality it relies upon, proves so intractably significant. It is in approaching this significance that what makes sport so appealing may in fact be the very inequity that it sustains and encourages. This is not to downplay or ignore those attempts that seek to tackle sporting injustices, especially those centred on encouraging wider participation at both global and local levels, rather it is to appreciate the fact that our very enjoyment in sport—the fantasies it sustains and the desire it evokes—is obstinately related to the contradictions it provides. In drawing out the significance of this contradiction, we briefly elucidate on the unconscious desires, fantasies, and fears that constitute our enjoyment in sport.

EXPLORING THE UNCONSCIOUS DESIRES, FANTASIES, AND FEARS OF SPORT

One way of developing a nuanced understanding of the unconscious processes that underlies our participation in sport is through the desire it evokes. Vaczi asserts, "Sport are a field of desire that is not limited to the desire for the goal" (2016, 300). In fact, despite the possibility of sporting success, every victory remains fleeting: we lose more than we ever win. Whether it be the prospect of the forthcoming fixture or the possibility of the knockout punch, success is haunted by its failure and an unconscious desire to tolerate, overcome, and repeat loss. This bespeaks the important contention that it is not necessarily the end result which underscores our interests in sport, but the unique way it maintains our enjoyment *through* failure and loss (Black 2023). Whereas desire can only be sustained in its repeated failure, in the case of sport, all sporting success is immediately and inevitably shadowed by the next event. Interestingly, the significance of desire and the realization of success may, for some, leave them without the desire to continue. Five-days after winning the 2016 Formula One World Title, Nico Rosberg retired from the sport. In his Facebook post, the driver noted, "I have climbed my mountain, I am on the peak," with the world title proving to be the "one thing" he had spent his career working towards (Hodgetts 2016).

Key here is the extent to which our enjoyment is not necessarily tied to overcoming the sporting "obstacle"—the impossible achievemen or the world-record—but to the obstacle itself. That is, what speaks to our sporting enjoyment is unconscious enjoyment we receive from the various obstacles that sport erects. Importantly, these obstacles are not simple prohibitions, but integral to the very purpose and nature of sport. All sporting activities require some obstacle for which the subject, or their team, must enjoy beyond the simple accomplishment of its overcoming—even if this overcoming results in sporting success.

Where the unconscious plays its role is in the act of disavowal that supports such enjoyment. Whether it be the personal-best, world-record, gold medal, match win, or break in a run of bad form, so much of sport is embroiled in the fetishization of this success ("this will be our year!"). In this way, the long-hoped for success is the fetishized object, for why else would one compete? However, to partake in such enjoyment is to disavow the very enjoyment that maintains such investment; an enjoyment that is achieved not just from the final sporting achievement, but from the failure and loss that maintains one's investment in the sporting obstacle. Where the unconscious resides is in the desire not to know this knowledge. Too often, this enjoyment is disavowed by being chalked-up to tired explanations . . . "the injuries haven't helped," "the referee was against us," "if only we'd signed *that* player." In doing so, our enjoyment depends on the desire that sport evokes, one which no sporting success, however trivial, can reconcile.

It is in this way that sport can speak to the paradoxes that the unconscious presents. What our unconscious belies in sport is our own self-interest. Nowhere is this more apparent than in the time spent training, watching, or participating in sport—activities which bear no social importance or significance beyond the competition they are put towards. In fact, despite the relative health benefits of competing in sport, benefits that we no doubt endorse, it is inevitable that at some point an injury, or worse, some life-threatening accident, will occur or will induce long-term damage. This is especially acute for former professional athletes, who all harbour and suffer from the lingering effects of an injury from their sporting careers. In many ways, it is against one's very self-interest that our enjoyment, desire, and disavowal come to bear: we disavow the unconscious sacrifice that sport requires in order to pursue our desire and enjoyment.

Fantasy helps to support this process. Where the obstacle proves constitutive of desire, fantasy is the frame through which the object's overcoming is formed. Sport is littered with fantasies of meritocracy, fair play, and underdog stories. This is not to say that these fantasies do not necessarily come true, but that in order to enjoy sport, adherence to the sporting fantasy is required. It is in our sporting fantasies for a past (nostalgia) or future (utopia) of plenitude that we are confronted with what we don't have. It is from this foundational place of the lacking subject that psychoanalysis begins theorizing and where every sporting endeavour begins. Whether one is a community centre basketball player, weekend coach for a youth hockey team, season ticket holder for the Los Angeles Lakers, fantasy sport enthusiast, or critical of the corrupting influence of the athletic world, sport always contains a transgressive fantasy, allowing us to push at the boundaries of "fair play," "sportsmanship," and "equality in competition," while, at the same time, balking at the remote possibility of these ideals ever being realised outside of sport itself.

In many ways, fantasy functions to allow the subject to avoid its own inconsistencies and social antagonisms. Here, fulfilment and loss are inextricably phrased in the desire of the Other, fantasies of the Other's enjoyment, and the obstructing or facilitating role the Other takes in the conscious pursuit of satisfaction. These obstructions present a transgression that always requires the fantasy of overcoming some presupposed limit. In sport, such limits may be erected in the final encounters of a close-run game, which require a decisive effort in order to overcome one's opponent. It is also there in the exaltation of those athletes who go beyond the limits of what is perceived to be possible; or, in the underdog story, where the capacity to overcome some internal limitation—a team of lesser ability, for instance—can, in their achievement, herald a moment of unexpected glorification. To achieve this, however, athletes must continually be working towards and going beyond the limits of the ordinary.

Nevertheless, what remains apparent is that such limits are never fixed but continually moving, always re-erected in the following game, i.e., the next obstacle. Where fantasy proves so alluring is in the extent to which these limits can be overcome—the promise land which can only ever be reached at the end of the final. With its massive global monetary and cultural appeal, contemporary sport provides an unlimited but underutilized resource for the theoretical exploration of how these fantasies serve only to compound our sense of incompleteness, fuelled that is by desires that are grounded within a social matrix that is undoubtedly contingent. For this reason, fantasy plays a key role in managing our sporting contingencies, most notably, the relative uncertainty that undergirds every sporting encounter.

Though not without exception, from Freud (primary narcissism, Oedipus complex), to Klein (depressive and paranoid schizoid positions), to Lacan (lack), psychoanalytic theorizing has centred on how individuals and groups relate to loss, whether actual, perceived, or fantasized. As stated earlier, losing forms the base of the sporting worlds of athletes and fans more than the achievement and mastery that scaffolds it. Sport provides opportunities to communally deny, displace, but also perform, the anxieties and fears that accompany the subject's origins relating to absence. The precarity and contingency that guides athlete and fan experiences is often expressed as opportunities squandered, shots or targets being missed, something or someone being taken away, points dropped, injuries robbing potential, victories stolen, and teams or organizations being raided for talent. Sport provides the content to fill in the form by which desiring what we don't have is marked by the fear of it being lost—with all its attendant fantasies of envy and ecstasy. Unsurprisingly therefore, a variety of superstitions, compulsive behaviours, and personal rituals come to characterize how we relate and partake in sport. Whether this be the well-known lucky pair of socks or the special shirt which ensures the team's win, what such actions reveal are the unconscious fears that continually confront and haunt the athlete and fan. In the case of the former, this can lead to eating disorders, troubles in over-training, or a reliance on performance enhancing supplements.

THE LINEUP

As has been detailed, this collection will seek to examine the unconscious processes that both maintain but also undermine our interests in sport.

Such enjoyment does not require some patronising detoxification, an assertion grounded firmly in the contention that sport presents some ideological mystification that its participants must be made aware of, and from which psychoanalysis can provide some sobering effect. Instead, the application of psychoanalysis in the following chapters will critically explore and examine the very antagonisms, tensions, and contradictions that dynamically pattern and shape our relation to sport. This includes both the subject and the social, cultural, and political institutions that frame our relations to sport and the social interactions it affords. Where psychoanalysis provides a novel opportunity to theoretically uncover these dynamics, sport, we argue, can play an important and facilitating role in uncovering the significance of these dynamics on both the subject and society.

Ultimately, we do not conceive of psychoanalysis as a one-stop shop to overcoming or ridding sport of its problems. As noted, our unconscious satisfactions and enjoyments are not so easily overlooked. Rather, what we draw attention to are the failures, disappointments, and unrelenting frustrations that underscore sport's appeal. Sport is not unique in eliciting such an appeal, yet it does provide a lens through which the contradictions inherent to its very appeal may be explored and the unconscious desires, fantasies, and fears that function to maintain some of its underlying injustices can be recognised. Psychoanalytically, the following chapters each provide their own distinct reflections on how the unconscious remains a relevant and important point of inquiry in the academic study of sport and its role within society.

In meeting this aim, the following chapters will be organised across five parts: Part I: The Athletic Body; Part II: Coaching; Part III: Fandom; Part IV: Identity; and Part V: Play. Together, each section will offer both theoretical and empirical support for examining sports from a range of psychoanalytic perspectives.

By investigating the psychoanalytic significance of embodiment in professional sports, Part I, "The Athletic Body," critically considers how the body remains a key site for cultural projection and fantasy within our sporting practices. The body, as a vessel of lived experiences, sensations, and expressions, emerges as a dynamic landscape under psychoanalytic investigation. While the psychoanalytic exploration of dreams, fantasies, and symbolism elucidates upon the various ways in which the body communicates by expressing unarticulated emotions and conflicts, it is in the somatic manifestations of repressed memories and the symbolic significance of bodily symptoms that the body becomes a canvas upon which the unconscious is expressed. This invites us to explore the rich interconnections between mental and physical states, which serve to recognize the body as both a source of insight and a site of conflict in our sporting experiences.

In Chapter 1, "Sport and the Erotic," David McIvor proposes that while psychoanalysis can offer valuable insights into the pervasive influence of sports on the collective psyche, conventional psychoanalysis reveals a cultural bias against "lower" cultural activities such as athletics—a judgment that inherently dismisses the body in its less sublimated expressions. In contrast to such bias, McIvor explores how sports, with its dynamic interplay of bodies in space, unveils both the tapped and untapped potentials of the human body for connection and transformation. For McIvor, these potentials possess an inherently erotic nature, best approached through Freud's exploration of infantile sexuality, which, he argues, helps to envision the broader emancipatory possibilities inherent in sports.

Drawing from a Lacanian framework, Chapter 2, "The Athletic Body: A Lacanian Perspective," involves Hub Zwart examining Lacan's conceptualization of three distinct registers of bodily experience: the Real, the imaginary, and the symbolic body. This dynamic interplay reinvigorates Lacan's conceptual perspective on the embodiment of individuals in the context of sports. With regard to historical examples, Zwart examines how this dynamic embodiment holds significance in contemporary discourses on sport, paying specific attention to a case study from the 2023 FIFA Women's World Cup. In doing so, Zwart's chapter asserts that a psychoanalysis of the body offers a valuable path to addressing the tensions, ambiguities, and paradoxes prevalent in modern sports, while also highlighting how sports practices can function as a captivating arena for psychoanalytical introspection.

It is widely accepted that effective coaching plays a pivotal role in sports, serving as a catalyst for athlete development, skill enhancement, and overall team success. Through implementing technical expertise as well as fostering leadership, motivation, and a positive team culture, the "successful" sports coach can help develop and progress an athlete's personal growth while also succeed in the achievement of collective goals. Trust in the coach is a crucial factor, with athletes needing to have faith that their coach possesses the expertise to enhance their athletic performance and the knowledge to win. Undertaking a critical perspective on the effects of coaching, Part II, "Coaching," explores how psychoanalytic theory can help identify inequalities in coaching as well as underlying discrepancies related to the coach as a figure of authority. While coaching operates on the premise of "progress," guiding individuals toward setting and achieving goals, unlocking their full potential, and fostering a proactive approach to life, psychoanalysis can offer a nuanced account of the tensions and complexities of coaching as it profoundly impacts the psycho-social well-being of athletes. Such an exploration invites us to reconsider the nature of coach-athlete relations: namely, the problems associated with the idealization of "the coach" ("the subject supposed to know"), and the effects of discrimination in coaching positions.

In this respect, Chapter 3, "The Racial Melancholia of Aspiring Black NFL Head Coaches," sees Bradley A. Thomas examine the National Football League (NFL), and, specifically, the significant underrepresentation of Black individuals in head coaching positions. Viewed through the lens of grief, Thomas provides a psychoanalytic intervention into examples of racial melancholia and implicit bias. In this context, the unattainable idealized White racial perfection serves as the lost object, compounded by various ongoing forms of loss, such as, discrimination, racism, assimilation, diaspora, and the challenges related to homeland and language. Thomas's chapter details how this collective experience underscores the need for broader societal recognition and action in order to address systemic issues surrounding diversity and inclusion in both professional sports and the larger societal context.

In Chapter 4, "Psychoanalysis, Mental Coaching, and Sports," Robert Samuels contends that achieving improvement in most competitive pursuits hinges on embracing profound self-honesty. Yet, as Samuels outlines, psychoanalysis reveals a striking paradox: individuals not only frequently deceive others but also engage in self-deception. That is, even though we presume to have the most intimate knowledge of ourselves, we often engage in self-deception to shield and stabilize our self-concept and perceived control. While examples of mental coaching frequently reinforce an idealized image of the coach ("the one who knows"), such idealization can reinforce a destructive mode of dependency. To this end, Samuels explains how psychoanalysis can contribute to the growing field of mental coaching, by paying specific attention to the world of poker.

Part III, "Fandom," considers how psychoanalytic accounts of fandom offer a space through which to explore how, as active participants, fans invest emotionally and intellectually in chosen narratives that become mirrors in reflecting the subject's aspirations, fears, and unresolved conflicts. For this reason, psychoanalytic concepts offer a unique opportunity to study the profound impact of fandom on personal development and the formation of cultural identities. As a prominent form of self-expression, offering a space for fans to grapple with the complexities of the world, what is left to be discovered is that sports fandom is no mere passive consumption of entertainment but a dynamic, participatory process that shapes and is shaped by the intricate workings of the subject and society. Accordingly, this section is supplemented with vignettes that survey the changing relationship between athletes and fans as well as the unique dynamics underpinning the individual sports fan and the larger sociocultural field—as well as the ambivalences therein. In doing so, the ethics of sport fandom and its association with anti-racist and feminist frameworks is considered.

In fact, while engaging in sports fandom can entail a form of imaginative play, where we immerse ourselves in the team's identity and hold the belief that our support wields an influence over the players, such 'make-believe' hinges on collective assumptions shared within the fan community and broader society regarding the acceptable behaviour expected from athletes, teams, and fellow fans. When these assumptions begin to fracture, as exemplified by athletes taking political stances, it disrupts the fan's fantasy world and can trigger conflict, as witnessed during recent instances like the U.S. national anthem protests. As a result, in Chapter 5, "Are We the Champions? Sports Fandom through the Lens of Pretend Play and Intersubjectivity," Ben Bernstein examines the psycho-social disruption that occurs when athletes' personal perspectives clash with fans' expectations of them as objects of play.

David G. Cushman's, "The Psychoanalysis of Basketball," occupies Chapter 6, where he considers that while professional sports have long been immersed in compelling morality narratives, sparking heated discussions on issues like right versus wrong, strength versus weakness, and loyalty versus disloyalty, this dynamic is notably pronounced in the National Basketball Association (NBA), the premier professional basketball league globally. Cushman argues that Basketball serves as a canvas onto which spectators project unspoken facets of their own psyche and broader cultural themes. Here, the act of watching a game can swiftly evoke themes of power, transformation, failure, authenticity, and masculinity, creating a multifaceted experience that involves both sensory engagement and a defensive organization marked by splitting and projection. By employing psychoanalytic thinking, coupled with the use of six vignettes, Cushman examines how the intersection of psychoanalytic thought, NBA fandom, and the on-court actions of NBA players, offers a nuanced exploration of the intricate processes underlying fans' experiences, shedding light on the motivations and behaviours of NBA players and coaches.

Indeed, while sports fandom is deeply woven into contemporary culture, carrying substantial psychosocial costs linked to excessive identification with teams, leagues, and individual players, in the realm of politics and sports, organizations and industries actively promote and sustain campaigns that foster a perpetual tension with the perceived "opposition." As a result, behaviours of a questionable nature, rooted in morally unjust premises, and driven by an us-versus-them mentality, have become fundamental pillars of raucous crowd conduct in stadiums and on social media platforms alike. It is against these tensions that Chapter 7, Monique S. Bowen's, "Cheering on Solid Ground: Plotting a Developmental Arc toward Ethical Fandom," serves to draw upon psychoanalytic theories spanning the past century, alongside modern approaches that integrate concepts of attachment and cultural positioning, in order to consider how a psychoanalysis of sports fandom can offer therapeutic frameworks. These frameworks, Bowen argues, help unravel the various motives underlying the phenomenon of sports fandom. By acknowledging the concurrent and reciprocal identifications occurring within a quasi-transference-countertransference milieu, we gain insight into our self/other representations as influential factors in shaping both distant and close attachment relationships.

The concept of identity remains a multifaceted tapestry woven from the threads of personal history, social influences, and unconscious motivations. Consequently, Part IV, "Identity," expounds upon how the nuances of identity formation in sport and through sport maintain a psychoanalytic importance. While our identities are dynamic and evolving entities, continually influenced by the interplay between conscious desires and unconscious conflicts, the internal struggles, and negotiations that individuals undergo in the process of constructing a cohesive sense of self through sport permits a deeper comprehension of the psychoanalytic significance of complex societal expectations and individual aspirations. Where unexplored desires, fears, and unresolved conflicts reside, sport offers an important insight into the nature of identity and its impact on the subject and society.

For this reason, sport serves as a rich canvas for exploring the complex nature of identity and its inherent contradictions. Following this, Chapter 8, "To Know of Manny Pacquiao . . . The Limits of Identity under Empire," by Joseph S. Reynoso, offers an extended analysis of the compelling appeal of Manny Pacquiao, the Filipino boxer-politician, both within the Philippines and as a broader symbol of Pan-Asian identity. Through exploring the potential for transcending our entrenched investment in identity, Reynoso contends that it is only by re-evaluating our attachment to figures embodying assertive forms of racial (and other) identity that a sustained examination of our unwitting involvement in perpetuating colonial and imperialistic mechanisms can be forged. Indeed, by delving into Asian-American identities and drawing insights from psychoanalytic perspectives, Asian political studies, and Filipino scholarship, Reynoso elucidates on the intricate connection between traumatic loss and racial identity

In Chapter 9, "Homosexual Football: Perspectives from Lou Andreas-Salomé," Rayyan Dabbous elucidates on how the psychoanalytic work of Lou Andreas-Salomé can shed light on the scarcity of openly gay and bisexual men in the realm of football. By establishing the argument that Andreas-Salomé's herself personified the athletic ideal throughout her life, Dabbous introduces Andreas-Salomé's theory of sublimation, before considering how footballers encompass various roles as free agents within the complex realm of probability. In doing so, Dabbous details how the responsibility of footballers extends toward truth and the unconscious, as opposed to focusing solely on conscious efforts to promote LGBTQ+ representation.

To conclude the collection, Part V, "Play," considers the significance of "play" as it pertains to sport and sporting practices. Indeed, from the games of childhood to the symbolic play of adulthood, psychoanalytic theory encourages us to unpick the profound connections between the ludic and the unconscious, shedding new light on the ways in which play comes to reflect the complexities of the human experience. Where play serves as a language through which the unconscious communicates—whether it is the tangible world of games or the intangible realm of fantasies—through play we navigate desire, conflict, and self-discovery, but also the creatives forces that provide insight into unarticulated emotions, unresolved conflicts, and hidden aspirations. This understanding elucidates on the clinical and social importance of play, which, with the support of clinical vignettes, allows us to identify how certain playful movements can invite new perspectives in therapy and in life.

To this extent, sports, such as baseball, can offer a rich terrain for psychoanalytic scrutiny, characterized by its tapestry of rituals, superstitions, and profound mental conditioning. While it remains amenable to a multitude of analogical interpretations, it can also yield insights of a more topological nature regarding the practice of analysis. Taking up this consideration, Chapter 10, "Turning Two: Psychoanalysis and the Poetics of Pivoting; Or Initial Thoughts for a Topology," sees Patrick Scanlon examine how Jacques Lacan's exploration of Borromean links—the Mobius strip and the torus—resonate within the realm of baseball: namely, how a distinctive event—the double play—mirrors the shape and motion of these geometric figures, while also sharing lexical parallels.

For Shani Samai-Moskovich, while psychoanalytic theory extensively explores the human body, a noticeable gap persists in understanding the development of the athletic dimension, which encompasses facets like the integration of body image into one's self-concept and the experience of competence and joy through the acquisition of athletic skills. Consequently, in Chapter 11, "Becoming-ball: A schizo-soma Ball Movement," Samai-Moskovich considers the athletic dimension within psychoanalytic theory through the application of Deleuze and Guattari's concept of "becoming." Indeed, while "becoming" can be easily grasped as a symbiotic process, an ongoing metamorphosis where individuals dissolve their boundaries and transform into something else, a continuous journey of "subjectification," it is through an illustration of the concept of "becoming-ball" that Samai-Moskovich provides an examination of the prologue to Don DeLillo's *Underworld* (1997) as well as a clinical case. In each example, Samai-Moskovich explicates upon the notion of "becoming-ball" by exploring the connection between the athletic body and its role in facilitating mental transformation.

Though perceptions of play often intertwine with a pursuit of instinctual satisfaction—an imperative for all individuals, regardless of age—the characterization of play is one that usually sees it as diverging from the routines of everyday life. While these distinctions suggest a clear separation between the joy of play and the mundane aspects of ordinary existence, they actually hint at a deeper understanding of the creativity inherent in play. Following this path, the final chapter of the collection, Chapter 12, "Play, Sport, and the Creativity of Sublimation: Understanding the Importance of Unimportant Activities," sees Jack Black argue that a crucial element shared between play and sport lies in the creativity they engender, particularly in how creative acts are intricately linked to the lack constituting the Lacanian subject. Drawing on the Lacanian concept of sublimation, Black explores how the structured rules and regulations of sport assert and demand a recognition of the inherent limitations they impose. Contrary to perceiving these limits as hindrances to creativity, sublimation reveals that these limits are constitutive of creativity itself. In other words, the capacity to sublimate—to creatively manifest distinct physical or artistic expressions—resides in the routine and profound significance of playful and sporting activities, along with the inherent restrictions and constraints these activities impose. Ultimately, Black contests that it is through embracing these limits that one's creativity can unveil an emancipatory potential within the realm of play and sport.

NOTES

1. For this, we recommend the reader consider the *Psychoanalysis, Culture & Society* Special Issue, "Just a Game? Sport and Psychoanalytic Theory" (Black and Reynoso 2024).

2. Across various disciplines and sub-disciplines, academic inquiries into sport have developed a wide array of topics, each employing their own theoretical and methodological approaches. All of this speaks to the physical, psychological, political, and sociological importance of sport and our relation to physical activity.

3. The *Marathon des Sables* is a six-day ultramarathon completed in the Sahara Desert (Morocco).

4. Thakur and Dickstein add, "Freud emphasized the border itself, the field in between, as what is really Other, this seeking to articulate what this Other entails; he called it the 'unconscious' and determined its characteristics by way of analyses of its various effects in situations intersecting the then nascent fields of neurology, psychology, sociology, and anthropology" (2018, 4).

BIBLIOGRAPHY

Auden, Wystan Hugh. 1940 "In Memory of Sigmund Freud." In W.H. Auden, *Another Time: Poems*, 118. New York, NY: Random House.

Black, Jack. 2021a. "Football Is 'the Most Important of the Least Important Things': The Illusion of Sport and COVID-19." *Leisure Sciences* 43, no. 1–2: 97–103.

Black, Jack. 2021b. *Race, Racism and Political Correctness in Comedy—A Psychoanalytic Exploration*. Abingdon, UK: Routledge.

Black, Jack. 2023. "Desire, Drive and the Melancholy of English Football: 'It's (not) Coming Home.'" In *Critical Issues in Football: A Sociological Analysis of the Beautiful Game*, edited by Will Roberts, Stuart Whigham, Alex Culvin, and Daniel Parnell, 53–65. Abingdon, UK: Routledge.

Black, Jack, and Joseph S. Reynoso. 2024. "Just a Game? Sport and Psychoanalytic Theory." *Psychoanalysis, Culture & Society*.

Cherrington, Jim, Jack Black, and Nicholas Tiller. 2020. "Running Away from the Taskscape: Ultramarathon as 'Dark Ecology.'" *Annals of Leisure Research* 23, no. 2: 243–263.

Freud, Sigmund. 1950. *The Standard Edition of the Complete Psychological Works of Sigmund Freud, Volume* I (1895): *Project for a Scientific Psychology*, edited by James Strachey, 281–391. London, UK: Hogarth Press.

Freud, Sigmund. 1953. *The Standard Edition of the Complete Psychological Works of Sigmund Freud, Volume IV (1900): The Interpretation of Dreams (First Part)*, edited by James Strachey. London, UK: Hogarth Press.

Freud, Sigmund. 1960. *The Standard Edition of the Complete Psychological Works of Sigmund Freud, Volume VI (1901): The Psychopathology of Everyday* Life, edited by James Strachey. London, UK: Hogarth Press.

Freud, Sigmund. 1961. "The Ego and the Id (1923)." In *The Standard Edition of the Complete Psychological Works of Sigmund Freud, Volume XIX (1923–1925): The Ego and the Id and Other Works*, edited by James Strachey, 1–66. London, UK: Hogarth Press.

Gabbard, Glen O., Bonnie E. Litowitz, and Paul Williams. 2012. *Textbook of Psychoanalysis*. American Psychiatric Pub.

Hanlon, Christopher, and Slavoj Žižek. 2001. "Psychoanalysis and the Post-Political: An Interview with Slavoj Žižek." *New Literary History* 32, no. 1: 1–21.

Hodgetts, Rob. 2016. "Nico Rosberg: World Champion Retires to Stun Formula One." *CNN*, December 2, 2016. https://edition.cnn.com/2016/12/02/motorsport/nico-rosberg-retires-formula-one-mercedes-world-champion/index.html

Hook, Derek. 2018. *Six Moments in Lacan*. London, UK: Routledge.

Lacan, Jacques. 2006. "Seminar on 'The Purloined Letter.'" In *Ecrits: The First Complete Edition in English*, translated by Bruce Fink, 6–50. New York, NY: W. W. Norton & Company.

Lacan, Jacques. 2023. *Le Séminaire Livre XIV: La Logique du fantasme*. Paris, France: SEUIL.

Maguire, Joseph. 2011. "The Global Media Sports Complex: Key Issues and Concerns." *Sport in Society* 14, no. 7–8: 965–977.

Miller, Jacques-Alain. 1995. "Context and Concepts." In *Reading Seminar XI: Lacan's Four Fundamental Concepts of Psychoanalysis*, edited by Richard Feldstein, Bruce Fink, and Maire Jannus, 3–18. Albany, NY: State University of New York Press.

Parker, Ian. 2023. "Psychoanalysts Unite . . . Against Trans." *Sublation Magazine*, February 21, 2023. https://www.sublationmag.com/post/psychoanalysts-unite-against-trans

Reynoso, Joseph S. 2021. "Boston Sucks! A Psychoanalysis of sports." *Psychoanalysis, Culture & Society* 26, no. 4: 591–607.

Thwaites, Tony. 2007. *Reading Freud: Psychoanalysis and Cultural Theory*. Los Angeles, CA: SAGE.

Vaczi, Mariann. 2016. "Dangerous Liaisons, Fatal Women: The Fear and Fantasy of Soccer Wives and Girlfriends in Spain." *International Review for the Sociology of Sport* 51, no. 3: 299–313.

Zirin, David. 2008. *A People's History of Sports in the United States: 250 Years of Politics, Protest, People, and Play*. New York: The New Press.

Žižek, Slavoj, and Renata Salecl. 1996. "Lacan in Slovenia." In *A Critical Sense*, edited by Peter Osborne, 21–46. London, UK: Routledge.

Zupančič, Alenka. 2008. *Why Psychoanalysis? Three Interventions*. Aarhus, DK: Aarhus University Press.

Zupančič, Alenka. 2016. "Power in the Closet (and Its Coming Out)." In *Lacan, Psychoanalysis, and Comedy*, edited by Patricia Gherovici and Manya Steinkoler, 219–234. New York, NY: Cambridge University Press.

Zupančič, Alenka. 2018. "12 Questions about Psychoanalysis: Answers by Alenka Zupančič." *European Journal of Psychoanalysis* 5, no. 1: 1–4.

PART I

The Athletic Body

Chapter 1

Sport and the Erotic

David W. McIvor

In the contemporary world, the dynamic relationship between sport and psychic life has reached a point of saturation historically reserved for the nuclear family and organized religion. In many respects, sport has eclipsed religion as a source of fantasy, meaning, drive, affect, and consolation, and "familial" questions of desire, aggression, and intimacy are clearly traceable within the dramas of identification and projection surrounding sport (Beneke and Remillard 2014; Mcleod 2023). Personally, I have seen (and felt) the seismic affective tremors that sport can induce—from manic elation to the deepest depression—along with accompanying psychic oscillations between insecurity and triumph, disintegration and omnipotence. All of this is ripe material for the analytic encounter, and also for psychoanalysis as social criticism. Perhaps if Freud were alive today to pen *The Future of an Illusion*, he would be writing about football (American or otherwise) rather than religion.

Psychoanalysis sheds valuable light upon the grip that sport has on the collective psyche. As Reynoso (2021) has catalogued, the intensity of involvement in sports touches upon a multitude of psychological concerns including the instability of psychic boundaries; the presence of fears and fantasies of destruction and triumph; the displacement or refusal of loss; Lack, desire, and the Other; fantasies of wholeness or plentitude, aggression, and violence—all intertwined with the psychic logics attending racism, patriarchy, and capitalism. Or, as Hirsch and Blumberg (2010) have argued from a somewhat more orthodox psychoanalytic position—sport seems to be a childish distraction or immature fixation, which represents carryovers from the affective significance that play has for children but which can serve a defensive function for adults protecting them from the "vulnerability and conflicts associated with more crucial life experiences" (2010, 477).[1] Greif, by contrast, emphasizes the Winnicottian idea that play is a "developmental achievement," and describes the spontaneity, playfulness, and fun that accompanied his lifelong involvement with sport (2010, 554). In this respect, a *lack* of engagement with sports might also serve a defensive function, protecting "some people from feeling anxious, insecure, or uncomfortable with their bodies" (Greif 2010, 558). Greif also notes that psychoanalytic reflection on sport often has betrayed a cultural bias against "lower" forms of cultural activity such as athletics, a judgment that contains its own rejection of the body in its less sublimated (or "refined") forms of expression such as dance or theater.

Sport is an overdetermined object, with many valences of motivation and meaning.[2] But overdetermination, as Norman O. Brown once argued, is "determination made into chance . . . meaning and absurdity reconciled" (1966, 248–9). In what follows, I want to tease out a few somewhat "absurd" ideas about sport, picking up on a challenge raised by Reynoso when he asked whether sports can "pose questions for psychoanalysis about the matters with which it concerns itself" (2021, 605). In particular, I want to explore the way that sport—with its dynamic movements of bodies in space—can reveal the human body's tapped and untapped potentials for connection and transformation. Such potentials, I will argue, are inherently erotic, and they can be best approached in the light of Freud's account of infantile sexuality, while also showing the limitations of Freud's official account. Exploring this path can inform psychoanalytic discourse and practice, but it can also allow us to envision the broader emancipatory potential of sport. The repressive logics surrounding and imbuing sport, from racial capitalism to patriarchy to the politics of shaming, do not exhaust sport's radical potential, which resides in the emancipatory kernel of plasticity and the erotic drive for union revealed in athletes' embodied enactments of dynamic vitality. Sport, I will argue, is a more accessible route to dynamic vitality than the highly sublimated activates of "high" culture (the very term betrays desexualization and a corresponding overvaluation of the intellect). The athlete hints at the possibilities for what Norman O. Brown called "love's body" or the mystical body of polymorphous perversity—which Freud glimpsed but could not adequately theorize—reconnecting us to a lost plentitude. In what follows, I explore these ideas by drawing upon the work of the psychotherapist Daniel Stern along with the mystical Freudianism of Brown. I begin, however, examining some of the reasons why this line of thinking might sound absurd from the perspective of the psychoanalytic tradition.

CAN PSYCHOANALYSIS EVEN THEORIZE THE BODY?

As many others have noted, psychoanalysis has a body problem.[3] Although Freud's concept of *das Ich* or the "I" (later "translated" by Strachey as the *ego*) was an inherently embodied concept, Freud himself could not fathom what he called the "mysterious leap" between mind and body (see Makari 2008, 351). Freud described psyche and body as different entities, with a kind of mysterious interface between the two that he largely left unexplored (Sella 2018, 16). Freud seemingly justified this gap by his observation that interpretations could have somatic effects, and if such "talking cures" were effective then it was unnecessary to focus on the body as an independent factor in analysis. Direct attention to the physical attributes of experience came to be considered as regressive, if not threatening, within analysis (Sella 2018, 17). Freud was very concerned about the early analysts who were "liberating" their patients' neuroses through sexual encounters, threatening—or so Freud feared—the scientific status of the fledgling enterprise (Makari 2008, 72). The possible intercorporeal interactions of the two bodies in analysis was thereby pushed to the side by Freud's insistence on analytic "abstinence" and "neutrality," including the specific positioning of bodies that made such connections less likely (see Sella 2018, 31). Exceptions to this tendency only seemed to prove the wisdom of the rule (i.e. Wilhelm Reich's obsession with character armor and the orgasm).

As a result of these assumptions and insistences, the mainstream of psychoanalysis has betrayed a lingering Cartesian split between mind and body, lavishing attention on mental life while leaving the body behind. The Cartesian split was reinforced by companion ideas such as the (immature and bodily) "primary processes" versus the (mature, representational) "secondary processes." Arguably, the leeriness towards embodiment also informed Freud's theory of infantile sexuality. The infant's "polymorphous perversity"—the erotic enjoyment of its entire body—is forsaken through the maturational pathway by which overflowing erotic energy comes to be channeled into specific areas and ultimately focused on the genitals (Freud 2011). Freud accepted this development as a matter of course, and it clearly influenced his understanding of childhood play. Freud rarely discussed play—and never, to my knowledge, discussed professional sports—but in his few treatments of the subject he theorized play within the economic dynamics of the pleasure principle (the building up of tension before the pleasures of release) and the mimicry of adult behavior ("playing house," etc.) (see Holowchak 2011). Once again childhood experiences of erotic embodiment are indexed to "mature," adult seriousness and the dictates of reality. Play is a preparation and a practice for the markers of healthy adulthood: work and love (i.e. reproduction).[4]

Freud's official or exoteric doctrine, then, reflects a split between body and mind informing a hierarchy of psychic functions that deprivileges embodied experience in the name of adaptations to the reality principle. However, while

Freud did not seem to value play on its own terms, he noted that the play of childhood is never fully renounced by the adult but, rather, lingers within the unconscious. When the adult stops playing, Freud says, they *phantasies* (2001 [1908]). Fantasy—conscious and unconscious—is a refuge for the erotic exuberance experienced in play, but if play is merely a practice for (re)production then it is unclear why such a refuge would be psychically necessary. Freud's idea here amounts to a confession: play cannot solely be seen as a preparation for adulthood but is rather an independent, *sui generis* experience. The energy of play may be forcefully adapted to the dictates of reality—just as erotic energy may be channeled and focused on specific organs—and fixations to lingering resonances of play may result in neurotic "symptoms" to be treated. But these symptoms could also be read as protests against both the analyst and the analytic tradition that refuses to take seriously the "lost" experience of erotic exuberance. Freud lets us read it both ways, which opens the door to an appreciation of embodiment that Freud himself could not articulate. The body problem of psychoanalysis—its "evasive unconscious" (Elisha 2010)—can be addressed by exploring the vital movements within sport and play, as well as the erotic resonances of such movements and the possibilities for plasticity they represent for human life.

THE UNCONSCIOUS OF SPORT? THE EROTIC BODY OF POLYMORPHOUS PERVERSITY

Psychoanalysts who have emphasized the relationship between sport and playfulness often still betray what could be called Freud's maturational bias, which sees the value of play in terms of preparation for adulthood. For instance, Greif, who otherwise reflects thoughtfully on the ways in which sport can enable experiences of spontaneity and joy, repeats the idea that "play is the work of children" and emphasizes how sport teaches "valuable life lessons" including "discipline, determination, focus, and sportsmanship" (2010, 553). Once again, this is a view of the sport and play of children from the (repressed) perspective of adulthood. Although children may mimic adults in their play, they do not obviously rationalize it as a preparedness for adulthood or a training in discipline and determination. Play is not work; it obeys the pleasure principle rather than the reality principle, which is why adults do not "play house," but, more and more, watch sports.

Of course, it is obvious that adult sport is a serious business. The financial rewards of professional sport have never been higher, and as a result the intensity of competition for participation in elite sports has perhaps never been greater. Sport is a profession, and as such a highly repressed form of activity that oftentimes little resembles play or playfulness. Athletes often reflect on the "grind" of a season and the bothersome aspects of the "job"; many of them view their participation in sports as primarily an economic opportunity—as a means not only of securing valuable employment contracts in an ever-growing industry but also endorsement deals that are oftentimes more lucrative than their professional contracts. The endless, nonstop commentary on sports focuses in large part on ranking the "greatness" of players or teams, or speculating about future possibilities, rather than re-living or poetically describing the experience of watching or playing the sport. Spectatorship itself increasingly becomes a status symbol relating to the proximity to power and wealth (see media stories each year about the cost of Super Bowl tickets, or the celebrity appearances courtside). Conscious understandings of sport—whether by observers or participants—by and large accede to the demands of the reality principle, and to suggest otherwise must seem like a willful exaggeration.

And yet we ought to recall Adorno's famous line that "in psychoanalysis nothing is true except the exaggerations" (2010 [1951]). As Norman O. Brown puts it, psychoanalysis begins from the radical claim that humans "do not know what we want," and that our lives are shaped by unconscious longings that are repressed or disavowed. If embodiment is the evasive unconscious of psychoanalysis, then sport too has an unconscious that must be outlined. Before turning more directly to the work of Brown to do so, however, there is another entry point to this argument in the work of the psychotherapist Daniel Stern. Stern was perhaps best known for his mother-infant studies and the ways in which those studies revealed the interpersonal nature of very early life, challenging orthodox positions about primary states of undifferentiation or narcissism (Stern 1985). In Stern's final published work, however, he expanded his view to reflect upon what he called "vitality forms," or the ways in which "dynamic forms of vitality" are among the "most fundamental of all felt experience" (2010, 3). For Stern, movement provides the primary sense of aliveness, or what Winnicott termed "going on being" (2010, 4; Winnicott 2005 [1971]).

Vitality is an aspect of experience "hidden in plain view," and vital movement has largely been left by the wayside in psychoanalytic approaches emphasizing "linguistically carried psychoanalytic meanings" (Stern 2010, 39). Stern asks, rhetorically, why the "word, the symbolic, was given such a remarkably elevated and protected status . . . and why were movement-related therapies split off from talking therapies for so long?" (2010, 120). As we have seen, part of the answer for this question had to do with the attempt to keep sexuality out of the analytic encounter (if not, of course, from analysis altogether) in order to protect the detached objectivity of the analyst and the scientific credibility of the movement. But the effect of this segregation is an underappreciation for how dynamic movement underlies all psychic life, including the development and expression of emotions, body concepts, language, intention, and cognition (Stern 2010, 19–21). All "psychological" events are inextricably linked with movement dynamics; as Stern puts it, "the mind is indeed embodied, and motion is key" (Stern 2010, 20). The psyche is, among other things, a body in motion: sadness rippling through causing a folding of the cervical spine and a bending forward in the chest, fear or desire intertwined with distinct patterns of breathing—all of these deeply communicative and intersubjective acts that are interpreted by other bodies spontaneously and non-discursively. Vitality, for Stern, is the process by which the embodied mind integrates internal and external events, subjective experiences, and phenomenal realities. For Stern, vitality is a gestalt or emergent property of action, and thereby the emphasis on vitality provides resistance to linguistic, mental, or neurological reductionism.

As an example of vitality forms, Stern describes how nuances of authenticity within interpersonal encounters can be differentiated based on specific vitality dynamics involving gestures, physical positions, muscular tonicity, and voice, alongside of language use. Vitality forms are most often received or introjected at a level below conscious awareness, implying that they are less susceptible to retrieval within an analytic session. Nevertheless, vitality forms are essential for understanding the pathways of identification or introjection—the ways in which a "charged other" occupies positions in our psychic life through their specific vitality forms: i.e., the way a head is tossed back in laughter or eyes rolled in dismissal, or the subtle somatic postures attending withdrawal, punishment, or seduction (Stern 2010, 145). For Stern, it is "forms of vitality as these relate to specific actions, feelings, attitudes, reactions . . . that are internalized and identified with" (2010, 144). Dynamic forms of vitality, therefore, are another path for psychotherapy to access non-conscious past experiences including what Stern calls the "implicit relational knowing" on which the narrative self is built (Stern 2010, 11 & 13).

Stern's account of vitality forms corrects a significant imbalance in the mainstream of psychoanalysis, which has largely carried forward Freud's split between body and mind and his official leeriness towards embodiment. Yet Stern's account suffers from significant limitations as well. First, although his account opens the door to seeing vital movement as a lodestar for "going on being," Stern replicates Freud's emphasis on adaptation to reality at the expense of emergence or creative flow. Vitality dynamics, on his reading, are crucial for "fitting a living organism into the world it encounters" (Stern 2010, 15). Moreover, from the perspective of this essay, Stern seemed unable or unwilling to extend his analysis of movement dynamics beyond the "high" culture of music, theater, and dance. He does not mention sport or athletic performance—or play, for that matter. More problematically, he does not refer to eros, barely mentions desire, and dismisses entirely the role of the drives in human motivation. As he puts it, the "dynamic terminology within psychoanalysis . . . forces being countered, blocked, displaced . . . is still with us as metaphors, but no longer as a scientific explanation" (Stern 2010, 34). If this is true, so much the worse for science—and for any scientific account of vital movement—since it can only fail to theorize the wishes or desires expressed, or countered, within movement.[5] Without an account of the drives, it is hard to explain or explore the full dynamics of vitality, especially as it might concern sport. It was the genius of Freud to see that the wishes of childhood *are* the wishes of the adult, albeit in altered or alienated form. As Brown puts it, "only a wish . . . can possibly set our psychic apparatus in motion" (1959, 8). Professional athletes are often said to be playing a "child's game," but more importantly they are reminders that we are all still playing a child's game—or at least a game to which children are more attuned.

I argue here that the "child's game" at the heart of sports—almost completely concealed by its other determinations—is a powerful, if largely unconscious, source of the fascination with athletic performance (for participants and observers), insofar as it holds space for repressed or forsaken desires for erotic embodied enjoyment. In making this somewhat absurd claim, I follow the lead of Norman O. Brown, for whom childhood wishes are the material not only of adult neuroses but of emancipated forms of life. The fact that this is denied reflects what Brown sees as the core observation of the "esoteric" Freud, i.e that neurosis is a general condition of the species, rather than an affliction of specific individuals. The key word in this analytic is repression, a term that unfortunately has fallen out of favor in relational accounts of psychoanalysis such as Stern's. As Brown states, the "Freudian revolution" begins with the radical idea that "the essence of society is repression of the individual, and the essence of the individual is repression of himself" (1959, 3). The concept of repression, in turn, implies the central role that desire plays within human life; the "essence of man" consists of "desiring" and not contemplation or cognition (Brown 1959, 7). Specifically, it is erotic desire—for union with self, other and world—that drives the species, a radical idea obscured by the utilitarian way in which Freud articulated the concept of the pleasure principle. Brown begins from Freud's radical account of infantile sexuality, but he argues that the radicalism of this theory is muted when adult sexuality is seen as the telos of erotic desire.

Young children, for Brown, are unrepressed, because they live in a space of "privileged irresponsibility" (1959, 25).[6] Freed from the demands of the reality principle, infants and young children can experience a blossoming of essential desires and moments of omnipotent indulgence in pleasure suspended from the dictates of social necessity. Freud loads the interpretive deck by calling this energy "sexual," but as Brown argues, "Freud's definition of the sexual instinct shows that he means something very general. It is the energy or desire with which the human being pursues pleasure [and …] he attributed the capacity of yielding such pleasure (an erotogenic quality, he calls it) to all parts of the surface of the human body and also to the internal organs" (1959, 26). From this perspective, it is clear that "infants have a sexual life [and] even that sex in this sense is their chief aim" (Brown 1959, 26). Infants, in fact, "have a richer sexual life than adults" (Brown 1959, 26). The delight made possible by the suspension from the reality principle is polymorphously perverse, i.e., many-formed or multi-sided: "delight in the active life of all the human body . . . includ[ing] the pleasure of touching, of seeing, of muscular activity, and even the passion for pain" (Brown 1959, 30). For Brown, there is no difference between Freud's theory of infantile sexuality and William Blake's ecstatic notion that "Energy is the only life, and is from the Body . . . Energy is Eternal Delight" (Brown 1959, 31). Erotic desire is the delight of the body in its plastic capacities to connect with itself in cooperation with the environment.

Over the course of early life, however, the loose and broad erotic desire of infants quickly becomes channeled into existing patterns of adult sexuality, reflecting a capitulation of the pleasure principle and the progressive narrowing of erotic enjoyment. Erotic energy becomes purpose driven, as opposed to a marker of freedom. The pleasurable life activity of the young child is "narrowed in range, concentrated on a particular (genital) organ, and subordinated to an aim derived not from the pleasure principle but from the reality-principle" (Brown 1959, 27). This reflects a tyrannical organization of desire, and the discarded elements of eros are thereby forced underground. Yet the desire for freedom—for joyful, purposeless activity—persists in the unconscious. The unconscious holds the essence of our being and is "secretly faithful to the principle of pleasure or, as Blake calls it, delight" (Brown 1959, 31). Although parental discipline, religious instruction, and cultural exaltations of the life of reason or sublimation inspire docility, in the unconscious we are "unconvinced, and therefore neurotic. [We] remain unconvinced because in infancy [we] tasted the fruit of the tree of life, and know that it is good, and never forget" (Brown 1959, 31).

Freud, as Brown notes, articulated this radical theory of human sexuality but did not see it as having any implications for re-writing the repressive script of the reality principle. Freud simply noted that "childhood remains man's indestructible goal," but argued that it is an unachievable goal in a tragic world where necessity will always outweigh desire (Brown 1959, 32). Freud's acceptance of repression marks the whole subsequent course of psychoanalytic theory and practice, with few exceptions. It is reflected in the accepted hierarchies between body and mind, primary and secondary processes, and immature vs. mature functioning. Stern, for example, in his discussion of the capacities for synesthesia—or the nondifferentiated enjoyment of the senses—refers to this as a "primitive sensibility" that only occurs at the "beginning of life" (2010, 35). He does not see these "cross-modal capacities" of infants as anything but relics of a lost past—a loss that is repeated with every new child (Stern 2010, 35). For Brown, however, they represent possibilities for the expression of a rich erotic life that remain latent in the human body and hence stored in the unconscious. Only a "divine naivete" takes these latent wishes as real, whereas orthodox psychoanalysis "bows down before the reality principle," which is based on desexualization (Brown 1966, 250).

Sublimation of synesthesic capacities for experience is a fragmentation of desire and of the possibilities for human life, but even sublimations are "substitute gratifications" that serve as storage containers for the "immortal desires of the human heart" (Brown 1959, 13). The hidden aim of sublimation is the "progressive discovery of the lost body of childhood" (Brown 1959, 170), and the aim of psychoanalysis—"still unfulfilled, and still only half-conscious"—is to overcome the state of self-alienation that fragments the senses, isolates spirit from body, and makes of adult life a rather dull affair of (re)production (Brown 1959, 158). The lost plentitude of synesthesia as a kind of polymorphous perversity is a misplaced inheritance susceptible to recovery. Or, as Brown might put it to Stern: who are you calling a "primitive"?

Brown follows the romantics, but he does not romanticize childhood as such, since the erotic desire set loose at that time "fails to reach the objective world" or alter the reality principle (1959, 39). Only when adult work becomes play, or when adult sexuality reconnects to its deeper roots, can the spontaneous spirit of embodied exploration come to fruition in a less repressive society. I argue that this is a theoretical vantage point that enables us to better understand the fascination and fanaticism surrounding sports—the ever-growing intensity of attachment, identification, and idealization of athletic performance across a variety of forms. Fanatics ("fans") are often seen as immature and delusional, but this can also be seen as testimony to the fact that the delusions of maturity or adulthood offer no effective consolation for the spurned longings of the species. The fascination with sport, as entangled as it is with exclusive or repressive logics, cannot be completely divorced from the experience of vital, dynamic movement, in which the plastic capacities of a body "fitted for many things" are stretched to the limits of existing imagination (Spinoza 1954, 277). Sport engages and enlivens the imagination, and the imagination is the means of tapping into the capacity for plasaticity— for expansion beyond what is presently possible. Imagination in this sense is better than the use of "fantasy," since the latter term implies that the esemplastic visions of wholeness are mere illusions or escapes from reality, as opposed to an attempt to resist the reality principle and imagine different forms of life. The reminders of erotic potential are clearly part of the appeal of sports, and yet sport—as play in the objective world—is still unconscious of itself, and hence still unattuned to its motivational headwaters.

The body fitted for many things, however, is not merely *a body*, because erotic embodied experience is a simultaneous refusal of "all the dualisms," including the mind-body dualism (Brown 1959, 53). As Brown puts it, eros is not merely about the free play of the individual body, but of a body in relation to a world that is no longer seen as *outside* (Brown 1959, 44). Erotic desire is "fundamentally a desire for union," and the polymorphous perverse body is a vehicle for connection and not merely a more organized arrangement of sinews and nerves, heart and lungs. There is a politics of physiology (Brown 1966, 225): a struggle over how we see the body, understand its potential, and its permeability—which is primarily carried out with metaphor. Poets, for Brown as for Shelley, are still the unacknowledged legislators of the world. What Brown calls "love's body" is a metaphor for the mystic body of erotic union, which polymorphous perversity prepares because it opens the sensorial and expressive capacities of the soma in ways that the metaphors of "skin-encapsulated egos" or "robots with nervous systems" fail to do. Here Brown resuscitates Freud's account of primary narcissism, as representing a moment of a full (embodied) ego feeling that embraced the entire world (1966, 45). Narcissism is a metaphor of blurred boundaries reflecting a broader truth of unrepressed sensuality.

Although contemporary sport may be said to idealize the body, it does not yet understand the body as such. The literal body is exceeded by the body as erotic energy. To be embodied is to be plastic, pliable, and in process; "the body" is a metaphor ("everything is symbolic") and the imagination is esemplastic (Brown 1966, 225–26). The imagination reaches for union, and it reaches with the body. Imagination sets the intention (from the Latin *intendere*: to stretch or extend), and imagination (as opposed to fantasy) is rooted in unconscious longings that remain repressed and unknown.

CONCLUSION: SPORT AND PSYCHOANALYSIS RECONCILED, AND FOR RECONCILIATION

If the arguments above sounded absurd, it is because they are (from the Latin *absurdus,* meaning discordant or out of tune). They fly in the face of common sense and sophisticated sense alike, and they sit uneasily next to my own more sober reflections on the way that sport serves as a vehicle for racialized fantasy, consumer capitalism, and patriarchal longings for control and mastery. Yet there is something else within sport that is irreducible to these logics. In short, capitalism does not need sport to function, even as it attempts to use the power of sport to conceal or compensate for the ravages of monopolistic power and the disciplinary regimes of market "rationality." Similarily, while racial and patriarchal fantasies surround and imbue sport, they cannot exhaust the latter's meaning. Insofar as these logics are perpetuated through sport, it is because they are preying upon a power that sport has to fascinate (from the Latin *fascinum*, spell or witchcraft). As described above, this is a power for connection and transformation—for plasticity—that limns the repressed experience of human longing for both a self and a world that enable perpetual (re)creation—a world in which we are all always playing, even while at "work."

In tracing this power, it seems we must follow Freud into the tricky subject matter of infantile sexuality, while understanding the latter in the broader terms described by poets and mythologists. As Brown argued, "psychoanalysis stands or falls on the expansion of the idea of sexuality to comprehend the entire life of the human body" (1966, 126). Sexuality is erotic play, not the other way around. And play is a transforming spirit: it is not about a paradise lost but the paradise that is already here, under the surface of life. Psychoanalysis above all rests on the ideas of childhood sexuality and the unconscious, and their intertwinement. Combined they reveal that sport is not yet conscious to itself, and that the work of making conscious the unexpressed longings for erotic union between self, other, and world—for ending "all the dualisms"—is a labor of the next century of psychoanalysts, poets and sportsmen and women. Movement and metaphor (embodiment and imagination) conjoined; or: sport and poetry reconciled, and fighting together on the same side of the culture war against repression.

NOTES

1. Although they do raise the question of the relationship between identifications and vitality ("what vital identifications and deserves are served by engagement with sport") as well as the possibility that adult play is "undervalued by psychoanalysis."

2. Robert Wälder (1936) was the first to introduce the concept of overdetermination to psychoanalysis. He argued that psychic acts emerge from separate domains with their unique pressures: instinct, the world, the superego, and the repetition compulsion.

3. See Sella for an excellent summary of the psychoanalytic view of the body across the various schools of psychoanalytic thinking (2018, 17–18).

4. There are moments, of course, where Freud's genius outstrips his narrowmindedness; for instance, where he discusses the allo-plastic possibilities of playfulness: "every child at play behaves like a creative writer, in that he creates a world of his own, or rather re-arranges the things of the world in a new way that pleases him" (1908, 42 cited in Holowchak 2011, 698).

5. Stern displays a bit of bad faith here, when he recounts a vital movement encounter between a mother and a child. The mother was raised in a "macho culture" (Stern's words) and she thereby models a dialectics of refusal, escalation, concession, and contempt to her child, to which Stern is certainly not neutral. Stern argues that this is a scene of negotiating the authenticity of desire, but he leaves the latter idea as a blank space in his argument. Why would desire pursue openness, reconciliation, assertion, and compassion as opposed to refusal, escalation, concession, and contempt, if each of these carries their own identifiable vitality form?

6. Of course, children also live in a space of radical vulnerability and dependency, and as such are subject to the stings of abuse, neglect and disregard. Brown does not tarry with these facts, except insofar as the he argues that they serve as the basis by which social authorities "extract submission" from individual subjects (1959, 25).

BIBLIOGRAPHY

Adorno, Theodor. 1951 (2010). *Minima Moralia: Reflections from Damaged Life*. London: Verso.

Brown, Norman O. 1959. *Life Against Death: The Psychoanalytical Meaning of History*. Middletown, CT: Wesleyan University Press.

Brown, Norman O. 1966. *Love's Body*. Berkeley, CA: University of California Press.

Elisha, Perrin. 2010. *The Conscious Body: A Psychoanalytic Exploration of the Body in Therapy*. New York: American Psychological Association.

Freud, Sigmund. 1908 (2001). "Creative Writers and Daydreaming." *The Standard Edition of the Complete Psychological Works, Volume IX*. Edited by James Strachey. London: Vintage Publishing.

Freud, Sigmund. 2011. *Three Essays on the Theory of Sexuality.* Eastford, CT: Martino Fine Books.

Greif, Don. 2010. "Revaluing Sports." Psychoanalytic *Perspectives on Intense Involvement with Sports.* London: Routledge.

Hirsh, Irwin and Phillip Blumberg. 2010. "Introduction: On Intense Involvement with Sports." *Psychoanalytic Perspectives on Intense Involvement with Sports.* London: Routledge.

Holowchak, M. Andrew. 2011. "Freud on Play, Games, and Sports Fanaticism." *The Journal of the American Academy of Psychoanalysis and Dynamic Psychiatry*. Vol. 39, No. 4 (December).

Makari, George. 2008. *Revolution in Mind: The Creation of Psychoanalysis*. New York: Harper Collins.

Murphy, Michael. 1992. *The Future of the Body*. New York: TarcherPerigree Publishers.

Reynoso, Joseph S. 2021. "Boston Sucks! A Psychoanalysis of Sport." *Psychoanalysis, Culture & Society*. Vol. 26, 591–607.

Sella, Yorai. 2018. *From Dualism to Oneness in Psychoanalysis: A Zen Perspective on the Body-Mind Question.* London: Routlege.

Spinoza, Benedict de. 1954. *Ethics: Preceded by an Improvement of the Understanding*. New York: Hafner Publishing Company.
Stern, Daniel. 1985. *The Interpersonal World of the Infant*. New York: Basic Books.
Stern, Daniel. 2010. *Forms of Vitality: Exploring Dynamic Experience in Psychology and the Arts*. New York: Oxford University Press.
Wälder, Robert, 1936. "The principle of multiple function: observations on over-determination." The Psychoanalytic Quarterly. Vol. 5, 45–62.
Winnicott, D.W. 1971. 2005. *Playing and Reality*. London: Routledge.

Chapter 2

The Athletic Body

A Lacanian Perspective

Hub Zwart

INTRODUCTION

While psychoanalysis traditionally focused on erotic bodies, multiple pathways of reflection have developed towards considering the vicissitudes of human bodies in other practices such as food intake or sport (*panem et circenses* if you like)—although these practices have an erotic dimension in their own right—while being politically relevant as well. Although other, e.g., phenomenological, approaches to sport received more emphasis during recent decades, and while the *philosophy of sport* has evolved into a full–fledged area of academic activity, psychoanalysis, notably Lacanian psychoanalysis, has something to say about it as well. Psychoanalysis is first and foremost a *clinical* practice, its "bed" (κλῖνη) being the famous couch, so that bodily passivity seems a precondition for analysis as a "talking cure"—in contrast with many forms of sports, which are physical and often are practiced in silence. Still, much is being *said* about sport, and psychoanalysis has something to add, not only about the discourse on sport, but also about the realities of sportive activities, wavering between the strive for *jouissance* and the strive for control, between pushing one's boundaries, and seeking one's balance.

My point of departure will be the three *registers* of bodily experience developed by Lacan in the course of his oeuvre, namely the *real*, the *imaginary*, and the *symbolic* body. After introducing these three dimensions, I will explore their relevance for deliberations and reflections about contemporary sport.

THE REAL, THE IMAGINARY, AND THE SYMBOLIC BODY

Throughout his oeuvre, Lacan develops three axes or registers of bodily experience; three basic ways in which the human body comes to the fore and may be encountered in various practices, including sports: namely, the *real*, the *imaginary*, and the *symbolic* body (Zwart 1998; Zwart 2019). Let me briefly outline what they entail. The *real* body is initially experienced as a fragmented body: a composite aggregate of organs, fluids, processes, and products. The *imaginary* body, by contrast, refers to the body as a meaningful, imposing, aestheticized *whole*. Now, the body is envisioned in terms of integrity or wholeness and seen as an integrated aesthetic unity. Finally, the *symbolic* body is the body as it emerges in modern technoscientific practices, the body as it is disclosed by technology and science: the body that is measured and quantified with the help of contrivances. In this section, I will explore these three registers or dimensions of human bodily experience somewhat further. Subsequently, I will outline how they are present in sportive practices.

The Real Body

In everyday adult life, we are hardly ever confronted with the real, fragmented body. Rather, the fragmented body ("corps morcelée" in French) is the body as it is experienced by very young children during early stages of development,[1] although we also recognise it in scenes of cannibalism and torture, especially when they are projected into a mythological past, where bodies are literally torn to pieces—e.g., the body of King Pentheus, dismembered by raging Maenads. Later in life, the real body is notably encountered under extreme circumstances, during boundary experiences—e.g., during childbirth, or in the case of serious bodily damage, or when a cancerous growth is suddenly detected. The real body tends to be hidden from view, wrapped in clothes and skin, although it may rise to the surface in the form of sweat, excrements, blood, tumours, etc. Yet, in the current era of technoscience, even blood and excrements are being measured and quantified ("symbolised")—for instance, in the context of microbiome research, focussed on analysing and sequencing human stool. The real body is that which resists efforts towards idealisation and symbolisation. It is unclean rather than clean, damaged rather than unviolated, destitute rather than wholesome, eerie rather than familiar.

The body as a *fragmented* body is played out in a rather provocative manner in Mary Wollstonecraft Shelley's classic novel *Frankenstein*, published in 1818. A science student named Victor Frankenstein (whose mother died during delivery) decides to find out whether deceased human bodies can be brought to life again with the help of experimental science. He visits cemeteries and mortuaries at night, looking for suitable bodily parts, organs, and tissues. From these collected parts, an organic amalgam is composed. Subsequently, by exposing it to high voltage electricity, this aggregate of organs is revivified, and the famous Monster is created, whose distorted torso suddenly starts to breathe and move. In other words, in Mary Shelley's novel, the body emerges as an *aggregate* of raw, semi–autonomous bodily parts (Zwart 2019). Removed from the body, such body parts arouse a particular experience, which Freud refers to as "the uncanny" (1919/1947): a typical ingredient of horror stories.

The Imaginary Body

A first effort to transform the fragmented body into a coherent whole is thematised by Lacan as the mirror experience (Lacan 1966, 93ff.). By recognising their image in a mirror, Lacan argues, building on contemporary psychological research, very young children for the first time learn to see themselves as individuals (literally: *undivided* beings). This "triumph" over fragmentation gives rise to an experience of "jubilation," Lacan contends. Yet, this newly acquired sense of unity is dependent on an external image: the *Gestalt* or *image* of the body as reflected in a mirror (or, before the development of mirrors, by the surface of a pond), and therefore remains highly vulnerable and image–dependent ("imaginary"), like the famous mythological image of Narcissus' body

The imaginary body can also be encountered in works of art, such as ancient Greek and Roman sculptures, or their Baroque or Neo-Classicist equivalents. An artistic rendering of the human body presents it as an integrated unity, as something admirable and whole. Moreover, through various body practices, such as bodybuilding, athletes (male or female) may sculpt their bodies into living works of art, thus mimicking or mirroring examples (either in marble or in the flesh) presented by others. Ancient Greek statues were basically the statues of athletes or gods, which amounted to the same thing—as gods were regarded as athletes and athletes as godlike humans. Moreover, as Lacan explains, statues of human beings, erected alongside major roads in ancient times, conveyed a normative ideal, a moral summons, presenting the athletic body as something to strive for (Lacan 1955–1956/1981, 328). Thus, statues of heroes, emperors, and other exemplary humans spread the ancient bodily gospel of human health, strength, fitness, and wholesomeness. They incorporated an idealised view of what embodied human beings should aspire to become. These statues were erected alongside public roads by way of ethical propaganda. They functioned like "missionaries in stone," whose unspoken sermons were meant to affect the anonymous masses of travellers and passers-by (cf. Sloterdijk 2009, 37ff.).

The idea of human bodily dignity (commanding admiration and respect) was thus carved into stone. Human physical perfection was a result of artistic *sublimation*, psychoanalytically speaking, turning real flesh into idealised marble. It was the celebration of the imaginary body: of a particular (normative) image of what our bodies ideally should look like. Turn thyself into a work of art, through sport and exercise! Ancient statues propagated a basic *idea* of what human bodies essentially *are*—even though there was always a tension between the real, empirical body and these imaginary ideals. Michelangelo's *David*, but also his impressive sculpture *Night* (in the *Sagrestia nuova* in Florence) may stand out as early modern counterparts of idealised male and female athletic bodies.

The beautified body was not only celebrated by pagan (Greco–Roman) artistic representations and their Renaissance or Baroque equivalents, but also by Christian views of embodiment. According to Thomas Aquinas for instance, the human body had once been beautiful and whole, during its state of innocence (*in statu innocentiae*, i.e., in Paradise), but this beautiful work of art, this gift from God, became damaged and corrupted due to the fall from grace (Aquinas 1922, Pars Prima, Q 96–97). And now, it is our duty to restore our body to its state of original splendour, though virtuous exercise. Yet, our earthly frame remains constantly under siege, exposed to corruptive forces, so that its vulnerable wholeness can never be taken for granted. Bodily existence entails a continuous dialectical struggle between good and evil, beauty and obscenity, consolidation and fragmentation.

The Symbolic Body

Modern anatomy, inaugurated by pioneers such as Vesalius (van den Berg 1961) revealed the presence of the real body beneath the idealised, imaginary body. Through dissection, the human body was opened up, so that the various parts and organs were exposed and presented as more or less separate entities. Initially, the *real* exposed interior of the human body must have seemed messy and inchoate. Hard scientific work was required to detect some degree of order in this fluid, fetid chaos. Modern science opened up a new and unprecedented experience of bodily existence, distancing itself, both from the chaotic and uncontrollable *real* body (experienced in early childhood and projected onto a distant, mythological past) and from the idealised and beautified *imaginary* body (reflected in the mirror experience, but also in classical sculpture as we have seen). Science created the *symbolic* body, describable with the help of mathematical, physiological, and biochemical symbols. Indeed, the emergence of the symbolic body is closely related to the rise of modern research practices (Brousse 1997). Now, the human body is measured, for instance in terms of height and weight. Gradually, a plethora of measurement practices have emerged, establishing normal standard values for various bodily functions, such as, oxygen saturation in the blood or systolic and diastolic blood pressure (120/80 mmHg). Outcomes of such measurements are represented with the help of specific *symbols* (kg, lbs, meter, cm, mmHg, and the like). Real blood is symbolised with the help of a small alphabet of symbols (A, B, AB, and O). Fat or skinny bodies can be characterised in terms of weight and height, with the help of the body-mass index (BMI) as an indicator of the general condition of a particular human body. All these numbers, units, symbols, technical terms, and acronyms constitute a symbolic ambiance, a symbolic environment referred to by Lacan as the *symbolic order*. It fosters particular ways of presenting the body, allowing it to emerge in a certain manner.

Various technical instruments have been designed, ranging from standard medical equipment to fairly advance high-tech devices or even self-tracking gadgets, to support this ongoing *symbolisation* of the body, in the context of biomedicine, but also in daily life. Moreover, these symbolic quantifications not only allow us to measure, represent and describe the body. Their purpose is to *enable and justify* effective manipulations and interventions—to reduce blood pressure or improve one's BMI for instance. Symbolisation is a practice of power, enabling and urging us to control our bodies.

THE GARDEN OF EARTHY DELIGHTS

There is an artwork where these three dimensions of bodily existence are brought together in a lively manner, namely, the famous triptych known as *The Garden of Earthly Delights* by Hieronymus Bosch, painted somewhere between 1490 and 1510. This collage of colourful scenes, projected on a triple screen, could be considered a late–medieval cinematic enactment of the ontological struggle over embodiment (Zwart 2019). The left panel is devoted to the idealised, *imaginary* body, depicting Adam and Eve *in statu innocentiae*, as Aquinas phrased it. The right panel, with its horrible scenes of warfare, torture, and prostitution, opens up a sadistic universe, where bodies are spoiled, exploited, pierced, and mutilated, and exposed to dismemberment and fragmentation. The central panel is the most sportive one, depicting the playful body, *homo ludens*, if you like. Here, the integrity of naked human bodies is endangered by various earthly temptations. Interestingly, we also notice the birth of biopower here, in the form of an animal experiment, involving a test tube and a rat, but multiple experiments can be detected on this panel once we begin to look for them. Various pieces of laboratory equipment, such as glass tubes and distillation vessels, can be discerned: a foreboding of the imminent *symbolisation* of the human body through technoscientific experimentation. Let me now explore the relevance of these three registers of bodily existence for sport, starting with the imaginary body.

THE IMAGINARY BODY AND THE OLYMPIC RENAISSANCE

The first modern Olympic Games took place in Athens in 1896, envisioned as an athletic renaissance: a rebirth of an ancient physical practice. Pierre de Coubertin, founder of the *Comité pour la Propagation des Exercices Physiques* in 1888, is considered as the visionary behind this revival, although teamwork was important. The plan to revive the Olympic Games took concrete shape during a conference in 1894 at the Sorbonne University in Paris. And although the subsequent Games in 1900 and 1904 still had some difficulty attracting sufficient international attention, 1896 is considered the heroic starting point of a periodic event that has become an indispensable part of the theatre of global sports.

Already in ancient Greece, Olympic Games were more than merely sport events. As religious festivities, they were *total works of art*. An Olympic Game was a *Gesamtkunstwerk*. It was a visual event (a spectacle) as well as a physical event (involving exercise and movement), but also an acoustic event. Pierre de Coubertin discerned a close relationship between sport and aesthetic practices such as architecture and music. Music had to make an important contribution to Olympic ceremonies, he contended. The Games should realise Wagner's concept of a *Gesamtkunstwerk* in which top achievements in music, dance, architecture, and sports were to join forces. There is an undeniable affinity between the return of Greek tragedy in Wagner's *Festspielhaus* in Bayreuth in 1876 and the return of the Olympic bodily ideal—between Wagner's dramatic and De Coubertin's athletic renaissance (Zwart 2023).

A striking difference between the Olympic Games as we witness them today and their ancient precursor (besides globalization) concerns the participation of women. De Coubertin himself was not in favour of it. His ideal was limited to the glorification of the muscular male body, and, in ancient Greece, Amazons had become a mythical category. They appeared on stage in tragedies (e.g., in *The Maenads* by Euripides), and female athletic bodies were visible as impressive statues, e.g., statues of Diana the Huntress, or on Grecian urns, as Atalanta the runner and wrestler, but these were imaginary models and women did not really physically compete during Olympic Games. In contemporary sports, the female athlete has resurged as a physical reality again, and spectators are impressed and challenged both by men and women, but this is the outcome of a long dialectical struggle.

Charles Baudelaire (1857/1972) already indicated how the dilapidated physique of the human body of the nineteenth century contrasted strongly with the robust, athletic physique of antiquity, also where women were concerned. Greek statues demonstrate how athletic men and women once enjoyed their strong, agile, and healthy bodies, training and caressing their "noble machines" (Baudelaire 1857/1972, 17).[2] In recent times, this has changed, as top performances by men and women are now on display. Athletes such as Penthesilea and Atalanta, who challenged and defeated male athletes, are once again making their appearance and the athletic imperative, the call to awaken physically, emphatically addresses both genders. As indicated, Wagner's music festival in Bayreuth was a decisive source of inspiration for the Olympic idea: it was its paradigm as it were,[3] also because characters like Siegmund, Siegfried, and Brunhild were top athletes.

The link between music and physical exercise has a long history. Plato's academy was established in a sports park and in *Republic* the formative role of physical exercise and music was emphasised. Top athletes and virtuosos had in common that, thanks to practices and self–edification, even unimaginable top performances were drawn within the domain of the possible. Sport and music were seen as educators, harmonising body and soul. For Plato, the ideal state was both a gymnasium and a symphony. Sport and music were considered an effective instrument for maintaining individual balance and public order.

Currently, the imaginary athletic body is presented and celebrated via commercials, again combining visual techniques with acoustics. They present the athletic body as a source of inspiration, something to imitate. Larger than life images of famous, iconic players, disseminated via social media and billboards, indicate how such icons function as normative mirrors. This is what many youngsters aspire to become. An iconic player apparently has "something" (referred to by Lacan as the *object a*) which youngsters also would like to have. Although it is difficult to tell what this something, this *must have*, exactly is. More often than not, it presents itself as a sense of deprivation or lack. And yet, "One day, this will be me," although something is missing as yet. Note that the object of identification is not a *real* person (facing financial troubles, health problems, relational crises, conflicts of interests, and other forms of malaise). The object of identification is an imaginary icon, an arte fact or construct, produced and disseminated by mass media and social media.

Lacan presented the first version of his famous paper on the mirror stage in 1936, during the Congress of the *International Psychoanalytical Association* in Marienbad. His contribution was a failure. He was not allowed sufficient time and forgot to submit his text, so that the original version of his paper was not included in the proceedings and was lost. From Marienbad, he travelled to Berlin to spectate on the Olympic Games, so as to witness the resurgence of the imaginary body, both spectacular and disconcerting. The 1936 Olympic Games, organised by National Socialism, are often seen as the beginning of the politization of sport, in close combination with its erotization. Indeed, a particular bodily ideal was enacted. In aesthetical terms, National Socialism staged a massive celebration of the imaginary body as "noble machines"—a bodily ideal exemplified by the work of sculpturer Arno Breker (1900–1991), who specialised in producing larger than life statues of male and female athletes, e.g., the statue *Die Partei* ("the Party") depicting a formidable male athlete, and *Die Siegering* ("the female champion," depicting a female body).[4]

Iconic athletes are typically seen from a distance, while proximity always entails a risk, because bodies close by tend to become too real. The modern stadium and the ancient amphitheatre were surrounded by walls, like cities inside a city. Walls were important, defining the place where certain rules applied. Initially, there was no amphitheatre. The competition between rivals took place outside the city walls, preferably in front of the walls, so that the audience (the non–combatants), situated upon those walls, could follow the course of events. In literary studies, this device, viewing the game from the walls, is known as *teichoscopy*: watching the rival armies or competing teams below.

This topology ("teichoscopy") can be found in Homer's *Iliad*, Book III, for instance, where Helen, situated on top of the wall (near the Skaian gates, Homer adds) follows the Trojans, playing a home game as it were, defending their city against the Achaeans, as Homer calls the invading Greek coalition. Like a commentator, Helen identifies the key players of the "other side," unbeknownst to the Trojan spectators on the wall: "that's Agamemnon, that's Odysseus, that's Ajax . . . ," etc. (Meeuwsen and Zwart 2023). After this scene, the duel commences, with both armies imploring Zeus and other gods to support them. In modern stadiums, the basic topology is still recognisable, I would argue, while other imaginary items can be discerned as well—e.g., the cup which the competing teams aspire to win, in the shape of a uterus.

SPORT AND THE SYMBOLISATION OF THE BODY

The symbolic is driven by a completely different logic compared to the imaginary body. Whereas the imaginary strives for an aesthetically compelling wholeness, as we have seen, so that even difference (e.g., the difference between the feminine and the masculine) is seen as complementarity, contributing to unity in the end, the symbolic relies on a logic of dichotomies: presence or absence, 1 or 0, prohibited or allowed, included or excluded. The symbolic becomes important in sport, first of all, in the form of basic rules, or rather: basic laws or prohibitions, such as the prohibition for soccer players to touch the ball with their hands, a prohibition from which only the goalkeeper is exempted (Meeuwsen and Zwart 2023). Such defining prohibitions constitute a space where a particular sportive practice can emerge and evolve. The rule is not visible directly, but rather becomes visible *indirectly*, namely through a punishable violation, when a referee intervenes, or fails to do so. In many ways, the virtuosity of professional soccer players compensates the prohibition against the use of their hands. It is not in spite of but *because of* this prohibition that soccer can evolve and thrive.

Another example of a prohibition is the rule excluding women from participating in soccer until quite recently. We already mentioned such a prohibition in the context of the Olympic Games. De Coubertin considered participation of women *impractical*, *uninteresting*, *unaesthetic*, and *inappropriate*, four pre–fixes allegedly justifying a bar, a No against participation of girls and women in sports. Women participated in soccer from the very outset, however, and were actively banned as participants in the course of the Twentieth Century, especially after the Second World War, when soccer evolved into big business, so that the masculinity of soccer may well be a symptom of a relatively recent process, namely commercialisation, while the recent resurgence of women's soccer can be seen as a return of the repressed, the return of the ancient Amazons if you like.

Weight classes likewise perform a symbolic role, entailing practices of inclusion and exclusion. Prior to the competition, the athlete's body (e.g., in martial sports) is weighed with the help of a scale. This is a first example of what was already referred to as *symbolisation*—the *real* body is subjected to quantification with the help of contrivances so as to determine whether or not participation is allowed (in accordance with the logic of binary thinking: yes or no). The outcome is determined with the help of symbols (e.g., kg or lbs).

Symbolisation (the emergence of the symbolic body in sport) is closely entangled with the scientific and industrial revolution. It is no coincidence that modern sports emerged in England, homeland of the industrial revolution par excellence (Brousse 1997). It was here that local folkish sportive practices were replaced by modern sports. The rise of modern sports is closely entangled with the arrival of machines and mechanised practices of mobility. Besides precision instruments for timekeeping, modern sports require a technoscientific understanding of bodily functioning. As Jacques Lacan explains in *Écrits* (1966), modern labour requires the availability of precision instruments for time management. Indeed, the pendulum clock invented by Christiaan Huygens in 1656 not only enabled the symbolisation of the real through physics research, but also made it possible to define and monitor working hours independently from natural phenomena, such as dawn and dusk: a form of "liberation," and an important turning point in the shift from quality (craftmanship) to quantity (machine-labour). Since then, labourers are put to work in a universe of discipline and precision (Lacan 1966, p. 313). Similar forms of precision measurement enabled the development of modern sports in industrialising countries.

In contemporary sports (in professional sports but also in leisure sports) a plethora of practices of symbolisation has proliferated. Athletes are not only monitored in terms of height and weight, but also in terms of heart rate and other quantifiable indicators. Amateurs use self–tracking devices to assess their performance. In short, in Lacanian terms, contemporary sport practices are under the sway of the symbolic. This also applies to the normative dimension. Metrics are used to contain doping use, while shifting views on gender (aspiring to move away from traditional binary conceptions) unleash normative debates on inclusion and exclusion. Yet, in the era of artificial intelligence and informatics, the symbolic is subject to a radical mutation, also in sport practices, due to the emergence of what Lacan referred to as *gadgets*.

Gadgets

Although self–monitoring and self–recording have been practiced since ancient times, in the era of wearable devices and sensor-saturated environments, a self–tracking culture has gained momentum that is increasingly bent on quantification (Lupton 2016). Indeed, the combination of digital devices and personalised health information has given rise to the emergence of a "quantified" Self (Lupton 2016). Self-knowledge is increasingly articulated in terms of measurements and numbers, so that bio–citizens are expected to measure and monitor their bodies and their everyday lifeworld in real time, continuously and automatically. More than anywhere else, perhaps, this development is visible in sport.

Personal data are never purely personal. Not only because, at least potentially, they may become available to others (developers of devices, data–mining companies, government agencies, and the like [Lupton 2016, 4]), but also because, for these measurements to make sense, they must be compared to transpersonal standards and performance levels, to sociocultural expectations, indeed: to a digital version of the superego, exposing the self-tracking bio–citizen to continuous surveillance and criticism (Zwart 2017). Lifestyle gadgets easily become a personalised panopticon, urging individuals to adapt themselves to societal expectations in their daily private lives. Their sportive performance is compared with the performance of peers (in terms of age and gender).

During the academic year 1969–1970, Jacques Lacan presented his famous *Seminar XVII*. Marxism was in the air, adopted by Maoist students and many of their teachers, arguing that the global proletariat should gain political control. Many considered psychoanalysis a bourgeois practice, focussing on affluent bourgeois families, using iconic gymnasium course materials (Greek tragedy, notably Oedipus) as frames of reference.

For Lacan, who himself came from a bourgeois catholic background, the traditional Marxist aim of establishing a proletarian dictatorship, eventually a communist society, was a questionable objective. Maoists, he argued, fail to notice that something has changed: a transition or mutation *within the symbolic order as such*, which outdated the traditional Marxist view on technology (Lacan 1991, 207). What struck him as a distinctive feature of Maoism was the emphasis on handbook knowledge, provided by "manuals," exemplifying the manual knowledge of the exploited. Lacan saw Mao's red booklet as a prototypical political manual for producing revolutions. Yet, he argued, something completely new has emerged in our world, little things called "gadgets," in which technoscience now objectifies itself—entities that are entirely forged by science. And now the question is whether in such a high–tech world, completely under the sway of information technologies, manual know–how can still carry sufficient weight to count as a subversive factor (Lacan 1991, 174). Manuals were written in order to operate machines, but for Lacan gadgets exemplify a completely new type of machine, involving brain work, information science, robotics, and cybernetics, rather than manual labour.

Gadgets, as an unprecedented technological phenomenon sui generis, not only poses a challenge to Marxism, but to Freudian psychoanalysis as well. Freud had famously claimed that (contrary to fear, which is object-directed) "anxiety" is without an object. Lacan now disagrees with this and claims that anxiety is instilled precisely by these little interconnected objects, which he refers to objects *a*, tending towards invisibility (*Verborgenheit*), but pervasive and omnipresent (Lacan 1991, 172 & 216), putting us under constant surveillance, and therefore generating anxiety. Big Brother is watching us. The imperative of this new symbolic order, generated by gadgets is: "Work harder!," but at the same time: "Enjoy life to the full!," "Never enough!"

These gadgets, together with their normative summons—Work harder! Enjoy life! Be healthy! Never enough!—have pervaded the practice of sport, both on a professional level and in the realm of leisure sports. Whether practitioners are running, jogging, hiking, or cycling, many of them are equipped with wearables offering real–time monitoring of their performance, comparing it to certain standards. Under the sway of neo–liberalism, everything we do is tainted by competition—even if it means competing with ourselves (relentlessly trying to improve previous performances).

Thus, in the global society of late capitalism, science is producing a new type of entities, functioning as objects of anxiety and desire, as objects *a*: electronic gadgets, pervading the lifeworld with their unnoticeable, vibrating, Hertzian waves, relying on the manipulation of symbols, creating a new, artificial environment. The world is increasingly populated by these gadgets (Lacan 1991, 185), these tiny objects *a*, which we encounter everywhere, pervading the global metropolitan environment, and coming very close, as wearables. These gadgets are objects of desire, offering *jouissance*, but proving unsatisfactory in no time. Sporting consumers want them, they desperately need them, and they desire the latest versions of them, but in the end these electronic commodities exploit and consume their consumers, rather than the other way around, continuously registering and disseminating information, without us being aware of them (Millar 2018; 2021). They produce and circulate data on a massive scale, offering insight into what consumers allegedly want. While allegedly supporting pleasure and freedom, they de facto confront consumers with normalcy standards and societal expectations, informing them that they must work harder on themselves and keep a close watch on themselves, to optimise psychic and somatic functioning as well as postpone the impacts of unhealthy lifestyles (e.g., competitiveness and stress) and ageing.

CONCLUDING COMMENT: THE RUBIALES CASE

This year's women's World Cup soccer tournament highlighted the emancipation of female athletes, notably through their impressive re–participation in soccer, now at a global level. The remarkable performances of national female soccer teams were overshadowed, however, by the scandal that ignited during the celebration of the world cup final, revolving around Luis Rubiales, a former male soccer player, now President of the Royal Spanish Football Federation, who claimed a leading role for himself in the event. A lot of ink has been spilled, both in newspapers and on social media, and my aim here is not to repeat what has been said by many others, but rather to outline, from a psychoanalytical perspective, why this event generated such an impact, drawing attention away from the Cup Final itself.

The scandal consisted of three events. First of all, in front of high–level global media attention, for all the world to see, Rubiales kissed the Spanish midfielder Jennifer Hermoso on her lips during the medal presentation: the central event as it were, sparking the initial outrage. Already during the match, however, Rubiales could be seen demonstrating his enthusiasm and arousal by grabbing his crotch while standing in the VIP box near Spanish Queen Letizia and her 16–year old daughter Infanta Sofia. Finally, shortly after the game, Rubiales had entered the field, where he lifted player Athenea del Castillo over his shoulder. Pictures of this scene were quickly added to the file.

How to assess these events, revolving around the athletic female body, from a psychoanalytic perspective? First of all, psychoanalytically speaking, the first scene indicates the sway of the symbolic. We have seen how the exclusion of women had turned male soccer (notably professional male soccer, performed as a global media event and involving astronomic salaries) into an exclusively male affair, a celebration of masculinity, if you like. President Rubiales here functions as the proverbial alpha male, representing patriarchy while dominating not only women but also the other males. In history, such father figures could claim ownership of women (e.g., phenomena such as the harem, the *ius primus noctis*, etc.). Rubiales kissed Hermoso not on her cheek or forehead, but straight on her lips—not at all an innocent gesture, but rather a gesture which carries a meaning: I still dominate you; I still own you; you may have come this far, but patriarchy, represented by me, is still in place; and I will remind you of that, right here and now.

The crotch scene is different and is played out in a different register. Here, Rubiales enacts a gesture of regression. While being positioned among the VIPs, including some aristocratic VIPs, standing upon a privileged part of the walls as it were, Rubiales enacts the resurgence of the *real*, brutal body, the body of hooligans, the body of bad taste: provocative, abominable, and rude, allegedly untamed, revolving around a phallic protrusion. This gesture likewise carries a message, something like . . . *I may have made my way up to the VIPs, wearing a smart expensive suit, but, in reality, I am still one of the guys. The hooligan in me has never been extinguished, and I openly demonstrate my sheer physical arousal.*

The third scene is different again. Here, the imaginary body comes into play. Images of Rubiales lifting Athenea del Castillo are reminiscent of Baroque or Mannerist sculptures, for instance, sculptures depicting a famous classical scene, the rape of the Sabine Virgins. After a competitive event between two cities, euphoric Roman athletes suddenly begin to grab and lift young Sabine women, a scene which became a beloved theme for sculpturers, particularly during the Mannerist era, with its predilection for powerful, muscular, wrestling male and female bodies (Zwart 2020).

In other words, these three events demonstrate President Rubiales's flawed attempt to reaffirm male superiority in the face of female athletic emancipation, played out along three different dimensions of bodily experience.

CONCLUSION

After this short comment on a recent symptomatic event, let me arrive at my conclusion. The aim of my contribution was to explore how Lacan's three registers of embodiment allow us to come to terms with the phenomenon of sport, in the past and in the present, while at the same time using this exercise to deepen and update our understanding of the real, the imaginary, and the symbolic body, as envisioned by Lacan. Let me now briefly summarise the results.

The *imaginary* body, to begin with, is enacted in sport as a *spectacle*. From the perspective of the spectator, positioned at a distance (teichoscopy), sport entails an *exhibition of spectacular bodies*. There is an element of continuity in the breath-taking movements of athletes, be it sprinters, high jumpers, or soccer players, and Luis Rubiales' gesture of lifting such a body, attempting to join the athletic ballet as it were, albeit after the symbolic whistle had sounded, turning his gesture into a transgression. A dialectic of desire emerges between the fabulous body on the one hand and the spectator's fascinated gaze on the other. Lacan used a short-hand formula for this dialectic, involving a fascinated subject (*$*, the spectator, somewhere in the audience) and the "lost object of desire" (the object *a*), suddenly re-emerging (miraculously, almost) right in front of the subject's eyes, albeit at a distance (although optical instruments may be used to enhance the spectator's voyeuristic gaze):

$ ◊ *a*

The athletic body seems to *have* something (seems to have "it"), or even seems to *be* "it," seems to embody "it," although it is difficult to articulate exactly what this "it" entails. It is captured or suggested by the image (be it a mannerist sculpture or a picture going viral on social media).

Lacan discusses the spectacular exhibition of bodies notably in the context of the Baroque Church as a spiritual Gesamtkunstwerk (Lacan 1975). In fact, psychoanalysis points to a topological congruency between the Baroque church and the sport stadium, although at first glance these two locations may seem incomparably different. In both localities, bodies are exhibited under exceptional circumstances: while being exposed to dramatic challenges, be it torture (the Baroque church) or the athletic track (the stadium). Both martyrs and top athletes are depicted as if experiencing unique mixtures of suffering and *jouissance*. To some extent, Saints were athletes (athletes of endurance, for instance). For Lacan, the Roman world was a world of builders, of masons and architects, erecting amphitheatres but also enormous baths, as localities of bodily pleasure. Christianity put an end to all this, but the Baroque church is the return of the repressed. If the Roman world (enamoured with exhibited bodies) is the first moment, and Christianity its antithetical negation, then both the Baroque church and the Olympic stadium constitute the negation of this negation.

The *symbolic* body involves a rather different stance. We have seen, for instance, how the symbolic aims to *symbolise* the tantalising "it" with the help of measurements. In the case of two athletes—say, two sprinters—the competition ends with a minimal difference, suggesting nonetheless that one of them *has* something, is endowed with something, which is decisive and which other competitors lack. A slight but nonetheless measurable difference allows us to differentiate between winner and losers. A minimal difference may also determine whether a ball is *in* or *out* (e.g., in professional tennis), and the symbolic gap between these two options may be quite significant.

In the case of Luis Rubiales, we noticed something similar. Had he kissed the athlete on her forehead or cheek, he would have stayed within the boundaries of what is considered acceptable, and the event would have passed without notice. The decisive difference, causing the turmoil, was that he kissed the athlete's mouth. This was what, in the end, forced him to step down, literally: to give up his privileged position of power, a position which offered proximity to *real* athletic bodies. He should have respected such boundaries, defining what is allowed and not allowed, but he could not resist the transgression, prompted by desire. But why was he so eager to kiss her mouth? Precisely because it is prohibited, Lacan would argue. We also noticed how the realm of the symbolic has been subject to a radical transformation, due to the emergence of gadgets, not only serving our quest for symbolisation and precision, but also supporting our voyeurism. From now on, everything is seen, no single offence will go unnoticed.

The *real* body, last but not least, is connected with bodily apertures, e.g., the mouths of athletes, the sweat pores of their sweating bodies, etc. Things like sweat and odour are absent from the imaginary body but are now coming to the fore. The real body is also the body of surgery (when surgeons have to repair top athletes' bones and tissues, their Achilles heel for instance). It is the body which resists, or lets us down, but it is also that which is better kept hidden, that which we do not want to be seen, i.e., the obscene (e.g., Luis Rubiales' obscene phallic gestures). In short, while psychoanalysis allows us to elucidate some of the paradoxes in contemporary sport, sport practices provide a fascinating laboratory for psychoanalytical reflection, allowing us to revivify Lacan's conceptual framework.

NOTES

1. This was already pointed out by Freud: "Die Pathologie lehrt uns [Fälle] kennen, in denen uns Teile des eigenen Körpers . . . wie fremd und dem Ich nicht zugehörig erscheinen [Pathology has acquainted us with cases where parts of a person's own body appear as alien and as not belonging to the ego]" (1930/1948, 423–424).

2. J'aime le souvenir de ces époques nues, / Dont Phœbus se plaisait à dorer les statues. / Alors l'homme et la femme en leur agilité / Jouissaient sans mensonge et sans anxiété, / Et, le ciel amoureux leur caressant l'échine, / Exerçaient la santé de leur noble machine [I love the memory of those bare times, / Whose statues Phoebus took pleasure in gilding, / When men and women in their agility / Enjoyed without lies and without anxiety, / While the loving sky caressed their spines, / Exercising the health of their noble machine] (Baudelaire 1857/1972, 17).

3. Alkemeyer notes, "Coubertin designed the Olympic ceremony as a Wagnerian synthesis of the arts. In Wagner's Bayreuth . . . the 'Olympic horizon' had opened to him for the first time before his mental eye" (1996a, 148).

4. Arno Breker was the artist who accompanied Hitler and Speer during their famous visit to Paris. For the importance of his work in the context of the Nazi version of the athletic Renaissance see for instance Maud de Belleroche's memoirs entitled *The Ballet of the Crabs* (De Belleroche 2001).

BIBLIOGRAPHY

Aquinas, Thomas. 1922. *Summa Theologica*. Torino: Marietti.

Berg, Jan Hendrick Van den. 1961. *Het menselijk lichaam: een metabletisch onderzoek 2: Het verlaten lichaam*. Nijkerk: Callenbach.

Brousse, Marie-Helene. 1997. "L'activité sportive à la lumière de la psychanalyse." In *Sport, Psychanalyse et Science*, edited by Marie-Helene Brousse, Francoise Labridy, Andre Terrise, and Marie-Jean Sauret. *Sport, Psychanalyse et Science*. Paris: Presses Universitaires de France.

Freud, Sigmund. 1919 /1947. "Das Unheimliche." In *Gesammelte Werke* XII, 227–268. London: Imago.

Freud, Sigmund. 1930/1948. "Das Unbehagen in der Kultur." In *Gesammelte Werke XIV*, 419–513. London: Imago.

Lacan, Jacques. 1966. *Écrits*. Paris: Éditions du Seuil.

Lacan, Jacques. 1981. *Le séminaire de Jacques Lacan III: Les psychoses, 1955–1956*. Paris: Éditions du Seuil.

Lacan, Jacques. 1991. *Le séminaire XVII: L'envers de la psychanalyse, 1969–1970*. Paris: Éditions du Seuil.

Lacan, Jacques. 1975. *Le séminaire XX: Encore,* 1972–1973. Paris: Éditions du Seuil.

Meeuwsen, Sandra, and Hub Zwart. 2023. "Hands, feet, eyes, and the object *a*: A Lacanian anatomy of football." *Sport, Ethics and Philosophy*. DOI: 10.1080/17511321.2023.2195681

Sloterdijk, Peter. 2009. *Du musst dein Leben ändern: Über Anthropotechnik.* Frankfurt: Suhrkamp.

Wollstonecraft Shelley, Mary. 1818/1968. *Frankenstein; or, the modern Prometheus.* Harmondsworth: Penguin.

Zwart, Hub. 1998. "Medicine, symbolization and the 'Real Body': Lacan's understanding of medical science." *Medicine, Healthcare and Philosophy: A European Journal* 1, no. 2: 107–117.

Zwart, Hub. 2017. "Extimate technologies and techno-cultural discontent: A Lacanian analysis of pervasive gadgets." *Techné: Research in Philosophy and Technology* 21, no. 1: 24–54.

Zwart, Hub. 2019. *Purloined organs: psychoanalysis of transplant organs as objects of desire*. New York: Palgrave Macmillan/Springer Nature.

Zwart, Hub. 2020. *Styles of thinking. Series: Philosophy and Psychology in Dialogue 2*. Berlin/Münster/Zürich: LIT Verlag.

Zwart, Hub. 2023. *Scores of Being: Opera and Dialectics. Series: Philosophy and Psychology in Dialogue 5*. Berlin/Münster/Zürich: LIT Verlag.

PART II

Coaching

Chapter 3

The Racial Melancholia of Aspiring Black NFL Head Coaches

Bradley A. Thomas

Cheng defines racial melancholia as a "theoretical model of identity that provides a critical framework for analyzing the constitutive role that grief plays in racial/ethnic subject-formation" (2001, xi). The grief is unresolved and originates from racial oppression that is an everyday part of lived group experience for Black people in general and aspiring Black NFL head coaches specifically. The nonpathological nature of racial melancholia challenges Freud's (1953) pathologizing conception of melancholia (i.e., mourning without end) as well as centuries-old deficit narratives of Blackness (i.e., drapetomania—a combination of the Greek words "runaway" and "madness"—was a supposed mental health condition given to slaves who wanted to flee their captors by American physician Samuel A. Cartwright in 1851) and embodies their unrelenting endurance of and resistance to racism (Grinage 2019).

Racial melancholia frames the collective and everyday racialization of Black people within White supremacist societies that continue to exclude and oppress them through the pervasive power of systemic racism (i.e., policies and practices in areas such as the criminal justice system, employment opportunities, housing practices, educational resources, and healthcare that advantage Whites and disadvantage Blacks) that underscores the reality that the cost of being Black is deeply rooted in the personal *and* the political. On the gridiron, the colonial ideology of the NFL predominates (i.e., its *owners* are almost entirely White men and their *players* are predominately Black men) with the rampant perpetuation of racist stereotypes about the intellectual ability and "fit" of aspiring Black NFL head coaches that significantly lessen the chances that they'll realize their dream of being accepted into such an ultra-exclusive club (Collins 2007).

Black people continue to experience racial trauma: race-based traumatic stress injurious to one's mental, emotional, and physical well-being due to racism and with symptoms (e.g., avoidance, intrusive memories, negative alterations in cognition and mood, and changes in physical and emotional reactions) that are similar to post-traumatic stress disorder (PTSD). Racial melancholia structures racial trauma in so far as it provides a non-pathologizing framework for how Black people experience racial injury—a grieving that is an ever-evolving negotiation between paralysis and agency that allows space for a more dynamic understanding of mourning and dismisses notions of an existence in which their identity is permanently damaged (Grinage 2019). Many foundational components of psychoanalysis have perpetuated racist and colonialist ideologies through a conceptual framework that largely neglects sociohistorical, political, and cultural concerns (Frosh 2013). Conversely, racial melancholia is a compelling and more comprehensive lens through which to explore the plight of aspiring Black NFL head coaches given its inherent post-colonial interest in accounting for the significant role that the historical exclusion of Black people through social norms and legislation has played in shaping their internal (i.e., affective) and external (i.e., physical) worlds. The purpose of this chapter is to encourage psychoanalysis to expand its theoretical repertoire by considering racial melancholia not only as a non-negotiable underpinning of its conceptualization of loss and resultant grief for people of color but also as a general approach to providing them with culture-centered care that is flexible and empathic enough to view some of their dysregulatory affect as not about them "not being enough," but rather a proportionate and natural reaction to systems of oppression that have defined them as "not enough." In order to move towards a fuller appreciation and understanding of the depths to which Black people have experienced racial melancholia, the impact and sources of such loss (e.g., colonialism, slavery, racism, implicit racial bias, and internalized racism) must be explored.

THE ERASURE OF AFRICAN HISTORY IN WORLD HISTORY

Historians, scientists, and scholars alike have identified Alkebu-lan (i.e., the ancient and indigenous name of Africa) as the birthplace of civilization (Ben-Jochannan 1989; Bower 2012; Shillington 2012) that began some 2.5 million years ago. All humans are genetically linked to an African woman who lived 200,000 years ago (Williams 1991). Thousands of years before Greece became an exemplar of Western civilization, Africans in ancient Kemet (Egypt) created the earliest recorded civilization approximately 6,000 years ago. It was so advanced that it established the foundation for modern-day society. Kemet (KMT), "the black land" was a nation founded by King Menes (c.3100 B.C. to 3038 B.C.), who established a centralized government while politically uniting the north (i.e., lower part) and south (i.e., upper part) with the Nile River flowing from the south to the north and connecting both regions (Zulu 1993). Kemetic rulers were divided into 30 time periods or African dynasties with 12 of them in power for more than 1,000 years (Hilliard 1992). Throughout Kemet's existence of nearly 3,000 years, a high culture was fortified (e.g., hieroglyphics [Mdw Ntru] were introduced, pyramids were built, and the first library and first university were founded) marking a record of achievement that few others could rival.

Kemetians created the world's first primary, secondary, and postsecondary schools (Clarke 1991; Mswazie and Mudyahoto 2013; Nobles 2008; Woldegiorgis and Doevenspeck 2013). Their scholars created curricula at institutions of higher learning that initially featured four foundational elements: language, science, mystic science (spirituality and religion), and philosophy (Ben-Jochannan 1989; Nobles 2008; Watkins 2008), before adding music, mathematics, and African history (Ben-Jochannan 1989; Heimonen 2008; Lee 2008). These core subjects became known as the seven liberal arts—the basis for modern education in Western civilization (Lee 2008; Mswazie and Mudyahoto 2013). African history was later eliminated from its position amongst the seven liberal arts during medieval times (≈ 476 A.D.≈1400–1450 A.D.) when its educators modified curricula to include the study of European history—a format later copied by American educators (Cohen and Kisker 2009; Wesseling 1998). The aggressive act of cultural erasure symbolized the burgeoning White supremacist ideology that would serve as a bellwether for the continued subjugation and dehumanization of Black people despite the painful irony that the history of the world begins with African history.

Historical whitewashing by Western educators also included distorted beliefs and teachings that intentionally omitted the fact that Nile Valley civilizations—which included ancient Kemet—contributed to the educational, scientific, and philosophical activities of ancient academicians and theorists from Europe, specifically the ancient Greeks (Muir 2015; Shugart 2013). James notes how "The Greeks didn't carry culture and learning to Egypt, but found it already there, and wisely settled in that country, in order to absorb as much as possible of its culture" (1954, 47). For example, Thales (624 B.C.–548 B.C.) studied under the guidance of learned Kemetic priests (i.e., scholars), before returning to Miletus in Ionia and opening the Ionian Institution of Science and Philosophy (Obenga 2002). His student Pythagoras (570 B.C.–490 B.C.) was also formally educated in Kemet (Finch 2002) which armed him with the requisite knowledge to further his efforts as an academician and teacher in Greece. The Egyptians also welcomed Aristotle

(384 B.C.–322 B.C.) to their schools of higher learning. He was there as the student, not the teacher.

The colonization of thought that manifested through its removal from the source created a false consciousness that began "in the fifteenth and sixteenth centuries during the rise of the Atlantic slave trade when the Europeans not only began to colonize the minds of the people of the world, [but …] also colonized information about the world" (Clarke 1991, 43). During this time, prodigious losses (e.g., freedom, life, culture, identity, and autonomy) proliferated and compounded at unrelenting speeds to form a synergistic dislocation of Africans across the globe (i.e., Diaspora).

The Transatlantic slave trade involved eight principal regions (e.g., Senegambia, Sierra Leone, Windward Coast, Gold Coast, Bight of Benin, Bight of Biafra, West Central Africa, and Southeast Africa) of West African activity and ports of embarkation (Eltis et al. 1999). The West African slave trade and its soul-crushing and deadly Middle Passage lasted almost 400 years (Kolchin 1993).[1] As far back as 1501, the Spanish were the first Europeans to import a modest number of African slaves into places like Hispaniola and Cuba (Davis 2006). Almost 12 million Africans were forcibly sold into slavery between 1619 and 1807, about 500,000 of whom found themselves in what is now the United States (Davis 2006). During this time, African men and women were treated as chattel (i.e., legal property of slave owners to be bought, sold, and owned in perpetuity) and considered partial human beings. This ideology was illustrated in the Three-Fifths Compromise of 1787 in which three out of every five slaves were counted to determine a state's population for legislative representation and taxation (Lynd 1966).

Negative racial stereotypes and derogatory images (e.g., dangerous criminal, licentious, intellectually inferior, dancing and shuffling buffoon, and lazy) were used to justify the bondage of Africans during slavery. Representations of Africans as dehumanized beings are almost as old as Europe's first interactions with West Africa (Ovington 1929). Early nautical writings of Europeans' experience with Africans described them as primitive people more closely akin to apes than to White explorers (Dapper 1688). As race theory moved from a theological perspective to a biological one, a racial hierarchy emerged to provide itself with a rationale and justification for its heavy reliance on the "Negro-ape metaphor," as Lott (1999) detailed it. Although this relationship existed before scientific racism (i.e., pseudoscientific study of techniques and hypotheses to support or justify the belief in racism, racial inferiority, or racial superiority), it gained in popularity when Franz Boas, the most renowned anthropologist of his era, and even Charles Darwin, speculated about the possibility of an evolutionary spectrum within primates (Lott 1999). They believed that the least evolved side of the spectrum contained monkeys and apes, and moved through savage and/or deformed anthropoids, culminating with Whites at the other end (as most evolved [Jahoda 1999]). It was speculated that African descendants were situated somewhere between the deformed and the simian (Goff et al. 2008).

The Emancipation Proclamation (January 1863) only freed slaves from the 10 confederate states (e.g., Alabama, Arkansas, Florida, Georgia, Mississippi, North Carolina, South Carolina, Texas, and sections of Louisiana and Virginia) who were rebelling against the Union during the Civil War. The 13th Amendment (December 1865) freed slaves throughout the United States but came with the dreaded caveat that slavery or involuntary servitude could be used as punishment for people convicted of crimes. The celebration of Juneteenth (June 19, 1865) finally marked the end of slavery in Texas where over 250,000 enslaved Black people were finally free after being the last Confederate state to be reached by the Union army.

Despite the abolishment of slavery, the persistent racial traumatization of Black minds and bodies continued unabated through the aggressive enforcement of formal and informal anti-Black segregation laws called Jim Crow (1877–1896)—a racial caste system that subordinated Blacks to Whites in southern states. These laws (i.e., black codes) legitimized anti-Black racism and were reinforced through a system of terror and violence (e.g., lynchings, beatings, and intimidation were common occurrences) meant to control the labor and behavior of Black people by denying them the right to vote and excluding them from public transport, facilities, juries, jobs, and neighborhoods.

IMPLICIT BIAS

Many of the distorted images and racist stereotypes about Black people that fuelled slavery and Jim Crow still exist today but also manifest in much more subtle, often unintentional forms known as implicit bias (i.e., modern racism). Implicit bias refers to the attitudes or stereotypes that affect our understanding, actions, and decisions in an unconscious manner that are triggered by the utter existence (actual or symbolic) of the object for which one has an attitude (Dovidio et al. 2004). People's implicit associations do not necessarily match their stated beliefs and may not indicate positions that individuals would explicitly endorse. On the other hand, explicit biases (i.e., "old-fashioned" racism) are conscious preferences for or aversions to a person or group. Both biases can occur at the same time and may even serve to reinforce each other. Implicit bias is harder to identify given the inherent challenge of identifying that which is not consciously known to someone. Lawrence states: "[M]ost of us . . . do not recognize the ways in which our cultural experience has influenced our beliefs about race or the occasions on which those beliefs affect our actions. In other words, a large part of the behavior that produces racial discrimination is influenced by unconscious racial motivation" (1987, 322).

The most popular way implicit bias has been assessed is through the use of the Implicit Association Test (IAT), which measures the relative ease with which people make associations between target categories (e.g., White faces and Black faces) and evaluations (e.g., pleasant words and unpleasant words) (Greenwald et al. 1998). Suppose one is quicker to associate pleasant words with White faces than Black faces and slower to associate unpleasant words with White faces than with Black faces. In that case, the test will report that you have a *slight*, *moderate*, or *strong* preference for White faces over Black faces or some similar language. The IAT has shown that approximately 70 percent of individuals implicitly prefer Whites over Blacks (Nosek et al. 2002; Sabin et al. 2009).

Implicit bias can have serious real-world consequences in the form of racial disparities in health care between Whites and Blacks. It has been widely documented that the racial disparities in the treatment of cardiovascular disease (Smedley et al. 2003) are alarming, with Whites up to two times as likely to receive treatment for thrombolytic therapy for myocardial infarction than Blacks (Allison et al. 1996; Canto et al. 2000; Petersen et al. 2002; Taylor et al. 1998; Weitzman et al. 1997). In what is believed to be the first study to assess implicit associations concerning mental health diagnosis, compliance, and treatment in medical students and psychiatric physicians, the study found that participants had a greater probability of associating Black faces with psychotic disorders (rather than mood disorders), non-compliance (rather than compliance), and antipsychotic medications (rather than antidepressant medications). Additionally, White participants who endorsed a higher level of training most strongly predicted the association of Black faces with psychotic disorders, even after adjusting for participant age (Londono et al. 2021).

Implicit bias has undoubtedly contributed to the unlevel playing field in the hiring of aspiring Black NFL head coaches. Two civil rights attorneys (Johnnie L. Cochran, Jr. and Cyrus Mehri) who believed that Black coaches were systematically disadvantaged in pursuing head coaching positions commissioned University of Pennsylvania labor economist Dr. Janice Madden to statistically analyze the win-loss records of the 5 Black head coaches (e.g., Art Shell, Dennis Green, Tony Dungy, Ray Rhodes, and Herman Edwards) who coached from 1986–2001 against the performance of the 86 White NFL head coaches who coached during the same period. Their damning report concluded that Black head coaches outperformed White head coaches (Cochran and Mehri 2002, 2). Dr. Madden's most compelling findings were: (1) Black head coaches won an average of 1.1 more games per season than White head coaches; (2) Black head coaches led their teams to the playoffs 67% of the time compared to 39% for White head coaches; (3) Black head coaches averaged 2.7 more wins in their first season than their White counterparts; and (4) Black head coaches averaged 1.3 more wins in their final season before being terminated than terminated White head coaches. Madden concluded, "No matter how we look at regular season success, African American coaches have performed better. This data is consistent with African Americans having to be better coaches than Whites to be hired as head coach in the NFL" (2004, 15).

Along with the announcement and publication of these statistically significant and peer-reviewed outcomes, many years of criticism, threats of legal action in response to the shortage of Black head coaches in the NFL (Lapchick 2004), and the firings of Tony Dungy and Dennis Green in 2002, the Rooney Rule was implemented ahead of the 2003 season. It was named after Dan Rooney, then-owner of the Pittsburgh Steelers and chairman of the league's diversity committee. The Rooney Rule operates as a quasi-affirmative action policy designed to address significant racial disparities in its hiring practices by diversifying its coaching fraternity. It initially mandated that all 32 teams with head coaching vacancies had to interview at least one minority candidate for the position.

In tribute to racial inclusion, support of the Rooney Rule, and galvanization of the NFL's community of color, the Fritz Pollard Alliance (FPA) was co-founded in 2003 by Cyrus Mehri and the late Johnnie Cochran. Its name honors Frederick Douglas "Fritz" Pollard. In 1919, the former chemistry major at Brown University turned pro following his service in the Army during WWI and then joined the newly founded APFA (American Professional Football Association)—now known as the NFL—as a running back from 1920 until 1926. Pollard was one of the league's first two Black players and became its first Black head coach in 1921. The FPA embodies the ethos of an affinity group in which all members share and are dedicated to realizing a common goal—equal opportunity of employment in coaching, scouting, and NFL front offices (Collins 2007).

It formed not too long after Cochran and Mehri's report was released when Floyd Keith, the Executive Director of the Black Coaches Association (BCA) (i.e., a support network for black college coaches interested in increasing their employment opportunities and fostering their professional development) advised Cochran and Mehri to reach out to John Wooten. Wooten was a former NFL All-Pro offensive lineman and NFL executive for the Dallas Cowboys, Philadelphia Eagles, and Baltimore Ravens spanning almost 30 years, and was well-regarded for not only his athletic prowess but also his persistence in making higher-level coaching opportunities available to Black coaches (Miller 2021). He became the Fritz Pollard Association's first chairman.

Over the subsequent years, the Rooney Rule has undergone a few changes to ostensibly create a more equitable and inclusive environment amongst its coaching ranks. In 2009, the rule expanded to include general manager (GM) positions and equivalent front-office roles and required each team to interview a minimum of two external minority candidates (NFL 2018). Seven years later, the NFL required that women be included in the process of interviewing for executive positions at the team and NFL office level (Reid 2016). In 2020, team owners approved a proposal designed to incentivize teams that developed minority talent into GMs or head coaches by rewarding them with a third-round compensatory pick. If a team lost a minority executive or coach to another team, they would receive a third-round compensatory pick for two years, and if that team lost both a coach and an executive, the third-round compensatory pick would be extended for a third year (NFL 2020). One year later, the NFL approved a proposal that required every team to interview at least two external ethnic minority candidates for available head coaching positions, at least one external minority candidate for a coordinator job, and at least one minority and/or female candidate for senior-level positions such as team president and/or senior executive (Bell 2020). In 2022, the latest change to the Rooney Rule was implemented, which required each team to interview an external minority and/or female candidate for available QB (quarterback) positions (NFL 2022).

Despite numerous tweaks, the measure designed to ensure the hiring of more Black coaches has produced mostly poor results two decades after its inception. The percentage of Black NFL coaches in 2003 was 9% and is currently 18.75% despite increases as high as 22% in four of the intervening years. One study found that when a coach's age, experience, and performance were controlled, the Rooney Rule failed to increase the number of minority head coaches in the NFL (Solow et al. 2011). Those numbers seem even more bleak when one considers that some owners don't respect the process. As Jones highlights, "[The Rooney Rule has] also . . . been circumvented and made a mockery of regularly by team owners who show no interest in deviating from their (pre-determined) plan at the head coach or general manager positions" (2020).

Implicit bias has influenced the selection and scarcity of Black NFL head coaches in at least three systemic ways: (1) through the internalization of negative stereotypes about their intellectual ability by those in high-level decision-making positions; (2) through the creation of "old boy" networks that perpetuate in-group (White)/out-group (Black) dynamics (Collins 2007); and (3) through their media framing (i.e., coverage) by NFL beat writers (Harrison et al. 2022). Each of these factors contributes to the racial melancholia of aspiring Black coaches in which the lost object is unattainable idealized white racial perfection (i.e., not only immunity from racism but also equitable treatment and access to employment opportunities) given other forms of continuous loss (e.g., discrimination, racism, assimilation, diaspora, motherland, and mother tongue). For aspiring Black NFL coaches, their efforts to assimilate into and be accepted by the dominant White NFL culture (i.e., 95.3% of team majority owners are White and 0% are Black) continue to remain at an unattainable distance —a primary catalyst for the production of profound racial grief and injury that is the hallmark of racial melancholia.

RACIST STEREOTYPES

Negative stereotypes about Black people's intelligence perpetuate racial discrimination and many of those who have the power to hire head coaches implicitly endorse similar stereotypes (Davis 1998). The negative feedback loop of implicit bias continues to thrive given the inherent uniqueness of the NFL's structure and culture that place such a premium on hiring intelligent head coaches. For comparison, the organizational structure of the NFL is considerably more complex and hierarchical than the National Basketball Association (NBA) (Thomas and Rich 2005), given its greater number of assistant coaches who make up the three main groups on every team: 1) *offense* is managed by the offensive coordinator and his assistants (e.g., quarterbacks coach, wide receivers coach, running backs coach, and passing game coordinator); 2) *defense* is managed by the defensive coordinator and his assistants (e.g., linebacker's coach, defensive backs coach, and defensive line coach); and 3) *special teams* are managed by the special team's coach and his assistant (e.g., assistant special teams coach). The number of assistant coaches averages out to be 15 per NFL team and for whom the head coach is responsible. A head basketball coach of an NBA team oversees an active roster of 12 players and typically has no more than six assistants (NBA 2023), who are mostly generalists with no formal area of expertise (Collins 2007).

Selecting an NFL head coach who is equally adept at creating an environment in which his assistant coaches are fully committed to implementing his philosophy (i.e., strategic pre-game and in-game planning of opponents), as he is at motivating all 53 of his players to reach their full potential in service of the team's overall success, demands the prioritization of high mental aptitude in a team leader. Hop to Gun King Trips Right Tear 52 Sway All Go Special X-Shallow Cross H-Wide is a staple West Coast (i.e., style of passing offense) play call (Doctor 2023) and just one example of the more than 100 play calls that a head coach must know (i.e., this number can easily increase to over 200 when the same play is run out of a multitude of different formations or new ones are added for a specific opponent depending on the particular style of passing offense (e.g., pro-style, spread, pistol, and option) that he chooses to employ. The responsibility of managing such increasing complexities (e.g., sophisticated play calling using high-tech headsets to communicate with staff and players in real-time and the constant substitution of players meant to afford rest and actively influence a game in progress by attempting to create more favourable matchups) makes it easier for decision-makers to implicitly associate Black head coaching candidates with being less capable of successfully executing these responsibilities.

"Old-boy" networks (i.e., predominately White social networking groups) also impede the upward mobility of aspiring Black NFL coaches as they maintain and reinforce traditional power structures that center Whiteness and stigmatize Blackness through the predominance of implicit bias. These types of exclusive in-groups severely limit the hiring pool of potential applicants for head coaching jobs to other high-status members or acquaintances within the system. The exclusion of Black people from these groups may be less linked to overt racism than the "tendency to recognize intellectual power and unusual capacity for [creativity] more easily in persons of one's sex and race" (Kay 1979, 140). While it makes intuitive and reasonable sense to hire people within one's social circle given the likelihood of a more intimate understanding of a potential coach's intellect, character, and competence, the disproportionate reliance on such networks even excludes the few Black people who have traversed the treacherous terrain of racism and rejection to be well-positioned for head coaching jobs that they most likely will never get. Some help may be on the way with the NFL's (2022) recently created accelerator program—a meet-and-greet event that puts qualified minority head coaches and front-office candidates in the same room as team owners (Reid 2023). It remains to be seen whether this new initiative will be a catalyst in creating sustainable growth and diversification in its head coaching ranks.

IMPLICIT BIAS IN MEDIA FRAMING

Media framing of race and racism by NFL beat writers covering head coaching searches has been relatively scarce, making the plight of Black coaches a more lonely existence given the inadequate supply of allyship and representation in sports media. Goffman's (1974) sociological approach to framing has been used extensively in sports media research and is primarily concerned with the media's predisposition to "select some aspects of perceived reality and make them more salient in communicating text" (Entman 1993, 52). White men are the overwhelming majority in the sports media industry and this imbalance affects the way that athletes of color are viewed, and how race and systemic racism are covered and communicated to the masses (Harrison et al. 2021). Research studies have examined the use of race as an identifier of Olympic athletes in print media (Hardin et al. 2004) as well as the pervasiveness of stereotypes and racial descriptors in the language of sports television commentators (Billings 2004; Bruce 2004; Eastman and Billings 2001; Lewis et al. 2020; Rada and Wulfemeyer 2005; Van Sterkenberg et al. 2019). The use of racial descriptors reinforces Whiteness as the norm given that they are often used exclusively to describe people from culturally, racially, and linguistically diverse backgrounds.

The framing practices of the sports media are not immune to the pervasiveness of racial stereotypes and biases. Ash and Cranmer (2020) showed that media framing of college athletes (i.e., highlighting either their intelligence, strength, or athleticism) affects the way that they are perceived by their non-athlete college peers. Research studies have shown that "brawn" vs. "brain" frames have been historically racialized with sports media more likely to focus on the intelligence and fundamentals of White athletes and the athleticism of Black athletes, which perpetuates racial bias in sports media coverage (Cranmer et al. 2014; Deeb and Love 2018; Eagleman and Martin 2013). Ferrucci and Tandoc (2017; 2018) found that patrons of sports media applied these same racial attributions to football quarterbacks, which is particularly relevant for aspiring Black NFL head coaches given that the ideal head coach is proficient at working with quarterbacks. If Black quarterbacks are stereotypically characterized as being less intelligent than their White counterparts, Black coaches may also be viewed as lacking the requisite intelligence to not only coach quarterbacks but lead football teams as well (Harrison et al. 2021).

A study by Harrison et al. (2021) examined the extent to which sports media coverage ignored or mentioned race and racism in their coverage of the 2020 and 2021 head coaching hiring cycles and whether there was a significant increase in the discussion of race year-over-year, given the prevalence of anti-Black bias, and used media framing theory as a means to explore this phenomenon. To answer these research questions, the authors conducted a content analysis of web articles written by NFL scribes covering specific teams during the aforementioned hiring cycles (N=374).

Results showed that while the overwhelming majority of articles written about the 2020 and 2021 NFL coaching searches weren't framed to mention race, beat writers mentioned race more than twice as much in 2021 than in 2020—a statistically significant increase. This gain may have been attributable to more minority candidates being interviewed in 2021 as a result of the NFL's new Rooney Rule mandate that same year, which required teams to interview minorities for not only head coaching jobs but also offensive coordinator and senior-level positions. The relatively small number of articles that mentioned race in both 2020 and 2021 may also be a product of White NFL beat writers' natural reticence in reporting racial injustices that reflect poorly on team owners who overwhelmingly represent society's most privileged class—wealthy White men (Harrison et al. 2021). By not bringing more attention to the NFL's lack of Black representation among its head coaches, sports media plays a significant role in the preservation and proliferation of implicit bias.

CONCLUSION

Aspiring Black NFL head coaches' experience of implicit bias—over their lifespans generally and in their professional lives specifically—is a constant reminder of the loss of idealized White racial perfection. The normalization and structuralism of oppression in daily life necessarily facilitate the internalization of the dominant White group's values, norms, and ideas by African Americans and other people of colour. Through its internalization, oppression becomes self-sustaining or domesticating (Watts et al. 1999). Watts-Jones explained that "when people of African descent internalize racism it is an experience of self-degradation and self-alienation; one that promotes the assumptive base of our inferiority" (2002, 592). According to Williams and Williams-Morris, "internalized racism refers to the acceptance, by marginalized racial populations, of the negative societal beliefs and stereotypes about themselves" (2000, 255).

Like all forms of internalized domination, internalized racism is not the result of some cultural or biological characteristic of the subjugated. Nor is it the consequence of any weakness, ignorance, inferiority, psychological defect, gullibility, or other shortcoming of the oppressed. The internalization of oppression is a multidimensional phenomenon that assumes many forms and sizes across situational contexts, including the intersections of multiple systems of domination (Padilla 2001). It cannot be reduced to one form or assumed to affect similarly located individuals or groups in precisely the same way. It is an inevitable condition of all structures of oppression (Schwalbe et al. 2000). Although internalized racism has been most studied in African Americans, it can also impact how other minority groups view themselves.

Research has explored the relationship between internalized racism and ethnic identity. One study found a negative relationship between internalized racism and ethnic identity in Black and Latinx college students (Cokley 2002; Hipolito-Delgado 2007). Internalized racism is so insidious that it has been known to be transmitted inter-generationally (e.g., children of color may be told by their parents to avoid socializing with others who have not embraced mainstream White culture). This sharing of historical oppression has been observed in Native Americans (Duran and Duran 1995), Jewish survivors of the Holocaust (Krell 1990; Moskovitz and Krell 1990; Solomon et al. 1988), and Japanese American WWII internees (Nagata 1990). Other groups that suffer from internalized oppression include women (Bearman and Amrhein

2014), LGBT (Nadal and Mendoza 2014), and people with disabilities (Watermeyer and Görgens 2014).

The dearth and exclusion of Black National Football League (NFL) head coaches continue to serve as an enduring symbol of systemic racism as evidenced by the employment of only six Black coaches (e.g., Mike Tomlin of the Pittsburgh Steelers, Todd Bowles of the Tampa Bay Buccaneers, DeMeco Ryans of the Houston Texans, Raheem Morris of the Atlanta Falcons, Jerod Mayo of the New England Patriots, and Antonio Pierce of the Las Vegas Raiders; Mike McDaniel of the Miami Dolphins identifies as bi-racial) out of the 32-team league heading into the 2024 season - a lowly 18.75%. Substantive changes in the NFL's overwhelmingly homogeneous coaching ranks remain an elusive fantasy for most aspiring Black head coaches. The psychic pain from the continuous loss of equitable employment opportunities and cumulative grief and trauma of exclusion and othering is repetitiously endured, resisted, and revealed in their collective experience of racial melancholia.

Racial melancholia serves as a powerful and symbiotic bridge between psychoanalysis and sport as a site of exclusion through an audacious reimagining that loudly protests White supremacist assumptions of homogeneity of lived experience for people of color by honoring their past and present histories of continuous racial loss (e.g., idealized Whiteness, assimilation, erasure, racism, and implicit racial bias) within the larger sociopolitical and cultural context. More specifically, racial melancholia allows for a more empathic and robust perspective-taking of the plight of aspiring Black NFL coaches by identifying their racialization (e.g., the social and political process of ascribing race to groups of people who invariably become the racialized "other") as a determining factor in their exclusion from head coaching opportunities.

Consequently, racial melancholia establishes itself as an "agentic mechanism of the psyche" (Grinage 2019, 231) that registers both adaptive and maladaptive responses to racial trauma in a never-ending negotiation between melancholia and mourning given losses that perpetually materialize and compound. As Moglen notes, "Analyses of socially induced loss must account for processes of grieving in which the bereaved sustain ongoing relations to the objects they are persistently losing and to the social pressures that are persistently injuring them" (2005, 160). Perhaps most importantly, racial melancholia encapsulates not only the adversity that aspiring Black NFL coaches face but also their enduring resilience to it.

NOTE

1. Approximately 2 million slaves died on ships headed to the New World from Africa from a combination of disease, suicide, and murder.

BIBLIOGRAPHY

Allison, Jeroan J., Catarina I. Kiefe, Robert M. Centor, J. Brent Box, and Robert M. Farmer. 1996. "Racial Differences in the Medical Treatment of Elderly Medicare Patients with Acute Myocardial Infarction." *Journal of General Internal Medicine* 11: 736–743.

Ash, Erin, and Gregory A. Cranmer. 2020. "Transcontextual Effects of Racialized Sports Media Framing: Students' Off the Field Perceptions of Student-Athletes." *Communication & Sport* 8, no. 3: 389–408.

Bearman, Steve, and Amrhein, Marielle. 2014. "Girls, Women, and Internalized Sexism." In *Internalized Oppression: The Psychology of Marginalized Groups*, edited by Eric John Ramos David, 191–226. New York, NY: Springer Publishing Company.

Bell, Jarrett. 2020. "NFL Approves Plans to Reward Teams for Developing Minority Coaches, GMs." *USA Today*. https://www.usatoday.com/story/sports/nfl/2020/11/10/nfl-minority-coach-general-manager-hiring-proposal-approved/6234064002/

Ben-Jochannan, Yosef A. A. 1989. *Black Man of the Nile and His Family*. Baltimore, MD: Black Classic Press.

Billings, A. C. 2004. "Depicting the Quarterback in Black and White: A Content Analysis of College and Professional Football Broadcast Commentary." *Howard Journal of Communications* 15, no. 4: 201–210.

Bower, Bruce. 2012. "Icy Isolation May Have Led to a New Human Species." *Science News 181,* no. 7:5–6. https://doi.org/10.1002/scin.5591810703

Bruce, Toni. 2004. "Marking the Boundaries of Normal in Televised Sports: The Play-by-Play of Race." *Media, Culture, and Society* 26, no. 6; 861–879 + 882.

Canto, John G., Jeroan J. Allison, Catarina I. Kiefe, Contessa Fincher, Robert Farmer, Padmini Sekar, Sharina Person, and Norman W. Weissman. 2000. "Relation of Race and Sex to the Use of Reperfusion Therapy in Medicare Beneficiaries with Acute Myocardial Infarction." *New England Journal of Medicine* 342, no. 15: 1094–1100.

Cheng, Anne. 2001. *The Melancholy of Race: Psychoanalysis, Assimilation, and Hidden Grief.* Oxford, UK: Oxford University Press.

Clarke, John Henrik. 1991. *Africans at the Crossroads: Notes for an African Revolution*. Trenton, NJ: Africa World Press.

Cochran Jr., Johnnie, and Cyrus Mehri. 2002. *Black Coaches in the NFL: Superior Performance, Inferior Opportunities*. Washington, DC: Mehri & Skalet, PLLC.

Cohen, Arthur M., and Carrie B. Kisker. 2009. *The Shaping of American Higher Education: Emergence and Growth of the Contemporary System*. Hoboken, NJ: John Wiley & Sons.

Cokley, Kevin O. 2002. "Testing Cross's Revised Racial Identity Model: An Examination of the Relationship Between Racial Identity and Internalized Racialism." *Journal of Counseling Psychology* 49, no. 4: 476.

Collins, Brian. 2007. "Tackling Unconscious Bias in Hiring Practices: The Plight of the Rooney Rule." *New York University Law Review* 8, no. 3: 870–912.

Cranmer, Gregory A., Nicholas D. Bowman, Rebecca M. Chory, and Keith D. Weber. 2014. "Race as an Antecedent Condition in the Framing of Heisman Finalists." *Howard Journal of Communications* 25, no. 2: 171–191.

Dapper, Olfert. 1688. *Naukeurige Beschryving der Eilanden in de Archipel der Middellandesche Zee* [Precise description of the islands in the archipelago of the Mediterranean Sea]. Amsterdam: J. Von Meurs.

Davis, David Brion. 2006. *Inhuman Bondage: The Rise and Fall of Slavery in the New World.* Oxford: Oxford University Press.

Davis, Timothy. 1998. "Racism in Athletics: Subtle Yet Persistent." *UALR L. Rev.* 21: 881. https://lawrepository.ualr.edu/lawreview/vol21/iss4/10

Deeb, Alexander, and Adam Love. 2018. "Media Representations of Multiracial Athletes." *Journal of Sport and Social Issues* 42, no. 2: 95–114.

Doctor, Robbie. 2023. "How to Break Down a Play Call in Football." SACMEDIA, January 10, 2023. https://sac.media/2023/01/10/how-to-break-down-a-play-call-in-football/

Dovidio, John F., Samuel L. Gaertner, Gordon Hodson, and Melissa A. Houlette. 2004. "Social Inclusion and Exclusion: Recategorization and the Perception of Intergroup Boundaries." In *Social Psychology of Inclusion and Exclusion*, edited by Dominic Abrams, Michael A. Hogg, and Jose M. Marques, 263–282. London, UK: Psychology Press.

Duran, Eduardo, and Bonnie Duran. 1995. *Native American Postcolonial Psychology*. Albany, NY: SUNY Press.

Duru, Jeremi N. 2014. "The Fritz Pollard Alliance, the Rooney Rule, and the Quest to Level the Playing Field in the NFL. In *Race in American Sports,* edited by James L. Conyers, Jr., 204–223. Jefferson, North Carolina: McFarland & Company, Inc.

Eagleman, Andrea N., and Tywan G. Martin. 2013. "Race Portrayals in Sport Communication." In *Routledge Handbook of Sport Communication*, edited by Paul M. Pedersen, 369–377. New York, NY: Routledge

Eastman, Susan T., and Andrew C. Billings. 2001. "Biased Voices of Sports: Racial and Gender Stereotyping in College Basketball Announcing." *Howard Journal of Communications* 12, no. 4: 183–201.

Eltis, David. 2000. "The Volume and Structure of the Transatlantic Slave Trade: A Reassessment." *The William and Mary Quarterly, Third Series 58,* no. 1: 17–46.

Eng, David. L., and Han, Shinhee. 2000. "A Dialogue on Racial Melancholia." *Psychoanalytic Dialogues* 10, no. 4:667–700.

Entman, Robert M. 1993. "Framing: Toward Clarification of a Fractured Paradigm." *Journal of Communication* 43, no. 4: 51–58. https://doi.org/10.1111/j.1460-2466.1993.tb01304.x

Ferrucci, Patrick, and Edson C. Tandoc. 2017. "Race and the Deep Ball: Applying Stereotypes to NFL Quarterbacks." *International Journal of Sport Communication* 10, no. 1: 41–57.

Ferrucci, Patrick, and Edson C. Tandoc. 2018. "The Spiral of Stereotyping: Social Identity Theory and NFL Quarterbacks." *Howard Journal of Communications* 29, no. 2:107–125.

Finch, C. S. 2002. "Critiquing the Critics: Advancing the Paradigm." In *Egypt vs. Greece and The American Academy,* edited by Molefi Kete Asante and Ama Mazama, 37–50. Chicago, IL: African American Images.

Freud, Sigmund. 1957. "Mourning and Melancholia." In *The Standard Edition of the Complete Psychological Works of Sigmund Freud*, edited by James Strachey, 237–258. London: Hogarth Press.

Frosh, Stephen. 2013. "Psychoanalysis, Colonialism, Racism." *Journal of Theoretical and Philosophical Psychology* 33, no. 3: 141.

Goff, Phillip Atiba, Jennifer L. Eberhardt, Melissa J. Williams, and Matthew Christian Jackson. 2008. "Not Yet Human: Implicit Knowledge, Historical Dehumanization, and Contemporary Consequences." *Journal of Personality and Social Psychology* 94, no. 2: 292–306.

Goffman, Erving. 1974. *Frame Analysis: An Essay on the Organization of Experience*. Harvard University Press.

Greenwald, Anthony G., Debbie E. McGhee, and Jordan LK Schwartz. 1998. "Measuring Individual Differences in Implicit Cognition: The Implicit Association Test." *Journal of Personality and Social Psychology* 74, no. 6: 1464–1480.

Grinage, Justin. 2019. "Endless Mourning: Racial Melancholia, Black Grief, and the Transformative Possibilities for Racial Justice in Education." *Harvard Educational Review* 89, no. 2: 227–250. https://doi.org/10.17763/1943-5045-89.2.227

Hampton, Ryan S., and Varnum, Michael E.W. (2020). "Individualism-Collectivism." In *Encyclopedia of Personality and Individual Differences*, edited by Virgil Zeigler-Hill And Todd K. Shackelford, 2231–2238. New York, NY: Springer International Publishing https://doi.org/10.1007/978-3-319-24612-3_2023

Hardin, Marie, Julie E. Dodd, Jean Chance, and Kristie Walsdorf. 2004. "Sporting Images in Black and White: Race in Newspaper Coverage of the 2000 Olympic Games." *Howard Journal of Communications* 15, no. 4: 211–227.

Harrison, Guy, Charli Kerns, and Jason Stamm. 2022. "Covering the Rooney Rule: An Exploratory Study of Print Coverage of NFL Head Coaching Searches." *Howard Journal of Communications* 33, no. 5: 435–451.

Heimonen, Marja. 2008. "Nurturing Towards Wisdom: Justifying Music in the Curriculum." *Philosophy of Music Education Review* 16, no. 1: 61–78.

Hilliard, Asa G. 1992. "The Meaning of KMT (Ancient Egyptian) History for Contemporary African American Experience." *Phylon,* 49, no. 1/2: 10–22.

Hipolito-Delgado, Carlos Porfirio. 2007. *Internalized Racism and Ethnic Identity in Chicana/o and Latina/o College Students*. PhD dissertation.

"Implicit Associations in Psychiatric Diagnosis, Treatment, and Compliance Expectations." *Acad Psychiatry* 45, no. 1: 23–33.

Jahoda, Gustav. 1999. *Images of Savages: Ancient Roots of Modern Prejudice in Western Culture*. New York, NY: Routledge.

James, George G.M. 1954. *Stolen Legacy: Greek Philosophy is Stolen Egyptian Philosophy*. New York, NY: Philosophical Library.

Jones, J. 2020. NFL's Rooney Rule Additions Are a Positive Step Forward, but More Teeth Needed. *cbssports*.com. https://www.cbssports.com/nfl/news/nfls-rooney-rule-additions-are-a-positive-step-forward-but-more-teeth-needed/

Kay, Herma Hill. 1979. "The Need for Self-Imposed Quotas in Academic Employment." *Wash. ULQ*:137.

Kolchin, P. 1993. *American Slavery, 1619–1877*. New York, NY: Hill and Wang.

Krell, Robert. 1990. "Holocaust Survivors: A Clinical Perspective." *Psychiatric Journal of the University of Ottawa: Revue de Psychiatrie de L'université D'ottawa* 15, no. 1: 18–21.

Lapchick, Richard. 2004. "The 2004 Racial and Gender Report Card: National Football League." https://www.tidesport.org/_files/ugd/7d86e5_d4e81d551510470ab133adcdff26c44e.pdf

Lawrence, Charles R. 1987. "The Id, the Ego, and Equal Protection: Reckoning with Unconscious Racism." *Stanford Law Review* 39, no. 2: 317–388. https://doi.org/10.2307/1228797.

Lee, Carol D. 2008. "Synthesis of Research on the Role of Culture in Learning Among African American Youth: The Contributions of Asa G. Hilliard, III." *Review of Educational Research* 78, no. 4: 797–827. doi:10.3102/0034654308320967

Lewis, Melvin, Travis R. Bell, Andrew C. Billings, and Kenon A. Brown. 2020. "White Sportscasters, Black Athletes: Race and ESPN's Coverage of College Football's National Signing Day." *Howard Journal of Communications* 31, no. 4; 337–350.

Londono, Tobon Amalia, Jose M. Flores, Jerome H. Taylor, Angeli Landeros-Weisenberger, Okoduwa Aboiralor, Victor J. Avila-Quintero, and Michael H. Bloch. 2001. "Racial

Lott, Tommy Lee. 1999. *The Invention of Race: Black Culture and the Politics of Representation*. Malden, MA: Blackwell Publishers.

Lynd, Staughton. 1966. "The Compromise of 1787." *Political Science Quarterly* 81, no. 2: 225–250.

Madden, Janice Fanning. 2004. "Differences in the Success of NFL Coaches by Race, 1990–2002: Evidence of Last Hire, First Fire." *Journal of Sports Economics* 5, no. 1: 6–19.

Manetho. 1940. *History of Egypt and Other Works*. Translated by William Gillan Waddell. Cambridge, MA: Harvard University Press.

Miller, Jeff. 2021. "East Texas's John Wooten on His NFL Career and Social Activism from 1967 to Today." https://www.texasmonthly.com/arts-entertainment/john-wooten-nfl-activism/

Moglen, S. 2005. On Mourning Social Injury. *Psychoanalysis, Culture & Society 10, no. 2:* 151–167. doi:10.1057/palgrave.pcs.2100032

Moskovitz, Sarah, and Robert Krell. 1990. "Child Survivors of the Holocaust: Psychological Adaptations to Survival." *The Israel Journal of Psychiatry and Related Sciences* 27, no. 2: 81–91.

Mswazie, Jonathan, and Tapiwa Mudyahoto. 2013. "Africanizing the Curriculum: An Adaptive Framework for Reforming African Education Systems." *Journal of Emerging Trends in Educational Research and Policy Studies* 4, no. 1: 170–177.

Muir, James R. 2015. "Overestimating Plato and Underestimating Isocrates: The Example of Thomas Jefferson." *Journal of Thought* 49. no. 3–4: 18–34, 71.

Nadal, Kevin L., and R. J. Mendoza. 2014. "Internalized Oppression and the Lesbian, Gay, Bisexual, and Transgender Community." In *Internalized Oppression: The Psychology of Marginalized Groups*, edited by Eric John Ramos David, 227–252. New York, NY: Springer Publishing Company.

Nagata, Donna K. 1990. "The Japanese American Internment: Exploring the Transgenerational Consequences of Traumatic Stress." *Journal of Traumatic Stress* 3, no. 1: 47–69.

NBA. 2023. New York Knicks Roster. *NBA Website*. https://www.nba.com/knicks/roster

NFL. 2018. NFL Expands Rooney Rule Requirements to Strengthen Diversity. *NFL Website*. https://www.nfl.com/news/nfl-expands-rooney-rule-requirements-to-strengthen-diversity-

NFL. 2020. NFL Owners Pass Resolution Rewarding Teams for Developing Minority Coaches, Execs. *NFL Website*. https://www.nfl.com/news/nfl-owners-pass-resolution-rewarding-teams-for-developing-minority-coaches-execs

NFL. 2022. NFL Owners Approve Rooney Rule Applying to Vacant QB Coach Positions. *NFL Website*. https://www.nfl.com/news/nfl-owners-approve-rooney-rule-applying-to-vacant-qb-coach-positions

Nobles, Wade W. 2008. "Per Aa Asa Hilliard: The Great House of Black Light for Educational Excellence." *Review of Educational Research* 78, no. 3: 727–747.

Nosek, Brian A., Mahzarin R. Banaji, and Anthony G. Greenwald. 2002. "Harvesting Implicit Group Attitudes and Beliefs From a Demonstration Website." *Group Dynamics: Theory, Research, and Practice* 6, no. 1: 101.

Obenga, T. 2002. "Thales of Miletus and Egypt." In *Egypt vs. Greece and The American Academy,* edited by Molefi Kete Asante and Ama Mazama, 165–178. Chicago, IL: African American Images.

Ovington, J. 1929. *A Voyage to Suratt in the Year 1689*. London: Oxford University Press.

Padilla, Laura M. 2001. "But You're Not a Dirty Mexican: Internalized Oppression, Latinos & Law." *Tex. Hisp. JL & Pol'y 7*: 59.

Petersen, Laura A., Steven M. Wright, Eric D. Peterson, and Jennifer Daley. 2002. "Impact of Race on Cardiac Care and Outcomes in Veterans with Acute Myocardial Infarction." *Medical Care* 40, no.1: I86–I96.

Rada, James A., and Tim K. Wulfemeyer. 2005. "Color-Coded: Racial Descriptors in Television Coverage of Intercollegiate Sports." *Journal of Broadcasting & Electronic Media* 49, no. 1: 65–85.

Reid, Jason. 2016. Rethinking the Rooney Rule. *The Undefeated*. https://andscape.com/features/rethinking-the-rooney-rule/

Reid, Jason. 2023. "The NFL's Accelerator Program Opens Doors, but Challenges Remain for Minority Employees." Andscape, May 23, 2023. https://andscape.com/features/the-nfls-accelerator-program-opens-doors-but-challenges-remain-for-minority-employees/

Sabin, Janice A., Brian A. Nosek, Anthony G. Greenwald, and Frederick P. Rivara. 2009. "Physicians' Implicit and Explicit Attitudes About Race by MD Race, Ethnicity, and Gender." *J Health Care Poor Underserved* 20, no. 3: 896–913.

Schwalbe, Michael, Daphne Holden, Douglas Schrock, Sandra Godwin, Shealy Thompson, and Michele Wolkomir. 2000. "Generic Processes in the Reproduction of Inequality: An Interactionist Analysis." *Social Forces* 79, no. 2: 419–452.

Shillington, Kevin. 2012. *History of Africa*. New York, NY: Palgrave Macmillan.

Shugart, Sanford. 2013. "The Challenge to Deep Change: A Brief Cultural History of Higher Education." *Planning for Higher Education 41, no.* 2: 7–17.

Smedley, Brian. D., Adrienne Y. Stith, and Alan R. Nelson. 2003. *Unequal Treatment: Confronting Racial and Ethnic Disparities in Health Care*. Washington, DC: The National Academies Press.

Solomon, Zahava, Moshe Kotler, and Mario Mikulincer. 1988. "Combat-Related Post-Traumatic Stress Disorder Among Second-Generation Holocaust Survivors: Preliminary Findings." *American Journal of Psychiatry* 145, no. 7: 865– 868.

Solow, Benjamin L., John L. Solow, and Todd B. Walker. 2011. "Moving on Up: The Rooney Rule and Minority Hiring in the NFL." *Labour Economics* 18, no. 3: 332–337.

Taylor Jr., Herman A., John G. Canto, Bonnie Sanderson, William J. Rogers, and Joseph Hilbe. 1998. "Management and Outcomes for Black Patients With Acute Myocardial Infarction in the Reperfusion Era." *The American Journal of Cardiology* 82, no. 9: 1019–1023.

Thomas, Robert E., and Bruce Louis Rich. 2004. "Under the Radar: The Resistance of Promotion Biases to Market Economic Forces." *Syracuse L. Rev.* 55:301.

Van Sterkenburg, Jacco, Rens Peeters, and Noortje Van Amsterdam. 2019. "Everyday Racism and Constructions of Racial/Ethnic Difference In and Through Football Talk." *European Journal of Cultural Studies* 22, no. 2: 195–212.

Watermeyer, Brian, and Tristan Görgens. 2014. "Disability and Internalized Oppress ion." *Internalized Oppression: The psychology of marginalized groups*: 253–280.

Watkins, William H. 2008. "Asa Grant Hilliard III: Scholar Supreme." *Review of Educational Research* 78, no. 4: 994–1009. doi:10.3102/0034654308320965

Watts, Roderick J., Derek M. Griffith, and Jaleel Abdul Adil. 1999. "Sociopolitical Development as an Antidote for Oppression—Theory and Action." *American Journal of Community Psychology* 27, no. 2: 255–271.

Watts-Jones, D. 2002. "Healing Internalized Racism: The Role of a Within-Group Sanctuary Among People of African Descent." *Family Process* 41, no. 4: 591–601.

Weitzman, Shimon, Lawton Cooper, Lloyd Chambless, Wayne Rosamond, Limin Clegg, Gretchen Marcucci, Fredric Romm, and Alice White. 1997. "Gender,

Racial, and Geographic Differences in the Performance of Cardiac Diagnostic and Therapeutic Procedures for Hospitalized Acute Myocardial Infarction in Four States." *The American Journal of Cardiology* 79, no. 6: 722–726.

Wesseling, H. 1998. "History: Science or Art?" *European Review* 6, no. 3: 265–267.

Williams, Allman F. 1991. "Who Are We." *U.S. News and World Report* 3, no. 12: 53–60.

Williams, David R., and Ruth Williams-Morris. 2000. "Racism and Mental Health: The African American Experience." *Ethnicity & Health* 5, no. 3–4: 243–268.

Woldegiorgis, Emnet Tadesse, and Martin Doevenspeck. 2013. "The Changing Role of Higher Education in Africa: A Historical Reflection." *Higher Education Studies* 3, no. 6: 35–45.

Zulu, Itibari M. 1993. "The Ancient Kemetic Roots of Library and Information Science." Newark, NJ: Black Caucus of the American Library Association.

Chapter 4

Psychoanalysis, Mental Coaching, and Sports

Robert Samuels

In my book *Bad Beat Therapy*, I argue that the key to getting better at most competitive activities is radical self-honesty (Samuels 2021). However, psychoanalysis tells us that people not only often lie to other people, but they lie to themselves. In fact, Freud's theory of repression is the key to understanding the unconscious and psychoanalysis itself; although few people fully accept this radical notion (Freud 1957). After all, if there is anyone we know, it must be ourselves, and yet, we deceive ourselves to protect and stabilize our self-image and sense of control. From this perspective, the unconscious is not simply the part of our mental world lacking awareness; rather, the unconscious is caused by self-deception, which itself requires a division of the self into a part that lies and another part that knows the truth (Von Hippel and Trivers 2011).

In terms of helping gamers and athletes improve their performance, they must be able to confront what they are doing wrong, and this demands that they stop hiding things from themselves. In fact, all other forms of therapy that do not embrace the principles of psychoanalysis are destined to be less effective since they do not begin with acknowledging the unconscious and repression. Moreover, as Freud discovered, the only way to gain access to repressed material is to allow for someone to speak without judgment or self-censorship, and this process is enabled by the neutrality of the analyst and the working through of the transference (Kris 1990). Unfortunately, most modes of mental coaching reinforce the transference by placing the coach or therapist in the idealized position of the one who knows (Rijken et al. 2016). This idealizing relationship functions to shift responsibility from the individual to the authority, thus establishing a destructive mode of dependency.

Following the tradition of Zen, in psychoanalysis, the student has to kill the master on a symbolic level in order to fully affirm freedom and responsibility (Moncayo 1998).

By refusing to gratify the demands of the patients, the analyst produces an optimal level of frustration, which can help them to deal with failure and dissatisfaction in a safe environment (Kohut 2009). This type of relationship also enables the working through of past expectations and desires as it allows for a direct access to the truth of one's memories and fantasies. As a blank screen, the analyst serves as a place for the mental projection of unconscious thoughts and feelings, and it is through this discovery of repressed material that one learns what one needs to know to improve one's performance.

To further elaborate on what psychoanalysis can contribute to the growing field of mental coaching, I will examine the world of poker. Although some argue that this game is not a sport, it does rely on skill, mental endurance, risk-taking, and strategy (Schoonmaker 2000). In fact, I argue that the main thing separating long-term winners from long-term losers in poker has to do with the psychology of the players. On the most basic level, to be successful in this activity, one needs to be patient, disciplined, rational, and in control of one's emotions. Moreover, like athletes and other gamers, poker players tend to be dominated by many superstitions and self-defeating tendencies that undermine their desired performance (Bersabé and Arias 2000).

THERE IS NO BIG OTHER

One of the hardest lessons for people to learn in life is that there is no super power watching over us and controlling the world. There is also no natural moral order or inevitable system of justice, but we can't help but believe that everything happens for a reason. In other words, there is no evil demon who caused you to suffer a bad loss, and even though there is much randomness in the world, you only have yourself to blame or reward (Guttentag and Havitz 2010). This is a very difficult and important life lesson that one can learn through poker and other competitive endeavors.

As a psychoanalyst who plays poker, one of the most interesting things that I have learned is how people are so deluded about their own personality and behaviors (Lubet 2002). For example, one time I was playing at the table with this guy who was winning most of the pots, and he had accumulated a huge stack. During one of the breaks, we started to talk, and he said to me, "I love every part of poker, every moment." I asked him if he still loved the game when he was losing, and he told me that it does not matter if he is up or down—he just loves the game. About an hour later, he had lost almost all of his giant stack, and I could see that he was becoming increasingly agitated and loud, finally after a bad beat, he screamed, and it looked like he was trying to tip over the table. Clearly this guy was not in touch with his own emotions and psychology.

As Tommy Angelo argues in his book *Painless Poker*, emotional 'tilt' can be reduced if you practice meditation; however, there is a negative side to this strategy (Angelo 2017). While I argue that one can learn a great deal from one's unexpected losses, the type of Zen meditation that Angelo discusses can lead to one simply denying the truth of one's own actions, thoughts, and desires. For instance, Angelo suggests that after a bad beat, which is the common poker term for losing when one should win, one should focus on one's breathing and try to remain still in order to remove oneself from the immediate emotions of one's situation. In contrast, I think that one has to learn from one's emotions and not escape into the bliss of meaningless nothingness.

To illustrate this last point about not using mediation or other practices to avoid the pain of bad beats, I once shared an apartment with a guy who spent hours each day meditating, but once he had a problem, he would fly off into a fit of rage. He had spent so much time trying to escape through Zen, that he was unable to deal with his problems, and he eventually had a nervous breakdown. The key then is not to deny one's emotions and feelings; rather, one has to seek out the causes for emotional pain, and one can do this through a practice of radical self-honesty.

PAIN AND PERFORMANCE

So far, most efforts to try to use psychology to help improve performance have been limited by the employment of a very unrealistic model of human thinking and behavior (Butler-Bowdon 2017). By turning to psychoanalysis, I show how we need to consider the ways that people receive satisfaction from suffering, and the only path to overcoming this basic masochism is to engage in a process of uncensored truth telling (Freud 1961). A key then to a psychoanalytic model of mental coaching is to realize that not only do people enjoy self-destructive actions, but they also enjoy lying to themselves about their own experiences.

Psychoanalysis tells us that we often can only learn something new and difficult if we learn it through a painful situation (Freud 1966). In other words, bad losses can help us to improve our game by searing new information into our resistant brains, but we have to be open to learning during a time of pain and confusion. Moreover, we can read a hundred books, but we will probably only learn from these books if we can match the abstract knowledge with our own specific experiences.

Another psychological lesson we can learn from poker is that people blame others for their problems, and they take total credit for all of their successes (Ahmed and Braithwaite 2005). This issue is evident when players blame the dealer for their bad luck and horrible cards, but they proudly praise themselves whenever they win (MacKay et al. 2014). Since people want to protect their positive self-image, they do not want to take responsibility when they make a mistake, and since they want to believe that they are better than other people, they have to blame someone else, or something else, when things go wrong. In fact, studies show that most people think they have above average looks and intelligence (Rahmani et al. 2017).

This positive belief in ourselves can help us get through the day and overcome obstacles, but it also can lead to a lot of self-delusion and an inability to learn from mistakes (Tolentino 2020). If a central aspect of my model of mental coaching is that we learn mostly by confronting reality in an open and truthful way, then people have to give up the need to always see themselves as good and effective. Once again, radical self-honesty is the key, and this is one of the hardest things to learn.

SELLING MAGICAL THINKING

As a psychoanalyst and teacher, I have learned that people often overestimate their ability to understand what other people are thinking. Since we like to believe that we are intelligent and great at mind reading, we often project our own thoughts onto other people (De Robertis 2022). Furthermore, psychoanalysis teaches us that we also do not always understand our own thoughts and behaviors and that we are often lying to ourselves in order to maintain a positive self-image. In terms of poker, players lie to themselves about how well they are playing or how good they are at predicting the actions of their opponents.

Not only do people over-estimate their own knowledge, but they also tend to over-value the knowledge of others (Saari 2020). Therefore, while it is clear that players often improve by hiring a mental coach, it is important to never over-estimate the ability of someone else to save you or fix all of your problems. In other words, just as you should not have an over-inflated sense of your own self, you should also not overly inflate the abilities of others because this over-estimation can also lead to self-blindness, a loss of perspective, and a lack of personal responsibility. Just like it is wrong to join a cult and think that some charismatic leader has all of the answers, one has to be careful not to be seduced by expert gurus who offer salvation at a reasonable or unreasonable price (Gedo 1975). Of course, it is ironic for someone like me who is writing about mental coaching to tell you to be wary of the advice of others, yet what I am trying to offer is not a set of guidelines from an all-knowing master but lessons derived from the study of psychoanalysis.

It is interesting to note that the type of emotional intelligence I am discussing here all relates to core ethical principles: one should be honest (with oneself), open minded, humble, and avoid prejudice. One should also take responsibility for one's actions and not blame others for one's own problems. It is also important not to seek out other people to save you from your own issues because you should not over-estimate anyone's ability to predict the future. Furthermore, since there is no inevitable moral order or big guy in the sky controlling everything, it is up to people to make their own destiny (Thompson 1998).

A huge problem of our culture is that people live in a state of anxiety because they do not want to look into the causes of their own emotions and the results of their own actions. Since we want to escape feeling shame, guilt, and anxiety, we turn to drugs and other forms of self-denial (Samuels 2020). Radical self-honesty is then essential to not only improving our athletic and gaming performance but also to improving our relationships and the world around us. For instance, many poker players who end up in debt, try to deny how much they owe, but the result is that they cannot sleep at night because they are full of anxiety and dread.

UNDERSTANDING EMOTIONS

What most people do not understand is that feelings are important sources of information, but they are incomplete in themselves (Parrott 2019). This means that when we have an emotional response to something, we are often repressing or denying our own interpretation of a specific event and focusing only on the bodily reaction to that event (Gobert 2016). For example, if I lose a big hand in poker, and I start to get angry, that anger is coming from the way I am interpreting the situation, but I am so overwhelmed by my emotions that I am not thinking about the cause and meaning of my reaction. I may be angry because I know that I made a bad move or I missed an important piece of information, or I lost again to a guy who I think sucks, but if I just focus on the emotion, I will learn nothing.

This topic of emotions is also essential to the notion that players should just go with their gut response. In the case of poker, some people say that math or logic does not matter because good players have an instinct for doing the right thing. The problem with these common beliefs is that they misunderstand how intuition and emotion work. When a player goes with his gut, it usually means that he has internalized a pattern of past situations and results on a non-conscious level, which do not require conscious attention (Gladwell

2010). This going with the gut does not mean that one is not thinking; it only means that one is doing automatic calculations and assessments. Players, then, are not relying on some animal instincts—they are simply processing information in a fast and automatic way. Therefore, when people say they are just playing on instinct, they are often simply saying that they don't like to think a lot about their own actions. Furthermore, since many of our unconscious intuitions deal with avoiding pain and dangerous situations in an automatic way, relying on your intuitions and emotions in poker and other competitive activities can get you in a world of trouble. What people need to do is to gain insight into the causes of their emotions and gut feelings, and once again the key is radical self-honesty.

OVERCOMING VICTIMHOOD

Psychoanalysis tells us that people not only blame others for their problems, but they enjoy seeing themselves as victims (Samuels 2016). Since the victim is good and pure, the victim cannot be criticized, and everything the victim does is justified (Cole 2007). After all, would you criticize someone with cancer or feel that they are unjustified in their anger and rage? While there are real victims of real events, what psychoanalysis tells us is that people actually fantasize about being victims and lie to themselves about their own history in order to take on a victim identity (Freud 1955). In fact, I would argue that victim identity is at the heart of most religions and political conflicts. Since the victim is always pure and justified, and you cannot criticize the victim. Victim identity allows people to act in horrible ways in order to seek revenge for their victimization, while they still see themselves as being innocent.

At the poker table, people use stories about unexpected losses to take on a victim identity, and this often blocks their ability to think through their past mistakes and current leaks in their game (Hayano 1983). As Bruce Springsteen wrote, you can hide in your bed and study your pain, or you can get in your car and escape. Actually, I am paraphrasing The Boss, but both of these reactions are really bad. One should not study one's pain: one should study what caused the pain and what one can do differently in the future. Radical self-honesty is, then, the key method for improving one's performance.

NARCISSISM AND COMPETITION

One of the main psychological pathologies affecting gamers and athletes today is called narcissistic personality disorder (Akhtar and Thomson 1982).

Although people think they know what narcissism is, it is actually more complicated than it first appears. Basically, a narcissist is someone who needs the recognition of others because he or she has a fragile sense of self (Samuels 2019). Therefore, one reason why these people seem so focused on showing off is that they constantly need the approval of others. Although, we all have this narcissistic need, in some people, it is exaggerated, and they are obsessed about what other people think about them. For poker players, gamers, and athletes, this obsession can be a big problem since it can not only block real self-awareness, but it can also lead to doing things only to uphold an ideal image. Thus, we find goaltenders who are afraid of staying in the middle of the net during a penalty kick because they will look bad if a goal is scored.

Psychoanalysts believe the cause for this disorder is that young people, who have either gotten too much or too little praise from their parents, grow up with an extreme desire to be praised by everyone they encounter (Kohut 1966). This form of narcissism explains why many people go on Facebook to post pictures of themselves or relate their latest activities. In our culture, there is a hunger for constant validation, and even though we are supposed to be a society of independent individuals, we have a culture of narcissism that pushes people to try to constantly have a positive image of themselves verified by others.

One of the negative effects of this narcissism is that when players do not win or do not receive recognition, they may enter into a spiral of self-hatred (Kennett 2020). A key then of overcoming this pathology, and its destructive effects, is to stop worrying about how other people think about you. This change is easier said than done, but it is an essential element of mental coaching. To be an effective and happy player, one has to give up the desire for recognition and approval. For instance, in many team sports, one has to check one's ego at the door and not focus on individual stats in order to help the team. Moreover, if one wants to improve, one has to be open to criticism, and this is the main thing that narcissists cannot tolerate. Since their self-image is so fragile, any criticism is seen as a direct threat to their identity (Atlas and Them 2008).

BORDERLINE PERSONALITIES

While narcissists are obsessed about what other people think about them, people with borderline personalities have a hard time controlling their impulses, and this causes them to be prone to addiction and failed relationships (Kienast et al. 2014). Many times, the driving force behind this impulsive behavior is a desire to escape shame, guilt, or anxiety. By engaging in self-destructive behavior, you can gain a temporary control over your life, and by using intense experiences of enjoyment, you can try to blot out the pain of having a conscience (Peters and Geiger 2016). The rush of winning can function to block self-awareness and flood the mind with pleasurable neurotransmitters (Beatty and Rush 1983).

WHY YOU CANNOT SLEEP

Anxiety and depression also affect how people sleep, and we know that it is very hard to play your A game if you do not sleep enough, but most people do not understand why they cannot sleep or what they can do to fix this issue (Vardar et al. 2007). In fact, the problem of not being able to sleep has become a national epidemic with many different causes, and unfortunately, the most common solution is to take sleeping pills, which can result in a self-destructive cycle where one takes a downer to go to sleep and then a stimulant to wake up and stay awake (Peng et al. 2021). These drugs can have a tremendous negative effect on your body and mind and should be avoided if possible (Machado et al. 2020).

The question remains why so many people cannot asleep, and one of the main reasons is they cannot stop thinking and worrying (Lundh and Broman 2000). A possible solution to this problem is to train yourself to change your thoughts and stop focusing on negative emotions in order to go to sleep. My advice here is the opposite of what I have been saying throughout this chapter: while meditative practices that train you how to stop thinking are bad for dealing with real problems and issues, when you need to sleep or rest, you have to train your mind how to stop processing information, and this can be done by establishing a "happy place" or fantasy world disconnected from your everyday reality. The goal then is to disconnect when you want to sleep and to re-connect when you want to learn and think.

Another reason why players cannot get a good night sleep is that they wake up in the middle of the night due to anxiety dreams (Meaklim et al. 2022). The main cause for these disturbing dreams is that when your conscious mind goes to sleep, your unconscious mind is able to bring up all of the things that you have been trying not to think about during the day. The solution to this problem is to deal with your issues through radical self-honesty during the day, so that you can have a peaceful sleep at night. However, most mental coaches and psychologists cannot help people with their sleep issues because they do not understand how the unconscious mind works, and they do not get their clients to practice radical self-honesty. Since people inside and outside of competitive activities are not really dealing with their problems, they take prescription medication and other drugs to regulate their anxiety and energy. In fact, we now have a giant medical-pharmaceutical complex that feeds off of people's vulnerabilities and provides alternative ways to silence thinking and difficult emotions (Samuels 2017). The problem with most of these medical solutions is that they only treat the symptoms (anxiety, lack of sleep) and not the underlying causes (the need to punish oneself, the fear of success, the aversion to risk).

FOCUSING ON RESULTS

Related to this distorted view of things is the outcome bias that relates to how we judge an event by the result and not the quality of the experience or decision-making process (Agrawal and Maheswaran 2005). In poker, we tell players not to be result-oriented because they cannot control variance, but they can control the quality of their decisions. Unfortunately, when someone loses money, the result often becomes the focus, and they are unable to learn from the experience.

This tendency to focus on outcomes affects all aspects of life and is very apparent in the field of education. I have found that many of my students are so focused on getting high grades that they are unable to learn something new (De Barros et al. 2021). For instance, I told students once "I want you to write the next paper without getting any help so I can see what you need to improve," but many of the students still got extra help because they were afraid of getting a bad grade. This problem stems from the conflict between external rewards (grades) and internal motivation (learning) (Covington and Mueller 2001). Related research has shown that when you give someone a raise or bonus, they often do a worse job because they no longer have an internal motivation, and they are simply working for the reward (Frey 1997).

One driving force behind outcome bias is loss aversion (Kahneman et al. 1991). Since people will often prefer holding onto something rather than taking the risk of gaining something new, they will avoid situations where they have to take a chance. In what is called status quo bias, people resist learning something new about themselves or opening themselves up to risks of losing what they already have, and so they tend to repeat what they already know and do (Samuelson and Zeckhauser 1988). Of course, to learn anything, you have to be willing to takes risks and give up on your present sense of what is right and wrong. Learning thus challenges how we see ourselves, and if we are not willing to see the world or our own identities in a new way, then we will be unable to learn in poker or in any other endeavor.

FINAL LESSONS

At the foundation of the model of mental coaching I am proposing is a practice of radical self-honesty. Drawing from Freud's theory of neutrality and free association, the goal is to create a space for people to confront their fears and desires in an open and truthful way. However, as we have seen, this method is rendered complicated because people not only lie to other people, but they also lie to themselves. Usually, these repressions are motivated by the desire to protect an idealized self-image, and so it is necessary to give up the desire for an idealized ego.

People also lie to themselves because they do not want to admit their guilt and shame, and thus it is easier to blame others for their own failures. In this process of transference, we transfer the locus of responsibility onto others. Part of this defence mechanism also entails idealizing the Other as the one who knows or understands. Since we do not want to be responsible for our own actions, we imagine a powerful higher power that is in control of everything. However, when we try to deny reality and rely on an idealized Other, we cannot help the truth from returning. Sports and games sometimes have a way of forcing people to confront a truth that they try to escape since these activities often have a clear winner and loser.

Instead of accepting the results on a competition, people often turn to magical thinking and superstitions. These uses of the primary processes show how our minds are able to go beyond material reality, and this form of mental autonomy not only makes us more creative and hopeful, but it also can leave us prone to delusions and distortions. Therefore, instead of relying on reason and a neutral assessment of results, people see the world through their fantasies. For example, many poker players believe that they never make mistakes; instead, they are just a victim of bad luck. Rather than admitting their faults, they cling to the fantasy of being an innocent victim.

Unfortunately, many of these lessons can only be learned though painful experiences, and some people will be unable to learn because of different cognitive biases. It is my hope that this chapter has helped to articulate a more realistic and effective form of mental coaching and performance improvement.

BIBLIOGRAPHY

Agrawal, Nidhi, and Durairaj Maheswaran. 2005. "Motivated reasoning in outcome-bias effects." *Journal of Consumer Research* 31, no. 4: 798–805.

Ahmed, Eliza, and John Braithwaite. 2005. "Forgiveness, shaming, shame and bullying." *Australian & New Zealand Journal of Criminology* 38, no. 3: 298–323.

Akhtar, Salman, M.D., and J. Anderson Thomson Jr. 1982. "Overview: Narcissistic personality disorder." *Am J Psychiatry* 139, no. 1: 12–20.

Angelo, Tommy. 2017. *Painless Poker*. Tommy Angelo Operations.

Atlas, Gordon D., and Melissa A. Them. 2008. "Narcissism and sensitivity to criticism: A preliminary investigation." *Current Psychology* 27, no. 1: 62–76.

Beatty, William W., and James R. Rush. 1983. "Spatial working memory in rats: Effects of monoaminergic antagonists." *Pharmacology Biochemistry and Behavior* 18, no. 1: 7–12.

Bersabé, Rosa, and Rosario Martínez Arias. 2000. "Superstition in gambling." *Psychology in Spain* 4, no. 1: 28–34.

Butler-Bowdon, Tom. 2017. *50 Psychology Classics Second Edition: Your shortcut to the most important ideas on the mind, personality, and human nature*. Nicholas Brealey.

Cole, Alyson Manda. 2007. *The cult of true victimhood: From the war on welfare to the war on terror*. Stanford University Press.

Covington, Martin V., and Kimberly J. Müeller. 2001. "Intrinsic versus extrinsic motivation: An approach/avoidance reformulation." *Educational Psychology Review* 13, no. 2: 157–176.

De Robertis, Daniela. 2022. "Mentalization promotion and affect mobilization in clinical work." *International Forum of Psychoanalysis* 31, no. 4: 218–225.

Freud, Sigmund. 1955. "'A child is being beaten': A contribution to the study of the origin of sexual perversions." In *The Standard Edition of the Complete Psychological Works of Sigmund Freud, Volume XVII (1917–1919): An Infantile Neurosis and Other Works*, edited by James Strachey, 175–204. London: Hogarth Press.

Freud, Sigmund. 1957. "Repression." In *The Standard Edition of the Complete Psychological Works of Sigmund Freud, Volume XIV (1914–1916): On the History of the Psycho-Analytic Movement, Papers on Metapsychology and Other Works*, edited by James Strachey, 141–158. London: Hogarth Press.

Freud, Sigmund. 1961. "The economic problem of masochism." In *The Standard Edition of the Complete Psychological Works of Sigmund Freud, Volume XIX (1923–1925): The Ego and the Id and Other Works*, edited by James Strachey, 155–170. London: Hogarth Press.

Freud, Sigmund. 1966. "Project for a scientific psychology (1950 [1895])." In *The Standard Edition of the Complete Psychological Works of Sigmund Freud, Volume I (1886–1899): Pre-Psycho-Analytic Publications and Unpublished Drafts*, edited by James Strachey, 281–391. London: Hogarth Press.

Frey, Bruno S. 1997. "On the relationship between intrinsic and extrinsic work motivation." *International Journal of Industrial Organization* 15, no. 4: 427–439.

Gedo, John E. 1975. "Forms of idealization in the analytic transference." *Journal of the American Psychoanalytic Association* 23, no. 3: 485–505.

Gladwell, Malcolm. 2010. *Blink: The Power of Thinking without Thinking*. Hachette Audio.

Gobert, Darren R. 2016. "Historicizing emotion: the case of Freudian hysteria and Aristotelian 'purgation.'" In *Emotion, Place and Culture*, edited by Mick Smith, Joyce Davidson, and Liz Bondi, 73–92. London: Routledge.

Guttentag, Daniel A., and Mark E. Havitz. 2010. "Superstition as a personal moderator in the development of commitment and loyalty to and within casinos." *Leisure/Loisir* 34, no. 1: 1–25.

Hayano, David M. 1983. *Poker Faces: The Life and Work of Professional Card Players*. California: Univ of California Press.

Kahneman, Daniel, Jack L. Knetsch, and Richard H. Thaler. 1991. "Anomalies: The endowment effect, loss aversion, and status quo bias." *Journal of Economic Perspectives* 5, no. 1: 193–206.

Kennett, Jeanette. 2020. "Blame, Reproach, and Responsibility." *Philosophy, Psychiatry, & Psychology* 27, no. 4: 395–397.

Kienast, Thorsten, Jutta Stoffers, Felix Bermpohl, and Klaus Lieb. 2014. "Borderline personality disorder and comorbid addiction: epidemiology and treatment." *Deutsches Arzteblatt International* 111, no. 16: 280–286.

Kohut, Heinz. 1966. "Forms and transformations of narcissism." *Journal of the American Psychoanalytic association* 14, no. 2: 243–272.

Kohut, Heinz. 2009. *How Does Analysis cure?* Chicago: University of Chicago Press.

Kris, Anton O. 1990. "The analyst's stance and the method of free association." *The Psychoanalytic Study of the Child* 45, no. 1: 25–41.

Lubet, Steven. 2002. "Lawyers' Poker." *U. Miami L. Rev.* 57: 283.

Lundh, Lars-Gunnar, and Jan-Erik Broman. 2000. "Insomnia as an interaction between sleep-interfering and sleep-interpreting processes." *Journal of Psychosomatic Research* 49, no. 5: 299–310.

Machado, Flávio V., Luciana L. Louzada, Nathan E. Cross, Einstein F. Camargos, Thien Thanh Dang-Vu, and Otávio T. Nóbrega. 2020. "More than a quarter century of the most prescribed sleeping pill: systematic review of zolpidem use by older adults." *Experimental Gerontology* 136: 110962.

MacKay, T. L., Nolan Bard, Michael Bowling, and David C. Hodgins. 2014. "Do pokers players know how good they are? Accuracy of poker skill estimation in online and offline players." *Computers in Human Behavior* 31: 419–424.

Macul Ferreira de Barros, Pedro, Maria Conceição do Rosário, Natalia Szejko, Natália Polga, Guaraci de Lima Requena, Beatriz Ravagnani, Daniel Fatori et al. 2021. "Risk factors for obsessive–compulsive symptoms. Follow-up of a community-based youth cohort." *European Child & Adolescent Psychiatry* 30, no. 1: 89–104.

Meaklim, Hailey, Malisa Burge, Flora Le, Sukjhit K. Bains, William Saunders, Stephen Ghosh, Moira F. Junge, Prerna Varma, Imogen C. Rehm, and Melinda L. Jackson. 2022. "Strange themes in pandemic dreams: Insomnia was associated with more negative, anxious and death-related dreams during the COVID-19 pandemic." *Journal of Sleep Research*: e13655.

Moncayo, R., 1998. "The real and symbolic in Lacan, Zen, and Kabbalah." *The International Journal for the Psychology of Religion* 8, no. 3: 179–196.

Parrott, W. Gerrod. 2019. "The social construction of emotions." In *The Second Cognitive Revolution*, edited by Bo Allesoe Christensen, 131–139. Champagen: Springer.

Peng, Yu-Ting, Ying-Hsin Hsu, Ming-Yueh Chou, Che-Sheng Chu, Chen-San Su, Chih-Kuang Liang, Yu-Chun Wang, Tsan Yang, Liang-Kung Chen, and Yu-Te Lin. 2021. "Factors associated with insomnia in older adult outpatients vary by gender: a cross-sectional study." *BMC Geriatrics* 21, no. 1: 1–12.

Peters, Jessica R., and Paul J. Geiger. 2016. "Borderline personality disorder and self-conscious affect: Too much shame but not enough guilt?" *Personality Disorders: Theory, Research, and Treatment* 7, no. 3: 303.

Rahmani, Kristin, Bonita Lee, and Decoding Human. 2017. "Cognitive bias on performance: Dunning-Kruger effect in collectivism culture." *Proceeding for ApsyA.*

Rijken, Noortje H., Remko Soer, Ewold de Maar, Hilco Prins, Wouter B. Teeuw, Jan Peuscher, and Frits GJ Oosterveld. 2016. "Increasing performance of professional soccer players and elite track and field athletes with peak performance training and biofeedback: a pilot study." *Applied Psychophysiology and Biofeedback* 41, no. 4: 421–430.

Saari, Antti. 2020. "Transference, Desire, and the Logic of Emancipation: Psychoanalytic Lessons from the 'Third Wave.'" In *Handbook of Theory and Research in Cultural Studies and Education*, edited by Peter Pericles Trifonas, 179–192. Champagne: Springer.

Samuels, Robert. 2016. *Psychoanalyzing the Left and Right after Donald Trump*. Champagne: Palgrave Macmillan.

Samuels, Robert. 2017. *Psychoanalyzing the Politics of the New Brain Sciences*. Champagne: Palgrave Pivot.

Samuels, Robert. 2019. *Freud for the Twenty-first Century*. Champagne: Palgrave Pivot.

Samuels, Robert. 2020. *Zizek and the Rhetorical Unconscious*. Champagne: Palgrave Macmillan.

Samuelson, William, and Richard Zeckhauser. 1988. "Status quo bias in decision making." *Journal of Risk and Uncertainty* 1, no. 1: 7–59.

Schoonmaker, Alan N. 2000. *The psychology of poker*. Two Plus Two Publishing LLC.

Thompson, M. Guy. 1998. "Existential Psychoanalysis." In *Psychoanalytic Versions of the Human Condition: Philosophies of Life and Their Impact on Practice*, edited by Paul R. Marcus and Alan Rosenberg, 332–361. New York: New York University Press.

Tolentino, Jia. 2020. *Trick Mirror: Reflections on Self-delusion*. New York: Random House Trade Paperbacks.

Vardar, Selma Arzu, Levent Öztürk, Cem Kurt, Erdogan Bulut, Necdet Sut, and Erdal Vardar. 2007. "Sleep deprivation induced anxiety and anaerobic performance." *Journal of Sports Science & Medicine* 6, no. 4: 532–537.

Von Hippel, William, and Robert Trivers. 2011. "The evolution and psychology of self-deception." *Behavioral and Brain Sciences* 34, no. 1: 1–56.

PART III

Fandom

Chapter 5

Are *We* the Champions?

Sports Fandom through the Lens of Pretend Play and Intersubjectivity

Benjamin Bernstein

How should we understand sports fandom? Or, put differently, what compels people around the world to spend their time reading about, cheering for, spending money on and emotionally investing in, sporting teams and competitions in which they themselves do not participate or impact the results in any meaningful way? This chapter posits that one helpful way of understanding sports fandom is as a form of pretend play, made possible by a shared consciousness among sports fans about explicit and implicit rules that govern this imaginary world. When fans engage with sports events, teams and players, they may imagine themselves as part of the team, with the capacity to influencing outcomes, in much the same way as children engaged in pretend play. Fandom-as-play can be thought of as a model for understanding different sports fan phenomena. This chapter will apply this understanding of fandom-as-pretend-play to a contemporary example of controversy in sports culture, the national anthem kneeling protests that began in the United States in 2016 as a way of drawing attention to racial injustice and police brutality, before spreading internationally to other sports such as association football/soccer. I will argue that inherent to the fandom-as-play model, is a difficult task in which fans must navigate the tension between the fantasy of athletes as play objects with the reality of them as subjective individuals whose opinions and actions might be opposed to those of the fans.

PRETEND PLAY AND SPORTS FANDOM

To understand why fandom is a form of pretend play for adolescents and adults, we must also define pretend play and understand how it functions for children.

Play is difficult to define, but a common and useful definition is that it is a pleasurable, voluntary, and engaging activity that has no contingent purpose other than enjoyment (Garvey 1990, 3). More specifically, *pretend* play, also referred to as symbolic or imaginative play, is a form of play in which children use objects, gestures, and words to represent people, animals, or events (Lillard et al. 2013, 2–3).

Pretend play sees children acting as though they live in imagined worlds where they may act as characters or take on roles that make sense within that world—such as, a pirate on a brigantine or a princess in a magical kingdom. In some cases, the playing child will dress up or use objects to symbolize objects in the make-believe world, like a pirate's hat or a stick that represents a pirate's sword, to continue with that example. Other times, children can pretend without any physical objects whatsoever. In any case, a key element of pretend play is that because the play occurs within a "pretend frame," any manipulation of these objects has no *real* impact on it (Weisberg 2015, 251).

In the context of this paper's premise, we can see these behaviors with fans who root for their team *as if* their cheering matters to the outcome, while simultaneously knowing it does not. We can think about superstitious fans (a recent poll indicated two thirds of fans identify this way) who might wear a specific jersey or sit in a specific place with the tentatively held belief that this action might impact the outcome (People Magazine 2021; Wann and Goeke 2018).

Winnicott writes about transitional space, noting that it occurs "in the exciting interweave of subjectivity and objective observation, and in an area that is intermediate between the inner reality of the individual and the shared reality of the world that is external to individuals" (1971, 64). This transitional space, which Winnicott believed develops in infancy, allows the infant to develop capacities for creativity and play.

The pretend play that emerges from this transitional space has been suggested to have myriad benefits for child development, both as the context for learning language (Vygotsky 2012, 29) and developing empathy (Brownell et al. 2002, 28), among other important milestones. From a child's conscious perspective, these benefits are immaterial—they play because they enjoy it. It also provides another key service to children, which is as a venue for expressing primitive feelings of aggression, desire, and fear.

As children grow up, they do not lose this primal need for pretend play, even if it can no longer occur as spontaneously or in this same form. It is rare, for example, to see teens or adults pretending to be cops and robbers, chasing each other around the factory or office floor with hands and fingers mimicking guns. And yet the desire for pretend play does not disappear, instead finding manifestation among adults in myriad forms, including the form of a sports fan.

While this chapter focuses on sports fandom, one might also see adult forms of imaginative play in political party affiliation, where we "root" for a certain candidate, regardless of their impact on our daily lives, or celebrity fan culture where fans might "root" for various outcomes of celebrity relationships, like a celebrity couple to stay together or split up. For example, warring groups of fans that became known as "Team Jen" and "Team Angelina" spent the early 2000s rooting for their preferred celebrity woman (Jennifer Aniston or Angelina Jolie) to win the heart of fellow celebrity, Brad Pitt (CNN 2012). Fans who wore shirts that read "Team Jen" or commented about the relationship did not affect the outcome of her romantic relationship, but were able to imagine, at least partially, that they were part of a pretend drama with real stakes. Similar examples can be found in politics where political supporters engage in fan rituals—like attending rallies or watching televised debates and cheering their candidate—which often have no clear connection to the election results.

Once we examine the origins and purposes of pretend play, the parallels with sports fandom become obvious. Fans dress in the uniforms of players who may look nothing like them and indeed might be 20 or more years older or younger than they are. Young fans, especially, may re-enact moments or moves in which they pretend to be the sports stars they cheer for. In extreme cases, groups of rival fans engage in violence towards each other as if their teams are truly at war.

Historically, we might look to the gladiator battles in ancient Rome as a precursor to the fan's experience of today. In those battles, the Roman people would attend real life or death battles between gladiators who were also slaves. Famously, these battles would often end when the spectators in the colosseum would cheer or jeer to influence the leading official, usually the emperor, to decide whether or not one gladiator should murder another (Allan 2005). The otherwise powerless people of Rome would get to experience omnipotent control over the actions and fates of these slave-athletes.

Do fans today continue to exert control over athletes like they did hundreds of years ago? The answer is complicated. On the one hand, the idea that fans can influence the events on the field, court, or pitch has never been less true than today, when multi-billionaires or sometimes entire nation states can buy players and act with impunity, changing the names of the teams, the colours of the uniforms, and even moving the teams to other cities. On the other hand, fan presence in the stadiums and arenas has been empirically shown to impact the performance of the players. A recent study during the Covid-19 pandemic found that European soccer stadiums without fans "decreased the home field advantage . . . as measured by goal difference, expected goal difference, and the probability of a home win" (Cross and Uhrig 2023).

Taken all together, the above theory and examples can form a conceptual model for thinking about sports fandom as a form of pretend play. In this model, fans are, ironically, "players." The play objects include the athletes, teams and associated paraphernalia, like jerseys and other athletic gear. In a less concrete sense, the fans use their imaginations to exist together in a sport-themed transitional space reminiscent of the one conceptualized and described by Winnicott.

Clinically, I have seen the pretend-play element of sports fandom in my therapy practice. With one patient, a 16-year-old boy struggling with anxiety, who is also a passionate basketball fan, we could sometimes spend a session imagining together the trades we might make if we were in control of his favourite basketball team, the Knicks. A shy and quiet kid in his typical social setting, he could become playful and creative when inhabiting his fan role. "*Oh man*," he would say, voice full of excitement, "*What if the Knicks got Dame and Embiid? Can you imagine that?*"[1] I might respond, "*Totally! They would be unstoppable. Who else would they need to round out the squad?*" And on we would go, imagining plays and victories while making jokes about players we both disliked. My patient could speak spontaneously and creatively, experiencing non-anxious social interactions and developing a playful intimacy that was impossible when others had tried to directly shift his anxiety through more behavioural or didactic interventions.

What makes actions like these not only possible but also enjoyable, is the transitional space, and what makes that space viable is an intersubjective frame: that is, a shared understanding of the rules, limits, and social practices of a particular population.

SPORTS FANDOM AND INTERSUBJECTIVITY

Psychoanalytic theories of intersubjectivity focus on how an individual's ability to communicate and share subjective experiences with one another leads to the co-construction of consensual reality (Stern 2005, 77–78). While various theorists have emphasized different aspects or forms of intersubjectivity, there is consensus that intersubjective processes help to fulfil an individual's epistemic and relational needs (Husserl 2013). That is, co-constructing and sharing in an experience of consensual reality promotes an ability to know about oneself and the world, as well as positive emotionality, play, intimacy, and bonding (Beebe et al. 2005).

While intersubjectivity is frequently viewed as an end-state or achievement of mutual understanding (Tomasello 2008), Husserl's initial conceptualization of the term suggested it was a condition in which social interaction and understanding became possible (Duranti 2010). Husserl's description of intersubjectivity emphasized the role of shared symbolism (e.g., language, culture) in allowing individuals to feel that they belong to a community or particular relationship, even when others are not present. He suggested that intersubjectivity could best be understood via the analogy of the possibility of Platzwechsel, translated as "Trading Places." This analogy is powerful, not only in describing the ways in which intersubjectivity pertains to taking the perspective of another, but also the capacity for intersubjective processes to allow for experiences that transcend one's physical position in time and space.

In sports fandom, the analogy of "Trading Places" pertains to the ways in which fans may identify with and embody the performances of athletes as their own, as a means of fulfilling their psychological needs. While this may not be inherently unique to sports fandom—certainly movies, TV shows, music, and video games provide individuals with a means transcending their physical state to experience that of another—several aspects of sports fandom stand out as distinct from these other arenas for intersubjectivity, likely contributing to their crucial role in human culture.

One distinctive feature of sports compared to the aforementioned activities, is the quality of fairness. That is, rules and officiating provide a structure for how sports are played to ostensibly make them fair and meritocratic. The quality of fairness suggests that those with the most talent, that put in the most effort, can succeed. This proposition is a far cry from the reality of many in the world. Particularly in a time when economic and socio-political inequity and injustice are salient and prevailing, much of reality includes the experience that it doesn't matter how talented or hardworking one is, it is nearly impossible to succeed.

Sports fandom addresses this sense of limitation in two seemingly contradictory ways. For many people, sports fandom may create a means for *escaping* a reality filled with oppressive forces and gross inequalities, via a reality in which hard work and determination give one control over their future and their success. A fan might think, "*even though I cannot triumph over my landlord who increases my rent in ways that feel unfair, in my fan-life I can cheer for and identify with players and teams who, due to the enforcement of rules, succeed or fail based on their hard work, talent and luck.*"

At the same time, sports fandom might be a way to dive more deeply *into* the inequities of our society, with fans actively engaging their identities as combatants against corporate interests and inequity. This latter way of being a fan can be seen in the reaction to the creation of a "Super League" by European football (soccer) teams in 2021, which fans perceived as an attack on fandom, itself (ESPN 2021). "Created by the Poor; Stolen by the Rich," read a fan banner at Old Trafford, the stadium of Manchester United. Fan outcry on social media and at the stadiums, themselves, led Oliver Dowden, the British Secretary of State for Culture, Media and Sport the British government to issue a statement: "With many fans, we are concerned that this plan could create a closed shop at the very top of our national game. Sustainability, integrity and fair competition are absolutely paramount and anything that undermines this is deeply troubling and damaging for football . . ." (Dowden 2021). The Super League project was soon abandoned by the British teams. In this case, fans had not participated in the fantasy of a world of fairness, but on the contrary had been able to use their fandom as a vehicle for exposing and battling injustice.

In a broad sense, regulative rules may be particularly related to establishing the parameters of a sport—what constitutes winning/losing; what actions are allowed, tolerated, and forbidden; who is the participant and how they participate. While essential to the game, many times breaking regulative rules (i.e., fouling an opposing player, getting a penalty) is widely accepted as within the boundaries of the game and does not compromise the integrity of the game or rupture the boundary between sport and ordinary life. In this way, minor breaks in regulative rules do not generally disrupt our perception of fairness or the capacity for individuals to experience the intersubjective benefits of fandom.

Conversely, constitutive rules are often quite central in maintaining the boundary between sport and real life. Particularly when focusing on fanhood, constitutive rules provide order and meaning to behaviour that would otherwise be socially inappropriate. That is, unlike "ordinary life"—where painting your face and body, believing that others behaviour is connected with your self, and/or acting antagonistically to others based on the logos on their clothing would be seen as bizarre and pathological—it is widely accepted in the context of sports fandom, on the condition that it fits within the boundaries of constitutive rules.

It is important to note that rules do not just pertain to the written, official rules of the sports but also the informal, "unwritten" rules that relate to etiquette or sportsmanship, meaning constitutive or behavioural rules (Kaluziński 2019). Further, rules in sport do not just apply to athletes, but often extend to and define the roles of coaches and staff, as well as fans/spectators. Rules are essential not only in defining the sport itself, but also in providing boundaries between what is sport and what is "ordinary life."

These unwritten rules, in particular, can be salient when fans seem to go beyond what is acceptable in their denigration of opposing team's players.

Fans violating the unwritten rules of etiquette have provoked some of the most notorious events in recent sports history. For example, in 2004, a fight on the court during an NBA game escalated to include fans in the crowd when one fan threw a drink at Indiana Pacers player, Ron Artest (now known as Metta World Peace). Known as the "malice at the palace," this massive brawl led to criminal charges against 12 players and fans, as well as changes to security procedures in order to better separate fans and players (Craig 2016).

Sports fandom is not the only fan culture to have trouble blurring the line between fan and player. In 1969, an armed fan at a Rolling Stones concert in Altamont, California, was killed by a member of a motorcycle gang who had been hired (famously paid in beer) to provide security (Austerlitz 2018). More recently, an attendee at a Dave Chappelle show rushed the stage and tackled the comedian before running backstage where he was apprehended. The attacker later said he was attacking Chappelle because he felt that his jokes about transgender people were "triggering" (Hernandez 2022). While these "fans gone wild" events can happen in non-sports fan settings, the sports arena seems particularly susceptible given that the athletes themselves are almost always engaged in their own competitions and battles in which their aggression must be channelled in appropriate ways. It is not surprising that sports fans, existing in a psychic space between reality and fantasy, find themselves negotiating the same tension.

THE ANTHEM PROTEST CONTROVERSY

Now, to further illustrate how this fandom-as-pretend play manifests, we will examine, in depth, the national anthem protest controversy of recent years. This example, chosen for both its recency and international relevance, demonstrates what happens when different groups of fans have different assumptions about the unwritten rules and intersubjective frame for the pretend world in which sports fandom exists.

The protests began in August 2016, when professional football player Colin Kaepernick of the San Francisco 49ers took a knee during the national anthem to protest racial injustice and police brutality. Kaepernick's action sparked a nationwide debate, with some praising his courageous stance against systemic oppression, while others criticized it as disrespectful to the U.S. flag and the military. The movement gained momentum as more athletes, from various sports and levels of competition, joined in solidarity, kneeling, or raising fists during the anthem.

Supporters argued that the protests aimed to draw attention to the urgent need for societal change and equality, while opponents viewed them as unpatriotic and undermining the spirit of national unity. Kaepernick himself said,

"I am not protesting the anthem or the nation, I'm protesting organized brutality. To me, this is much bigger than football and it would be selfish to look the other way. There are bodies in the street and people getting paid leave and getting away with murder" (Branch 2017).

The line between sports fandom and racial politics became blurrier a year later. In September 2017, at a rally, then President Trump said, "Wouldn't you love to see one of these NFL owners, when somebody disrespects our flag, to say, 'Get that son of a bitch off the field right now, out, he's fired!'" (Diaz 2017). A month later, on October 8, 2017, during an NFL game between the Indianapolis Colts and the San Francisco 49ers, Vice President Mike Pence attended the game and left abruptly after several players knelt during the national anthem. Pence later released a statement, receiving wide media coverage, explaining that he left the game as a gesture of respect for the flag and the anthem, stating that he would not "dignify any event that disrespects our soldiers, our flag, or our national anthem" (Pence 2017).

Critics viewed the incident as a political stunt orchestrated by the Trump administration to further polarize the debate surrounding the anthem protests and to appeal to their conservative base, noting that the costs for Pence's travel and security topped $350,000. (Deadspin 2018). Regardless, sports fandom was now explicitly and intimately intertwined with political power. In short, the executive branch of the most powerful government in the world conceived of itself and its mission, at least partially, through the lens of sports fandom. Importantly, fans themselves began to respond, with 33% of fans claiming to have stopped watching the NFL games in response to the protests, according to one poll in 2018 (Yahoo Finance 2018).

The protests were not limited to football and soon what began with Kaepernick was spreading to other sports around the world. In 2020, prompted by the murder of George Floyd and inspired by Kaepernick's kneeling, English soccer teams began taking a knee before every match as part of the "No Room for Racism" campaign. At first, the practice was widely supported but eventually some English fans began to boo the kneeling players and when the practice spread internationally, it was met with boos during a game between England and Hungary (Black et al. 2023). By the start of the 2022–23 season, the kneeling practice was discontinued with many team captains reportedly feeling that the practice had lost its impact as it had been too ritualized (Mather 2022).

On the surface, it appears as though the nature of the fan reaction to the anthem protests is simply about the rising importance of political identity in public life. That is, fans' political identities have superseded their identity as sports fans, in much the same way that partisan politics has infected many other areas of life, such as, the government's response to the Coronavirus pandemic (Rothwell and Makridis 2020). This idea connects to social identity theory, which posits that people tend to view the world through the lens of their group affiliations, making their identity a significant influence on their perception of new information and situations (Tajfel 1982). Consequently, individuals often rely on their social identity as a guiding principle when forming judgments in the face of contentious issues. Perhaps political identities have become more salient than other identities and sports fandom is just the latest arena to be infected with partisan political identities which trump everything else. While this theory can explain why fans might react with one opinion versus another, I do not believe it sufficiently explains why they react to events like player protests in the first place. For that we need to look at the pretend-play nature of fandom.

When applied to the anthem controversy, we can imagine that fans who agree that police brutality and/or racism is a major problem are supportive of the kneeling and fans who feel that this issue was not only overblown but also that kneeling is unpatriotic are against the kneeling (Mirer and Grubic 2020; Moritz and Zenor 2022). There is certainly some truth to this understanding, but there is a deeper understanding to be gained from seeing this through the lens of sports fandom as play. That deeper understanding is that fans found the protests to be disruptive—or not—to their ability to immerse in the intersubjective playspace.

As explained in the first section, sports fans enter a transitional space when they activate their fan identity. It is a space where they can imagine themselves to be something other than they are in a world other than the one they inhabit. What makes that space viable is that it is not invaded or polluted by a disagreeable version of reality.

For those fans who do not believe that the problem of racist policing exists, the anthem protests break the framework of their playspace by inviting the parts of "real life" that they are either trying to ignore or don't believe are real. In their fantasy, it is possible to leave behind the conflicts and tensions associated with race, as if they had moved to an all-white suburb. In this fantasy, they can pretend as if there is a world free from racial identity. Their fandom and whiteness allow them to imagine a frictionless existence, where any friction feels intrusive, with them no longer able to "escape" into the world of pretend play. The protests shatter their playspace. Indeed, one research study found that Black fans are more likely to support anthem protests and believe that protesting athletes should not be punished by their leagues (Intravia et al. 2018). While we might understand this as racial solidarity, there is something curious about the support for not only the players protesting but the belief that players should not be punished. In other words, the fans are saying that, in protesting, the players were still playing fairly.

For those fans in support of, or indifferent to, the kneeling, perhaps the kneeling does not rupture the frame of the playspace because these fans do not fantasize about leaving racial tensions behind. A fan whose schema of the world includes race, even a white fan, cannot move to a white suburb and forget that schema. The insisted absence of racial politics appears to be a childish act of denial. If anything, the introduction of political protests, and racial awareness, make the playspace feel more real. "*Oh*," this fan might say, "*this is similar enough to reality for me to still buy into it*." This points to the fact that it is not about the intrusion of reality that makes it assaultive to a sports fan, but instead the intrusion of a reality *disagreeable* to them. This experience is true across the political spectrum. For example, the fly-over of military jets before football games presents a form of reality that can intrude into fan enjoyment of sporting events, even if a more stereotypically "patriotic" fan might applaud it. One military veteran, a Boston Red Sox fan, described the experience of seeing military jets flying overhead before games, "That's not something that I see should be flying over a sports stadium . . . You know, these are weapons of death . . . they certainly shouldn't be celebrated and applauded" (WBUR 2018).

Analogously, if a group of children was playing cops and robbers and one child wanted to pretend to be a robber's brother who tries to persuade him to turn himself in, the children would have to somehow decide if this story line would make sense. Do robbers have brothers? Would the brother act this way? Is the departure from the main narrative—that of cops chasing robbers—too disruptive to the other children, or can they integrate it into their playspace? These are the questions we are confronting when sports fandom intersects with racial politics. Essentially: can anti-racism protests be part of a pretend play scenario without disrupting the frame that makes that pretend play possible?

If we start to think about sports fandom as pretend play, we can also imagine that the athletes are versions of our toys. As fans we semi-accept that we cannot control their athletic performance on the field. I say, "semi-accept," because indeed we still have the fantasy that our rooting and cheering can make them run faster ("*Go! Go!*" we yell as a player sprints down the field or around the bases) or defend better (the chant of "*de-fense! de-fense!*"). We become severely disappointed when our toys break, that is, when our favourite players get injured, but still, we can persist in the fantasy. However, we can't play pretend if our toys suddenly have consciousness and rebel.

When players began to kneel and protest, and some subset of fans get upset, part of the problem is a breaking of the illusion of control of our now conscious toys, that is, athletes who suddenly have consciousness. The wildly popular movie *Toy Story* (1995) and its sequels imagines a world where toys are alive with their own consciousness and will, but that, in the presence of those that play with them, namely children, the toys appear and act as lifeless objects to be controlled and manipulated. Our fantasy is that as fans, we can do the same with the athletes. Athletes whose actions appear to be fully self-possessed and act in opposition to our desires, can provoke big emotions in us from dismay to rage.

That rage was on display when a Michigan state police director Col. Kriste Kibbey Etue wrote on social media in response to the anthem protests that the players were, "millionaire ingrates who hate America" and "a bunch of rich, entitled, arrogant, ungrateful, anti-American degenerates" (Egan 2017). Notably, her police department was under investigation at the time for the assault of a 15-year-old black teenager.

This more sinister version of the sports fan-pretend play analogy was put forward by William C. Rhoden in his book, *Forty Million Dollar Slaves: The Rise, Fall and Redemption of the Black Athlete* (2006). Rhoden writes about how sports fans expect that black athletes "should be more grateful than their white peers for the money they make" (Rhoden 2006). The high salaries athletes earn should essentially buy their silence, like the toys in *Toy Story*. Early in the book, which traces black athletes' journey from "literal plantations" to "figurative ones" on sports fields and courts, Rhoden recalls a conversation with Bob Johnson, at the time the only Black majority owner of an NBA team (as of this writing, there are none, with Michael Jordan agreeing to sell the Hornets). At first, Johnson disputes Rhoden's plantation analogy but eventually concedes that, "The owners are white, the coaches work for white owners and the industry is run by white commissioners. Anyone who exercises power over them is white" (Rhoden 2006). Rhoden argues convincingly that summer camps and academies run largely by white men begin to separate black athletes from an early age, thus turning black athletes into assets that produce far more for their owners in terms of profit than most of these athletes receive themselves.

Much of psychoanalysis deals with how people navigate tense inner conflict. At the heart of sports fandom is one such tension: how can sports fans simultaneously exist in a transitional space in which they view players as their projective objects (heroes, villains, etc.) while also remembering the subjective, human nature of the players? These transitional objects, unlike toy soldiers and Barbie dolls, have the capacity to do everything from protesting unjust governments and laws, to voting for extremist candidates, and committing crimes. Fans often manage to contain this tension, as long as the subjectivity of the players is not *too* apparent. However, in moments of heightened political tensions, when players begin to act outside the norms of their role as athletes, and especially when those actions clash with the attitudes of fans, the tension can become unbearable, and fans feel ripped from their playspace and thrust back into reality.

It would be nice if it were as simple as reminding fans to remember that professional athletes are not our toys (or slaves). That, despite this somewhat disappointing reality, we can still enjoy the fantasies of omnipotent control as a fan if we change our frame to include the possibility that athletes can have political opinions different from our own. However, sports fandom, like the rest of life, is more complicated than that. There are actions an athlete can take, on and off the field, that cause us to awake from our fan dreams. In those moments, we fans are no longer members of the team, controlling the players, but fellow human beings, navigating an imperfect and unpredictable world.

CONCLUSION

To be a sports fan is to pretend. As sports fans, we pretend we are members of the team, that the team's victories are our own. We pretend that our cheering—even from behind a television screen—influences the players. Not only is this kind of pretend necessary for being a sports fan, but this make-believe quality of fandom is also why sports fandom appeals to so many people. Observationally, it is possible to see the many parallels between fandom and the kind of pretend play children participate in. Indeed, I argue in this chapter that sports fandom is a continuation of that childhood form of play, a way of satisfying a human need for a forum in which to express and potentially work through important emotions that might otherwise be unexpressed.

However, it's not enough to say that sports fandom appeals because of its pretend quality. In addition, we should acknowledge that to pretend there must be an intersubjective frame for this pretend quality to exist. That is, when sports fans pretend—for example, that they influence results from their couch or that it is permissible to jeer at opposing fans without meaningful consequences—they share certain assumptions with other fans and with society about what is allowed to happen in the service of fandom (Black 2021). These shared assumptions form a boundary that makes the play element of sports fandom possible. When these assumptions are no longer shared, the play, in a sense, cannot go on. That is, fans are taken out of their play when they cannot agree on the rules of their game.

If the teams or players break the rules, broadly defined, it becomes very difficult for fans to stay immersed in the transitional space required for play. One intersubjective area that commonly presents a challenge for fans and the intersubjective frame is fairness (see examples above). But the assumption more salient to this chapter's argument is that the players should act in ways that seem to have them "come to life." We want players who have subjectivity on the field or court, but it can be disruptive to our fantasy when that subjectivity includes political positions. When players seem to have a socio-political consciousness, especially one that is in opposition to ours, we may no longer feel as fans that we can participate in the make-believe required for fandom.

In this chapter, I argue that this understanding of fandom can meaningfully explain fan reactions to major events in the world of sports, focusing specifically on the anthem protests of the late 2010s. I argue that during those protests, fans who complained about or boycotted the NFL, including political figures, were not only upset because of tribal affiliation with a particular party or position, though certainly this is part of it, but also, and more deeply, because the athlete's protest disrupted the fantasy that the athletes are the fan's toy objects. A tension between the fantasy of the athletes as play objects and the reality of them as subjective people, became, for some fans, too dissonant once the athletes began to express opinions and rebel in the way that they did. The use of the term "woke" to apply to protesting athletes is relevant (Black et al. 2023), because it is as if the previously unconscious playthings became conscious, upsetting the fantasizing fans. There is obviously a racialized component to this phenomenon as well, as in some leagues, like the NFL and NBA, the majority of the athletes are black and the fans and owners, white, mirroring exploitative racial power dynamics with a long and violent history.

In conclusion, the intricate dance of sports fandom hinges upon a delicate interplay of pretense and shared assumptions, offering supporters a sanctuary to express and navigate profound emotions. Yet, it is the tension between the fantasy of athletes as play objects and their reality as subjective individuals, exacerbated by socio-political consciousness, that forms the crux of fan reactions to monumental sporting events, exemplified by the anthem protests. In this paradox lies the essence of sports fandom: a dynamic fusion of make-believe and reality, underscored by the ever-present spectre of racialized power dynamics, all of which continue to shape the experience of being a sports fan today.

NOTE

1. At the time of this writing, Damian Lillard is a player for the NBA's Milwaukee Bucks and Joel Embiid is a player for the Philadelphia 76ers.

BIBLIOGRAPHY

Allan, Tony. 2005. *Life, Myth, and Art in Ancient Rome*. Los Angeles: Hudson, Christopher.

Austerlitz, Saul. 2018. *Just A Shot Away: Peace, Love, and Tragedy With The Rolling Stones at Altamont*. New York: Thomas Dunne Books.

Beebe, Beatrice, Steven Knoblauch, Judith Rustin, and Dorienne Sorter. 2005. *Forms of Intersubjectivity in Infant Research and Adult Treatment*. New York: Other Press.

Black, Jack. 2021. "Football is 'the most important of the least important things': The Illusion of Sport and COVID-19." *Leisure Sciences* 43, no. 1–2: 97–103.

Black, Jack, Thomas Fletcher, Mark Doidge, Colm Kearns, Daniel Kilvington, Katie Liston, Theo Lynn, Pierangelo Rosati, and Gary Sinclair. 2023. "'Let the tournament for the Woke begin!': Euro 2020 and the Reproduction of Cultural Marxist Conspiracies in Online Criticisms of the 'Take the Knee' Protest." *Ethnic and Racial Studies*.

Branch, John. 2017. "The Awakening of Colin Kaepernick." *The New York Times*, September 7, 2017. https://www.nytimes.com/2017/09/07/sports/colin-kaepernick-nfl-protests.html

Brownell, Celia A., Stephanie Zerwas, and Geetha Balaram. 2002. "Peers, cooperative play, and the development of empathy in children." *Behavioral and Brain Sciences* 25, no. 1: 28–29.

Bryant, Howard. 2018. "Veterans Speak Out Against the Militarization of Sports." *WBUR*, July 20, 2018. https://www.wbur.org/onlyagame/2018/07/20/veterans-speak-out-against-militarization-of-sports.

Craig, Richard. 2016. "Malice in the Palace: The Incident." *Spectrum: A Journal on Black Men* 4, no. 2: 21–41.

Cross, Jeffrey, and Richard Uhrig. "Do fans impact sports outcomes? A COVID-19 natural experiment." *Journal of Sports Economics* 24, no. 1 (2023): 3–27.

Diaz, Hector. 2017. "Failed USFL owner Donald Trump offers explanation for NFL's issues with player safety and protests." *SB Nation*, September 23, 2017. https://www.sbnation.com/2017/9/22/16353394/donald-trump-nfl-colin-kaepernick-rally-speech-alabama

Dowden, Oliver. 2021. Twitter post. April 18, 2021. https://twitter.com/OliverDowden/status/1383828560972902401.

Duranti, Alessandro. 2010. *The Anthropology of Intentions: Language in a World of Others*. Chicago: University of Chicago Press.

Egan, Paul. 2017. "State police director's FB post: NFL players who take knee during anthem are 'degenerates.'" *Detroit Free Press*, September 26, 2017. https://eu.freep.com/story/news/local/michigan/detroit/2017/09/26/nfl-anthem-protest-michigan-state-police/705511001/

Fernandez, Gabe. 2018. "Report: Mike Pence's Gutless Political Stunt At A Colts Game Last Year Was Expensive." *Deadspin*, October 7, 2018. https://deadspin.com/report-mike-pences-gutless-political-stunt-at-a-colts-1829583176

Garvey, Catherine. 1990. *Play*. Cambridge: Harvard University Press.

Goldberg, Stephanie. 2012. "'Team Aniston,' 'Team Jolie' or 'Team Over It'?" *CNN*, August 15, 2012. https://edition.cnn.com/2012/08/14/showbiz/celebrity-news-gossip/jennifer-aniston-angelina-jolie/index.html

Hamilton, Tom. 2021. "Super League collapses: How fan reaction, revolt helped end English clubs' breakaway." *ESPN*, April 22, 2021. https://www.espn.co.uk/football/story/_/id/37616441/how-fan-reaction-revolt-helped-end-english-clubs-breakaway

Hernandez, Marjorie. 2022. "Accused Dave Chappelle attacker Isaiah Lee reveals why he tackled comedian." *New York Post*, May 22, 2022. https://nypost.com/2022/05/22/isaiah-lee-says-he-was-triggered-by-dave-chappelles-jokes/

Husserl, Edmund. 2013. *Cartesian meditations: An introduction to phenomenology*. The Hague: Springer Science & Business Media.

Intravia, Jonathan, Alex R. Piquero, and Nicole Leeper Piquero. 2018. "The racial divide surrounding United States of America national anthem protests in the National Football League." *Deviant Behavior* 39, no. 8: 1058–1068.

Kaluziński, Bartosz. 2019. "Rules and games." *Philosophia* 47: 1165–1176.

Lillard, Angeline S., Matthew D. Lerner, Emily J. Hopkins, Rebecca A. Dore, Elizabeth M. Smith, and Christina M. Palmquist. 2013. "The Impact of Pretend Play on Children's Development: A Review of the Evidence." *Psychological Bulletin* 139, no. 1: 1–34.

Mather, Victor. 2022. "Premier League Players Will No Longer Take a Knee Before Every Game." *The New York Times*, August 3, 2022. https://www.nytimes.com/2022/08/03/sports/soccer/premier-league-kneeling-racism.html

Mirer, Michael, and Adrianne Grubic. 2020. "Promotional Space of Public Forum: Protest Coverage and Reader Response in Team-Operated Media." *Communication & Sport* 8, no. 4–5: 489–506.

Mirer, Michael, Megan A. Duncan, and Michael W. Wagner. 2018. "Taking it from the team: Assessments of bias and credibility in team-operated sports media." *Newspaper Research Journal* 39, no. 4: 481–495.

Moritz, Brian, and Jason Zenor. 2022. "Damaged Goods? Perspectives on the Dehumanization of NFL Players by Fan Typology." *Journal of Sports Media* 17, no. 1: 25–49.

Pence, Mike. 2017. "Statement by Vice President Mike Pence on Leaving Colts Game after Players Disrespect Flag and National Anthem." *National Archives*, October 8, 2017. https://trumpwhitehouse.archives.gov/briefings-statements/statement-vice-president-mike-pence-leaving-colts-game-players-disrespect-flag-national-anthem/

People Magazine. 2021. "Sports fans admit they're so superstitious they've asked 'bad luck' family members to leave during the game." November 23, 2021. https://people.com/sports/sports-fans-superstitions-survey/.

Rhoden, William C. 2010. *Forty million dollar slaves: The rise, fall, and redemption of the Black athlete*. New York: Three Rivers Press.

Roberts, Daniel. 2023. "Survey: 33% of NFL Fans Boycotted League in 2017, for Various Reasons." *Yahoo Finance*, January 8, 2023. https://www.yahoo.com/news/poll-33-nfl-fans-purposely-stopped-watching-season-split-trump-kaepernick-110215783.html.

Rothwell, Jonathan T., and Christos Makridis. 2020. "The real cost of political polarization: Evidence from the COVID-19 pandemic." *VOXEU CEPR*, July 10, 2020. https://cepr.org/voxeu/columns/real-cost-political-polarisation-evidence-covid-19-pandemic

Stern, Daniel. 2005. "Intersubjectivity." In *The American Psychiatric Publishing Textbook of Psychoanalysis*, edited by Ethel S. Person, Arnold M. Cooper, and Glen O. Gabbard, 77–92. Arlington: American Psychiatric Publishing, Inc.

Tajfel, Henri. 1982. "Social Psychology of Intergroup Relations." *Annual Review of Psychology* 33, no. 1: 1–39.

Tomasello, Michael. 2008. *Origins of Human Communication*. Cambridge, MA: MIT Press.

Vygotsky, Lev S. 2012. *Thought and Language*. Cambridge, MA: MIT Press.

Wann, Daniel L., and Mary E. Goeke. 2018. "Sport Fan Superstition: The Importance of Team Identification, Sport Fandom, and Fan Dysfunction." *Journal of Sport Behavior* 41, no. 2: 227–244.

Weisberg, Deena Skolnick. 2015. "Pretend play." *Wiley Interdisciplinary Reviews: Cognitive Science* 6, no. 3: 249–261.

Winnicott, D. W. 1971. *Playing and Reality*. London: Tavistock Publications.

Chapter 6

The Psychoanalysis of Basketball

David G. Cushman

Professional sports have long been saturated with strict morality tales. Issues of right versus wrong, weak versus strong, loyalty or disloyalty become objects of fierce debate and vitriol. These narratives are fed by wider unformulated cultural desires and upheld by generations of fans. The all-encompassing nature of fandom and the way it intersects with family dynamics and expectations, and with socio-cultural-political pressures, can be rich terrain for understanding interpersonal unconscious landscapes and wider cultural themes.

This dynamic is particularly apparent in the National Basketball Association (NBA), the top professional basketball league in the world. Basketball is a more intimate experience than most other team sports. A smaller number of players are on the court at the same time, players are forced to play both offensive and defensive positions, and fans are close to the court. The possibility of grasping something intimate and real about the player's own psyche seems close at hand, yet inevitability unformulated aspects of the spectators' own psyche become projected onto these athletes. Themes of aggression, power, failure, and masculinity can quickly surround the experience of watching an NBA game, creating both a sensory experience and a defensive organization featuring splitting and projection. Psychoanalytic thinking can help us understand the process of the fans' experience, including projecting unformulated and dissociated aspects of themselves onto an individual player's behavior, and can bring new understanding to the actions of the players and coaches themselves.

In what follows, I use psychoanalytic theory to explore various situations, players, and fan reactions within the NBA landscape. The first three vignettes feature Lebron James, considered by many the greatest basketball player of his generation and perhaps of all-time (Mannix 2023). LeBron James has had one of the sport's most interesting and original careers, not just from his play on the field but also from his decisions during free agency. He was drafted by his home town team, the Cleveland Cavaliers, then shockingly left them during free agency to play for the Miami Heat along with two other all-star players, Dwayne Wade and Chris Bosh. Journalists and sport analysts called them the first "superteam" (Armant 2023). After winning two championships in four years with the Heat, he then again shocked the world by returning home to the Cleveland Cavaliers and battled with another super team, the Golden State Warriors, for four consecutive NBA Finals, winning the first championship in Cavalier franchise history. He then left the Cavaliers for the Los Angeles Lakers, changing his career trajectory again and winning an NBA championship during the COVID lockdown season. I use the following three vignettes to explore key moments in his career via psychoanalytic theory in an attempt to better understand his own decisions and the reaction to them by NBA fans and analysts. The final three vignettes in this chapter describe moments of tension and uncertainty within the careers of prominent NBA athletes, and tensions within NBA fan narratives.

LEBRON JAMES—PART 1: LEBRON JAMES AS BELOVED (AGAIN): NBA FANDOM AND THE IMPORTANCE OF FOLLOWING THE SCRIPT

The 2012–13 Miami Heat season was legendary; 27 wins in a row. A dramatic come-from-behind victory in the NBA finals. Revolutionary offense and overwhelming defense (Amick 2020). This was Lebron James and the Miami Heat's second consecutive championship. After James and Chris Bosh, another all-star player, moved to Miami in 2010 to join fellow all-star Dwayne Wade, they experienced vitriol after falling short in the NBA finals to the Dallas Mavericks. Animosity, both for the Heat and particularly James, had overshadowed everything that happened to Miami after "The Decision."[1] However, after losing in the NBA finals in 2011, Miami defeated the Oklahoma City Thunder and then the San Antonio Spurs in back-to-back championship series. Suddenly, for much of the NBA fan base, James morphed from the villain, which he never played well, back to the beloved Greatest of all Time (GOAT). Why did this change occur? The short answer is America always loves a winner. But I believe there were deeper issues, tied to dynamics inherent in sports fandom: in how we react to change and how frightening it is when the script we've come to rely on is challenged and a new reality emerges.

Melanie Klein described two basic stages in life that everyone goes through: the paranoid-schizoid and the depressive positions (Klein 1946).

These stages take place very early in the infant's life and occur before the Oedipal stage, the key moment in Freudian developmental theory. The paranoid-schizoid position is the first and most startling; it proposes a world of extremes, with people, emotions, and objects completely merged or attacked. In this position the infant splits the mother into two—the good caregiver who protects and nurtures, and the bad caregiver who ignores its cries and allows the infant to suffer. In reality, mothers contain both good and bad, yet the infant cannot bear to know that the same mother who protects it is also the mother who torments it. Frustration cannot be tolerated, as it is a threat to existence. The paranoid-schizoid position describes life in a polarized lens, where danger lurks everywhere, bad things must be kept apart from good things and life exists in black and white. The depressive position, which develops only after the infant has become able to integrate good and bad, seeks the gray, the in-between of life. It arises when the infant discovers that the two separate caregivers they have been dealing with are in fact the same—the caregiver who protects is also the caregiver who torments. This realization is depressing (as its name indicates) and destroys the infant's fantasy of a perfect caregiver. However, it allows the complexity and frustration of the real world to be tolerated. The depressive position ultimately carries a less exciting reality—there isn't the perfect mother waiting for us, and there isn't an evil mother we can direct all our bad actions and thoughts to—instead we must grapple with an inconsistent, limited, and ultimately frustrating world.

So, what does the paranoid-schizoid and depressive position have to do with the fans' attitude toward James? Sport fandom naturally exists in the paranoid-schizoid world. The sports fan lives in a world of extremes and paranoia, where one's chosen teams are unblemished, referee biases target only your team, and the other players on the opposing team are cruel and undeserving of any appreciation or empathy. Sports taps into unprocessed and raw emotions: hate, love, despair, and exhilaration. Sports narratives almost universally stay in the paranoid-schizoid position (Reynoso 2021), where early fears of cataclysmic destruction are alleviated through splitting of experience into good or bad. Fandom is prone to this type of thinking, where more primodial fears, desires, and wishes can be displaced through the splitting of affections and hate towards athletes.

James' initial narrative was as a potential savior of the NBA, which had been losing viewership since the retirement of Michael Jordan (Chatelle 2008). He was seen as blessed with the scoring ability of Michael Jordan, the court vision of Magic Johnson, along with the marketability of Shaquille O'Neal, a complete package that could reinvigorate the NBA. A basketball prodigy from an extremely young age (Windhorst 2018), his high school basketball games were shown on national television and he entered the NBA as the most anticipated prospect perhaps ever. To cap it all off, he was drafted by his hometown team, the Cleveland Cavaliers. Suddenly, the best player to enter the league in decades had the potential to fulfill the often naïve and racist ideas of the "right way" to play ball (Colas 2012). James was polite and approachable—the anti-Allen Iverson.[2] He represented the ideal of a perfect player; the superstar who made teammates better without making white NBA fans uncomfortable, unlike many of the best players of the post-Jordan era, including Iverson. He was made into what corporate and white NBA fans wanted, based on their own fantasies of the perfect modern-era basketball star.

Once James demonstrated a more complex and nuanced personality by declining to resign with his hometown team the Cavaliers, signing with the Miami Heat, along with two other top NBA players, Dwayne Wade and Chris Bosh, and announcing the decision on an hour-long TV special, fans responded with shocking speed, switching from loving to hating him without a moment's pause (Givens 2010; Heisler 2010; Jackson 2011). NBA fans, when forced to consider a different James, one with his own motivations and his own idea of success, responded by eliminating much of their previous adoration towards him. The script they had created for him, the approachable yet dominant superstar, became muddled. They could not see James' decision as holding both selfish and selfless purposes—after all, he decided to take less money to play with other dominant NBA players to try to win an NBA championship, a decision that fits much of the traditional narratives of team-first ideals. His pass-first mentality went from a positive to a negative—he was suddenly seen as scared of the spotlight (Bleacher Report 2011), selfish for not wanting the ball, arrogant and stubborn. Instead of questioning the script they had created, fans simply decided that LeBron never actually fit it. He became all-bad, representing all that was wrong with modern sports.

While one can view this switch by many NBA fans as linked to paranoid-schizoid thinking (Reynoso 2021), another possible reason for this switch is the difficulty in the United States of seeing marginalized groups, in this case an African-American man, as having authority and desires unrelated to the majority-white NBA fans. This difficulty stems from racist beliefs and actions linked to need of the dominant group to avoid their own feelings of weakness, lack of agency, split-off feelings of inadequacy, and the accumulation and maintenance of power through dehumanization (Dalal 2006; Hamer 2006; Moss 2001).

After winning back-to-back championships, James was still fundamentally the same player and person he was in Cleveland. He was the game's best player, a mash-up of an ungodly amount of talent, incredible work effort, extremely high intelligence, and a natural unselfish tendency. From Cleveland to Miami there was some evolution—he became increasingly efficient in his offense, a dominant perimeter defender (Wallace 2012), and, likely the most important change, became much more comfortable handling the extreme pressures directed at him. After two consecutive championships, many NBA fans and analysts started to shift their opinion of James back closer to the original script they had of him—James as the greatest of all time, an unselfish version of Jordan, a likable Kobe (Beck 2013; Fromal 2013; Helin 2013; Mahoney 2013; Washington Post 2013). This shift did not represent a movement towards the depressive position, in which the vast NBA fandom started viewing Lebron James and other athletes in more complex ways, but instead indicated that sports narratives are most often designed to confirm what the collective fan unconscious already wants to believe. Part of the reason the paranoid-schizoid position dominates in sports plotlines is due to how complicated and perhaps unsatisfying the depressive position can be. Sports allow us to avoid the gray and stay in a black-and-white, good and bad world. James isn't the savior or sinner we described him as, and our inability to see him as both only limits our understanding of him.

LEBRON JAMES—PART 2: GHOSTS, ANCESTORS, AND LEBRON

In 2014, LeBron James, after four years with the Miami Heat, returned to the beginning of his professional career, his original and hometown team, the Cleveland Cavaliers. He returned to where he began; where he was drafted; where his specious innocence fell apart when he broke hearts across Akron and Cleveland by leaving; in which he seemed shockingly unaware of how his made for TV special announcing he was leaving would come across; where he went from beloved to hated in the span of a sentence; where he failed to win a championship for seven painful years; where he was not just seen as a basketball savior for a team whose most memorable moment involves Craig Ehlo collapsing to the ground (Herbert 2020),[3] but a savior with the weight of being literally born and raised in North Ohio. James, in an odd twist to his story, arrived back to Cleveland after four short, dramatic years with the Miami Heat, where he won two championships, lost two championships, and had his most dramatic failures (Neiman 2011) and successes (NBA.com 2013). Why would he go back to a place where he has known only heartbreak, of disappointment, of impossible to meet expectations? Why would he decide to possibly recreate an experience where he ended up becoming the ultimate bad object (Davies 2004)?

Hans Loewald, a psychoanalyst ahead of his time, was an extremely creative thinker (Whitebook 2004), in a psychoanalytic environment dominated by a rigid adherence to Freud. In his article "On the Therapeutic Action of Psycho-Analysis" (1960), Loewald compares the indestructible nature of unconscious thoughts and desires to the unsatiated need of ghosts, who haunt because they have not found peace:

> Those who know ghosts tell us that they long to be released from their ghost-life and led to rest as ancestors. As ancestors they live forth in the present generation, while as ghosts they are compelled to haunt the present generation with their shadow-life . . . In the daylight of analysis the ghosts of the unconscious are laid and led to rest as ancestors whose power is taken over and transformed into the newer intensity of present life, of the secondary process and contemporary objects. (1960, 29)

In this provocative description, Loewald proposes a distinction between how our memories stay with us. Ghosts are the memories that dissociate from our awareness. Instead, they stay and "haunt," they search for what he called "blood," such as remembrances and history. They cannot be satisfied because they are static, unchanging. Ancestors are the memories that we can tolerate as part of ourselves. They are free to live in our present as they have become part of our narrative. They do not have to haunt because they are not dissociated away, like ghosts. Loewald believes that we ultimately want our "ghost" memories to be transformed and integrated into our lives, to become "ancestors" that are content to live out their old age with us.

So can one understand James' decision to return to Cleveland as a desire to re-engage with his ghosts? To stop their haunting and blood sucking and transform them to benevolent ancestors? His Miami Heat period often felt dissociated from his Cleveland days. Outside of the intense backlash his move produced, there was little sense of continuity. He went from hometown hero to international playboy, with no in-between period. Perhaps James ultimately felt the pull to deal with the ghosts from his Cleveland days, that no matter how many championships he won in Miami the blood-sucking ghosts would not be satisfied. At the time it was unclear if it was a wise decision, as he left an extremely professional and coherent Miami Heat organization for a Cleveland franchise known mostly for disappointment and chaos. Some ghosts are best left alone, and if two championships did not transform his ghosts into ancestors while in Miami, it was difficult to imagine what could do the trick. However, during James' next four years with Cleveland, the sports world saw perhaps the most dramatic transformation of ghosts to ancestors in modern sports history. In the second year of his return to Cleveland, LeBron James' Cavaliers became the first team in NBA history to overcome a 3–1 deficit in the NBA Finals to win Cleveland's first-ever NBA championship (Windhorst and McMenamin 2017). Furthermore, James did so against a team that won the most regular season games in NBA history, and which was led by perhaps his one true rival, Stephen Curry, the player who has most fundamentally transformed how basketball is played since Wilt Chamberlain (Morse 2021).

It was impressive that James chose to come back in the prime of his career to a place that clearly haunted him. Perhaps by welcoming these ghosts, talking to them, dealing with them face to face, James began to transform them from dissociation into present day awareness, which helped him achieve, two years later, his crowning athletic accomplishment (Windhorst and McMenamin 2017). Loewald states that the "analyst helps to revive the repressed unconscious of the patient by his recognition of it; through interpretation of transference and resistance, through the recovery of memories and through reconstruction, the patient's unconscious activity is led into preconscious organization . . . " (1960, 29). If we relate this to the world of the NBA, while James may have lacked the safety of the therapeutic relationship, he was trying to do what Loewald recommends—recovering and reconstructing old memories, through his return to Cleveland.

It is a bit of a fallacy that ghosts and ancestors cannot coexist. We cannot transform everything into awareness, and in a particular vantage-point, feeling haunted can become a motivating factor. Ultimately, there needs to be room for both to live within us and around us.

LEBRON JAMES—PART 3: ON APPRECIATING BEAUTY: THE AESTHETIC CONFLICT WITHIN NBA FANDOM

The Warriors and the Cavaliers played in four consecutive NBA Finals, from 2015 to 2018, four years in which LeBron James confirmed his greatness by orchestrating the greatest comeback in NBA Finals history (Windhorst and McMenamin 2017), and Stephen Curry and the Warriors stamped their legacy as one of the great teams in NBA history (McCauley 2017). But, to my mind, the most interesting of their confrontations was their third meeting (Cacciola 2017). This series found both teams at the peak of their performance, with no major injuries to any of their key players, and a classic clash of styles between the freewheeling creativity of the Warriors and the physical dominance of the Cavaliers. The narratives surrounding this series also seemed to dredge up defining moments for both franchises—in 2015, the Warriors overcame LeBron James and a 2–1 deficit, winning the franchise's first NBA championship since 1975, and in 2016 the Cavaliers overcame 3–1 deficit, which had never been done before in an NBA finals series, and defeated a Warriors team who had won the most games ever in an NBA single season. After the 2016 series, Kevin Durant, one of the greatest players of his generation and in the prime of his career, joined the Warriors in a shocking and controversial free agency decision (Chau 2016; Gallo 2016) that challenged many of the tropes around talent, masculinity, and what qualifies as success (Lee 2019). At this point it was most intense and all-consuming rivalry since the Lakers and Celtics dominated the NBA in the 1980s.

Yet, there was an intense edge of negativity surrounding the finals (Felt 2017; Future 2017; Nadkarni 2017). Fans bemoaned the lack of drama during the 2017 playoffs, while journalists and former players complained (ESPN.com 2016) that Kevin Durant's decision to join the Warriors in free agency was cowardly (Gallo 2016), and made the outcome of the playoffs a matter of course and reduced interest in the NBA as a whole.

Within each respective fan base, Warriors and Cavaliers, there was a constriction of thought that led to simple narratives of "good" and "bad," with an abundance of paranoid schizoid thinking (Klein 1946). Gone was any discussion of the incredible play and individual and collective achievements from each team. Instead, players became transfixed into their most simple and obvious selves depending on which team one followed or which narrative felt most appealing. Sports fandom is based on projections, split off parts of our own aggression and fear, aspects of ourselves we are not allowed to express in normal society. So while this was not exclusive to this series, what I found interesting was that the longer these particular playoffs went on, the more the discourse from fans and the media became detached from what was unfolding: the beautiful and inspiring play of both teams, the truly outlandish individual accomplishments of multiple players during the playoffs (Kawakami 2017; Manning 2017), how each team dominated their respective divisions, and the likelihood that this moment represented an elevated plane of basketball not likely to be matched in this decade and perhaps for several more to come (Tinley 2017).

Donald Meltzer, a British analyst, has written extensively about the idea of the "aesthetic conflict" (Meltzer 2008), that the lack of capacity to have an authentic, immediate, and powerful interaction with beauty indicates a sign of deeper, powerful and troubling issues. Here, we had two teams that were playing beautiful, compelling basketball, yet somehow it seemed difficult for the larger NBA community to not only acknowledge this but allow itself to be stunned and overwhelmed by it. Did the incapacity to be animated by this moment in NBA history say something about our current society? The hypercritical nature of internet discourse, the increased amount of money and time fans invest in their teams, and a general skepticism from White America towards black athletes making free agency decisions all likely played important parts.

However, Meltzer (2008) might argue that it demonstrates a limitation of thinking, that if we were able to truly take in the beauty of what we're witnessing, to be stunned by the magnificent play of both teams, that it may open up room to experience deeper questions within ourselves and in our current culture. It may be safer to avoid such uncomfortable and uncertain terrain and dismiss this moment with skepticism and cynicism. However, this denies us this moment of beauty, which in turns limits our connection with ourselves and each other.

The alternative to the cynicism that dominated much of the conversation within the 2017 NBA finals was to try to keep in mind the opportunity to witness beauty, to see the genius in LeBron James' passing, Steph Curry's immense creativity, Kyrie Irving's gorgeous drives, and to be inspired by Dryamond Green's hustle and desire. The beauty showcased by both teams was rare. The challenge to fans of the NBA and in sports in general is to try to allow oneself to be stunned and awed by what they witness, and not, as Meltzer writes, "retreat in order to protect oneself from the impact of the beauty of the object" (2008, 150).

The last three vignettes describe moments of tension and uncertainty within the careers of prominent NBA athletes and tensions within NBA fan narratives. Various psychoanalytic theories are used that may help elaborate and illuminate these strains.

DWIGHT HOWARD AND FEAR OF BREAKDOWN

Dwight Howard was the first pick of his draft in 2004, one of the best defense centers ever, and is now out of the league despite tremendous talent. He played for several franchises and yet ended up frustrating each one (Scoloa 2012; Toback 2011). A theme of his career seemed to be a need to constantly begin anew, again. One example was when he was traded to the Los Angeles Lakers from the Orlando Magic after he become embroiled in a feud with his head coach (AP 2012). Soon after a very disappointing period with the Lakers, his free-agency ended with him leaving the Lakers and joining the Houston Rockets. He seemed confused and hesitant about the reasons behind his decision, which was similar to his prolonged exit from the Magic (Swartz 2013). Howard often appeared uncertain where he wanted to play and how he wanted to be portrayed by the media and the larger NBA fan-base (Bresnahan and Simers 2013). Each time he has left a team and a city, there is a sense that he was running away, leaving behind a chaotic mess (Scola 2012). Angry and hurt feelings from all parties were abound. Why did this same dynamic keep recurring?

Donald Winnicott, the British psychoanalyst and pediatrician, developed an idea he described as the "fear of breakdown" (Winnicott 1974). Winnicott believed that some patients, overwhelmed by fear and hopelessness, become frozen with unthinkable worry over experiencing a breakdown.

This breakdown is un-defined but central to the patient's fears and behaviors. Winnicott believed that the patient's fear is actually "the fear of a breakdown that has already been experienced" (1974, 104). The patient's overwhelming anxiety of breaking down, whatever idiosyncratic meaning that has to each person, has already happened to them when they were very young. They experienced a primitive agony that was so threatening to their existence they were unable to integrate it into their consciousness. They are haunted by the shadow of a trauma that was both experienced and not experienced. Paradoxically, the patient will maintain this paralyzing fear of a breakdown due to an unconscious hope that they will find a way to process their previous yet split-off breakdown.

So, what could Howard fear? What was his breakdown? There is no way to know, of course. Yet there is a sense that he kept running from something. When leaving various teams Howard struggled to layout his intentions and desires. He appeared to both want to stay loved by the fans yet be allowed to leave them without any repercussions. He tried to avoid being disliked yet his indecision left fans in several separate cities despising him. Howard seemed to struggle tolerating falling short or feeling disappointed with his situation. His tendency to run from these moments likely only increased their intolerableness.

Winnicott (1974) felt that the patient must find a way to experience what has already occurred yet was lost to conscious memory. The patient will continue to be overwhelmed by their fear of breakdown until they are able to experience it again through their relationship with the therapist. Or, as Winnicott wrote, "if the patient is ready for some kind of acceptance of this queer kind of truth, that what is not yet experienced did nevertheless happen in the past, then the way is open for the agony to be experienced in the transference, in reaction to the analyst's failures and mistakes" (1974, 105). By the patient finding the therapy incompetent and hopeless and surviving the analyst's futility, they can get in touch with their previous breakdown without completely breaking down themselves.

Did Howard try to create a breakdown, seen in the frantic nature of his vacillation at each choice on where he wanted to play, as an attempt to integrate what until now has been dissociated? Following Winnicott's idea of the patient re-experiencing a breakdown through the transference, Dwight may have needed to live out his fear of breakdown with teammates, owners, fans, and not run away, to tolerate disappointment and being disappointing, and realize that he has already survived his worst fears. If he had been able to experience this without needing to abdicate and leave, he may have found that his fear of breakdown wasn't as overpowering as he imagined it to be. Which might have been part of the key toward Howard becoming the franchise-changing player he aspired towards.

TRANSFORMATION THROUGH KLAY THOMPSON

Often patients come into the therapy room seeking something akin to transformation. They may know what they want changed in their life, or only have a vague sense of discontent and frustration. The drive to have something in one's life be transformed often exists beyond conscious speech. Therapy as a profession is largely dependent on the idea of transformation, and yet within psychoanalytic thought there is both an embrace of transformation and a weariness of this idea. Bollas (1978) writes about how the aesthetic experience with an early caregiver is the first source of transformation, and how the clinician needs use the poetics of interpretation to foster a transformational-object. Charles (2003) writes about how Bion saw understanding as a function of transformational experiences, mainly through metaphor and myth, and that transformation can lead to greater or lesser knowledge. Eagle (1999) importantly points out that even when clients claim they want to change, there is often a deep-seated fear of what they may lose by going through a transformation.

In a strange way, there is similarity between the therapeutic paradox of transformation and the increased wish of NBA teams to locate and understand the transformation potential of individual players.. In the NBA, athletes are increasingly coming into the league as unformed potential, rather than polished certainties. Thus, the idea of transformation is central to evaluating players and team potential. Some players drafted with high expectations may quickly be out of the league, such as Anthony Bennett (Hoffman 2017), or find their place as an excellent role player instead of a main scorer, such as Andrew Wiggins (Thompson 2022) or Aaron Gordon (O'Donnell 2023). Others confirm everyone's expectations or become even greater then what was anticipated, such as Luka Doncic (Pina 2023). Others may become all-stars from completely unexpected places, such as Giannis Anketokounmpo (Fader 2021), Ben Wallace, Draymond Green or Nikola Jokic (Rafferty 2023). As players are drafted into the NBA, the conventional wisdom is to not view them as their current form, but in year three or four of their career. This makes player projection increasingly complex. How can you determine someone's potential for transformation?

To expand on this discussion of transformation for both basketball and therapy, I will focus on NBA superstar Klay Thompson. Thompson, now four-time NBA champion, five-time All-Star, and likely hall-of-famer, was not always seen in such a light. In the summer of his fourth season, there was an active debate about his value and fit with his team, the Golden State Warriors. There were those who saw his potential (Kawakami 2012) and believed that his impressive size for his position, his excellent shooting, and potential as a strong defender indicated he would become a special player who was crucial to the teams' future. Yet, there were many basketball analysts at this time who believed his stats had not backed up the idea of Thompson as future star. Advanced stats largely showed that he had been an average starter (Lowe 2014). A discrepancy appeared to be emerging between his potential and his actual results. During the summer of 2014, rumors were abound that Kevin Love, an all-star power forward, wanted to leave his team, and that the Warriors were interested (Burns 2014; Stein and Shelburne 2014). Thompson was reportedly the player that Love's team wanted from the Warriors, and there was a general expectation that the Warriors would agree to trade him. Yet, the summer came and went, the Warriors steadfastly refused to consider trading Thompson (Helin 2015; Thompson 2014), and Love was eventually dealt to another team. If you went by both players' stats at that point, it seemed obvious that the Warriors had missed an opportunity (Lowe 2015). Many NBA observers were genuinely shocked and confused at the Warriors decision (Hughes 2014).

Once Thompson's fourth season started, all these concerns vanished quickly. His play took off to a new level, and he posted career highs in points, rebounds, assists, steals, blocks, free throws attempted, and shooting percentage, all while playing fewer minutes than the year before. The Warriors won 67 games and the NBA championship. Since then, he has become a multi-time champion and all-star while surviving two career-threatening injuries (Spears 2022), and is now beloved by the fanbase (Crowley 2022).

Psychoanalysis is often viewed as a theoretical and clinical endeavor that casts a harsh view of the human condition. Yet, psychoanalysis is a discipline that in many ways is dependent on the idea of transformation. In Freud's (1924) original conception of the Oedipal process, one succeeds by transforming erotic thoughts and feelings to parents by turning them towards peers. Klein (1946) viewed therapeutic growth through transforming from the paranoid-schizoid position (where splitting and projection rule) to the depressive position (where good and bad co-mingle). Relational psychoanalysis relies on the idea of patients transforming through the creation of new relational experiences between therapist and client (Barsness 2017). Psychoanalysis generally views transformation in complex light, where one struggles through a variety of complications, fears, and uncertainty to approach something akin to transformation (Eagle 1999).

What led hompson to transform from good to superstar? Some have argued that his time with the USA national men's basketball team between this third and fourth season increased his confidence (Cooper 2014). Others argue that was due to a new head coach at this same juncture (Taylor 2014). Like clinical work, it can be difficult to pinpoint the exact cause or reason for change, for patients in treatment or for NBA players in the prime of their career.

Possibilities are endless, and we often know little of what leads to a player's transformation.

Gerald Green is an example of the complications of knowing—he was a first-round pick who became a household name for the dunk contest, only to quickly struggle with consistency and focus and ultimately was out of the NBA by the age of 24. He then came back after two years of playing overseas and became a reliable and regular role-player, playing a crucial role in the playoffs for the Houston Rockets at age 32. Like Green's own roller-coaster career (Abrams 2012), transformation in the therapy room often arrives unexpectedly, on the patient's own timeline. The therapist is often most effective by simply maintaining curiosity, sustaining contact, and witnessing the client's own journey. The therapist's own desire for transformation from the client can actually get in the way of the patient process (Searles 2017). In the NBA, with the pressures of fans expectations, payroll demands, and ownership instability and incompetence, it is extremely difficult to wait, pause, and reflect. Perhaps the question should be turned around: how long can one wait for transformation to occur?

CONCLUSION: THE FRUITLESS SEARCH FOR AUTHENTICITY WITHIN NBA LORE

Authenticity is a strange quality, often mysterious to the individual who is searching for it within themselves, and between people who are locked in an interpersonal exchange. Often it is something akin to a "gut" instinct—you know it when you feel it. The search for authenticity has been an aspect throughout psychoanalytic history. Freud's conception of the id as a person's true wishes/instincts can be viewed as an attempt to identify authenticity within an extremely conservative Victorian society. Early psychoanalysis was defined by an attempt to uncover deeply repressed unconscious fantasies and wishes, and that through the careful silence and detachment of the analysis, the patient would eventually regress and reveal their true uncensored thoughts (Mitchell 1993). Jung's (1981) idea of individuation, Kohut's investigations into narcissism and the development of his self-psychology theory (Havens 1986), and Winnicott's (1965) conception of a True and False self, are further examples of psychoanalysis' attempt to define what authenticity looks like. A lack of authenticity often brings clients into the therapy room—a common reason is an uncertainty about who one truly is and hoping that therapy can help them uncover their authentic self.

In addition to the therapeutic process, authenticity is a searched-for feeling within the NBA. Much of the discourse within sports media and fandom is identifying if a player or coach is genuine. In the NBA, authenticity is prized but frequently questioned. Players gather a particular reputation around authenticity early in their career, but it can change and shift, often in relationship to their success or failure on the court. Dwight Howard's humor and frivolity was initially seen as charming and forthright, but soon became seen as evidence of his insincerity (Sharp 2012). Tim Duncan's aloofness made it difficult for NBA fans to relate to him, but by the end of his career this same characteristic was seen as proof of his indisputable nature (Murphy 2012).

NBA fans tend to forgive much if they feel a player is being authentic. For example, Giannis Antetokounmpo, former NBA champion, former MVP and one of the top NBA players of his generation, lost in first round in the 2023 NBA playoffs, a huge shock and disappointment. When asked if he considered his season a failure, he launched into a criticism of the very nature of the question, discussing how he sees success and failure in a very different light and that progress is not linear (Collier 2023). This response brought out mostly praise from NBA fans, seeing his response as an authentic reaction to a bitterly disappointing moment and also reflecting his unique path to the game (Fader 2021). If he had not been regarded as authentic and instead was viewed as avoiding responsibility or shaming the reporter for asking a question on everyone's mind, the response from the larger NBA community would likely have been very different.

Within the fans search for a player's authenticity, they often see it as a singular fact, and much of what is considered authentic is related to a sense of if the player is successful. Win in the playoffs or championships, and the player is seen as real and honest. Lose, and questions about their veridicality come fast and furious. However, the same aspects of the player that leads them to being successful are often the same characters that can lead to pain or disappointment. Fans misunderstand authenticity and ascribe aspects of a player's identity to authenticity that have nothing to do with it.

Stephen Mitchell articulates a different vision of authenticity then has historically been discussed within psychoanalysis (Mitchell 1993). Adopting temporal metaphors, Mitchell counterbalances the historical idea of there being a true, core authentic "self" by articulating authenticity as ever-changing. In his view, authenticity is often a relational experience. How one is authentic can depend on who they are with, the period of their life they happen to be in, what values they hold at in that moment, and so on. Authenticity can shift and evolve and contain multiple possibilities and represent a variety of different self-states. As Mitchel explains:

> A particular act or self-expression . . . may feel extremely authentic at one point and extremely inauthentic at another. In the first case, it feels "right" suites both the external, interpersonal context and the internal emotional context. In the second case, it feels "off," forced, contrived, out of "sync" interpersonally,

> internally, or both. The degree to which an act or feeling represents or misrepresents the personal self depends not on its content (not on what is in it) but on its place in the context and configuration of experience as it is continually organized, disorganized, and reorganized in time . . . The sense of authenticity is always a construction, and as a construction, it is always relative to other possible self-constructions. (1993, 131)

Mitchell is laying out a view of authenticity that is less about what the person says or does, but more about the context of the situation, the particular developmental point the individual is in, and how the person feels afterwards. This version of authenticity is ever fluctuating and adjusting due to the context surrounding the words the person utters or action the person took. It is held as a relational experience and can evolve and change as the individual does. This vision runs counter to the narratives often found around NBA players, where deeds or words are viewed as unchanging and permanent reflections of the inner-core of the individual. Two NBA all-star players, Draymond Green and Russell Westbrook, demonstrate the ineffectiveness of this approach, and the way NBA fan narratives limit and undercut a true understanding of authenticity.

Both Draymond Green and Russell Westbrook are known for their aggressive play, intense competitive energy, and a willingness to use their aggression and force to help propel their play and teams forward. Draymond Green came into the league as a second-round pick after a four year career at Michigan State. He was seen as a tweener, not big or strong enough to be a power forward, not quick or skilled enough to be a small forward. His first year was spent playing limited minutes as a defensive specialist, and his second year was spent surprising his critics by continuing to earn more minutes during the playoffs as an unanticipated starter. An injury to the starting power forward, David Lee, in his third year allowed him to become a permanent starter and he thrived, helping the Warriors earn the most wins in the NBA, being selected as a first-team defensive player, and helped the Warriors win their first NBA championship since 1975. Since then, he has won the NBA Defensive Player of the Year in 2017, been a four-time all-star, and viewed as one of the greatest defensive players of his generation and a central component of multiple NBA championships.

Russell Westbrook was a high draft pick who managed to succeed all expectations. His play is known for relentless aggression that allows him to trample over his limitations, which include an inconsistent outside shot. Initially seen as a player without a natural position, he became an icon, winning the NBA MVP award in 2017 and setting the NBA record for most triple-doubles of all time. A multi-time all-star, he was the face of the Oklahoma City Thunder for over a decade.

Green's intensity and physicality were seen as huge aspects of how despite not being graced with incredible athletic abilities he became one of the best defensive players of his generation (Thompson 2019). Westbrook's nonstop motor and refusal to backdown led to one of the greatest individual seasons in NBA history (*New York Times* 2017). Green can be expressive in his language on the court, bating players with trash talk to gain an advantage. He often gets into conflict with opposing players and referees, using these battles to charge himself up and his team. These conflicts at times have crossed lines and led to Green getting suspended in the playoffs (Zillgitt 2016) and getting into verbal and physical altercations with his head coach (Sherwood Strauss 2016) and teammates (Botkin 2023; Cash 2018). Westbrook's stubbornness and competitive fire can intimidate opposing players. His intractability has also led him to struggle to adapt when his athletic skills started to slightly dimmish (Grimes 2022), created conflict with coaches (Wojnarowski 2023), and led to an entire fanbase blaming and bullying him for the team's struggles (Faigen 2022). For both Westbrook and Green, when their teams were seen as successful, their pugnacity and emotion were viewed by fans as authentic and necessary. When their team struggled, or their behaviors led to negative consequences, they were seen as hostile, narcissistic, arrogant, and out of control.

The reality for Green is that the same behavior that propelled his incredible play also led to behavior that dimmish his ability to stay on the court and maintain relationships with his teammates. The same behavior for Westbrook that led to his MVP award also led to an inability to acknowledge his growing limits and adjust his game to reflect his capacities on the court. Both Green and Westbrook are authentic—their authenticity contains incredible heights and immeasurable lows. It's understandable if NBA fans and the media debate if their actions are worth it. But what is missing in many of these discussions is the acknowledgment that both Green and Westbrook are authentic in either direction—their competitive will and undisciplined reactions, their brash arrogance and impulsive destructiveness are the different sides of the same coin. They are authentically themselves, and like most of us, struggle to find the right balance that will propel them forward while minimizing the carnage below.

In viewing authenticity in the manner Mitchell suggests, one can glimpse the complexities inherent in all NBA players and create a more well-rounded understanding of what drives and facilities success and failure on the court. Without this understanding, NBA fans quickly turn towards a static idea of authenticity that fluctuates based on the outcome of the court and offers little towards understanding the particular player they are examining. It flattens discourse and limits players motivations and actions to a capitalistic lens, where success equates to genuineness, failure equates to counterfeit, and no one learns anything real.

NOTES

1. "The decision" was a live television special in which James announced he was leaving the Cavaliers and joining the Miami Heat. It was quickly panned as arrogant, awkward, and insensitive to the Cavaliers fans (Windhorst 2011). It is now seen as a marker of the era of player empowerment (Eluemuno 2022).

2. Allen Iverson, one the best players of his generation, introduced style and attitude from black and hip-hop culture, and was often the target of racist attacks from primarily white middle-class NBA fans who did not understand Iverson and were uncomfortable with urban black America (Wilson 2005).

3. Ehlo was part of a very talented Cavaliers team in 1989 who played and lost to Michael Jordan's Chicago Bulls on a last-second shot by Jordan. Ehlo, who was guarding Jordan, collapsed to the ground while Jordan and the bulls celebrated, creating an iconic moment that defined the futility of the Cavaliers and Cleveland sports team in general until James came.

BIBLIOGRAPHY

Abrams, Jonathan. 2012. "Refound youth: Gerald Green's importable return to the NBA." *Grantland*. April 19th, 2012. http://grantland.com/features/the-improbable-return-nba-new-jersey-nets-gerald-green/

Amick, Sam. 2020. "The 25 Most Dominant NBA Teams Ever." *The Athletic*. May 20th, 2020. https://theathletic.com/1822805/2020/05/20/the-25-most-dominant-nba-teams-ever

Armant, J. 2023. "LeBron James, Dwyane Wade Headline Miami Heat's 2010s All-Decade Team." *Sports Illustrated*. July 28th, 2023 https://www.si.com/nba/heat/miami-news/lebron-james-dwyane-wade-headline-miami-heats-2010s-all-decade-team

Associated Press, 2012. "Magic Man No More: Dwight Howard Dealt to Lakers." *The Florida Times-Union*. August 10th, 2012. https://www.jacksonville.com/story/sports/nba/2012/08/11/magic-man-no-more-dwight-howard-dealt-lakers/15858048007/

Barsness, Roy. E., 2018. *Core Competencies of Relational Psychoanalysis: A Guide to Practice, Study, and Research*. Edited by Roy E. Barsness. Routledge/Taylor & Francis Group: London, England.

Beck, Howard. 2013. "Pushed to Limit, James and Miami Repeat as N.B.A. Champions." *New York Times*. June 20th. 2013. https://www.nytimes.com/2013/06/21/sports/basketball/miami-heat-repeat-as-nba-champions.html

Bleacher Report. 2011. "Miami, We Have a Problem: Maybe LeBron James Isn't Wired to Take the Last Shot." *Bleacher Report*. March 3rd, 2011. https://bleacherreport.com/articles/626267-miami-we-have-a-problem-maybe-lebron-james-isnt-wired-to-take-the-last-shot

Boktin, Brad. 2023. "Draymond Green Admits Jordan Poole Punch Screwed Up Warriors' Season: 'We Would Still Be Playing.'" *CBS Sports*. May 17th,

2023. https://www.cbssports.com/nba/news/draymond-green-admits-jordan-poole-punch-screwed-up-warriors-season-we-would-still-be-playing/

Bollas, Christopher. 1978. "The Aesthetic Moment and the Search for Transformation." *Annual of Psychoanalysis* 6: 385–394

Bresnahan, Mike. & Simers, T.J. 2012. "Dwight Howard Leaves Lakers for Houston Rockets." *Los Angeles Times*. July 5th, 2013 https://www.latimes.com/sports/la-xpm-2013-jul-05-la-sp-0706-rockets-dwight-howard-20130706-story.html

Burns, Scott. 2014. "Would Kevin Love Trade Automatically Make Golden State Warriors a Title Threat?" *Bleacher Report*. May 26th, 2014. https://bleacherreport.com/articles/2075366-would-kevin-love-trade-automatically-make-golden-state-warriors-a-title-threat

Cacciola, Scott. 2017. "Warriors Win N.B.A. Title, Avenging Themselves Against the Cavaliers." *New York Times*. June 13th. 2017 https://www.nytimes.com/2017/06/13/sports/golden-state-warriors-win-nba-championship.html

Cash, Meredith. 2018. "Warriors' Kevin Durant and Draymond Green Exchange Heated Words for Nearly 3 Straight Minutes in OT Loss to Clippers." *Business Insider*. November 13th, 2018. https://www.businessinsider.com/kevin-durant-draymond-green-yelling-video-2018-11

Charles, Marilyn. 2002. "Bion's Grid: A Tool for Transformation." *Journal of the American Academy of Psychoanalysis* 30 (3): 429–445

Chatelle, Justin. 2008. "Lebron James: A King Is Born." *Bleacher Report*. October 16th, 2008. https://bleacherreport.com/articles/69653-lebron-james-a-king-is-born

Chau, Danny. 2016. "By Adding Kevin Durant, Golden State Scorches the Earth." *The Ringer*. July 4th, 2016 https://www.theringer.com/2016/7/4/16039652/by-adding-kevin-durant-golden-state-scorches-the-earth-d38bdd54e711

Colas, Yago. 2012. "What We Mean When We Say 'Play the Right Way': Strategic Fundamentals, Morality, and Race in the Culture of Basketball." *The Journal of Midwest Modern Language Association,* no. 45 (2): 109–125.

Collier, J. (2023). "Giannis Antetokounmpo Says Bucks' Early Exit 'Not a Failure.'" *ESPN.* April 27th, 2023. https://www.espn.com/nba/story/_/id/36301434/giannis-antetokounmpo-says-bucks-early-exit-not-failure

Cooper, Scott. 2014. "Experience with Team UA Changed Klay Thompson." *NBA.com*. December 11th, 2014 http://www.nba.com/2014/news/features/scott_howard_cooper/12/11/experience-with-team-usa-changed-klay-thompson/

Crowley, Kerry. 2022. "Why Warriors Fans Love Klay Thompson and Why His Return Will Bring Tears." *The Mercury News*. January 29th, 2022 https://www.mercurynews.com/2022/01/09/why-warriors-fans-love-klay-thompson-and-why-his-return-will-bring-tears/

Dalal, Farhad. 2006. "Racism: Processes of Detachment, Dehumanization, and Hatred." *The Psychoanalytic Quarterly,* no. 75, (1): 131–161,

Davies, Jody. 2004. "Whose Bad Objects Are We Anyway?: Repetition and Our Elusive Love Affair with Evil." *Psychoanalytic Dialogues,* no. 14 (6): 711–732

Eagle, Morris. 1999. "Why Don't People Change? A Psychoanalytic Perspective." *Journal of Psychotherapy Integration,* no. 9 (1): 3–32.

Eluemuno, C. 2022. "How LeBron James Championed the Start of Player Empowerment in the NBA with 'The Decision' on This day in 2010." Sportsskeeda. November 8th, 2022. https://www.sportskeeda.com/basketball/how-lebron-james-championed-start-player-empowerment-nba-the-decision-day-2010

ESPN.com News Service. 2016. "Charles Barkley Not High on Kevin Durant Going to Superteam." *ESPN*. July 6th, 2016. https://www.espn.com/nba/story/_/id/16825851/charles-barkley-thinks-stars-kevin-durant-cheating-get-title

Fader, Mirin. 2021. *Giannis: The Improbable Rise of an NBA MVP*. New York: Hachette Books.

Faigen, Harrison. 2022. "Russell Westbrook Feels Like This Has All Crossed a Line." *SB Nation*. March 8th, 2022. https://www.silverscreenandroll.com/2022/3/7/22966742/russell-westbrook-lakers-fans-criticism-death-threats-wife-tweets-westbrick

Felt, H. 2017. "Warriors' Sweep Reveals the Ugly Truth: These NBA Playoffs Have Been Awful." *The Guardian*. May 9th, 2017 https://www.theguardian.com/sport/blog/2017/may/09/golden-state-warriors-sweep-nba-playoffs

Freud, Sigmund. 1924. "The Passing of the Oedipus Complex." *International Review of Psycho-Analysis,* no. 5, 419–424.

Future, Young. 2017. "Cavaliers and Warriors Dominance in the NBA Playoffs is Ruining the NBA??!!." *Sportsblog*. May 21st, 2017 https://www.sportsblog.com/sportsblog_bigfutureblog45/cavaliers-and-warriors-dominance-in-the-nba-playoffs-is-ruining-the-nba/

Gallo, D.J. 2016. "How Kevin Durant Lived Long Enough to See Himself Become a Villain." *The Guardian*. July 6th, 2016. https://www.theguardian.com/sport/blog/2016/jul/06/kevin-durant-golden-state-warriors-villain

Givens, Kelsey. 2010. "Lebron James Decision: From Hero to Villain with One Decision." *Bleacher Report*. July 8th, 2010. https://bleacherreport.com/articles/417576-lebron-james-decision-from-hero-to-villain-with-one-decision

Grimes, Prince J. 2022. Russell Westbrook Blaming Bench Role for His Injury is a Bad Sign for Lakers. USA Today. October 19th, 2023 https://ftw.usatoday.com/2022/10/russell-westbrook-lakers-bench-injury-darvin-ham-trouble

Hamer, Forest M. 2006. Racism as a Transference State: Episodes of Racial Hostility in the Psychoanalytic Context. *The Psychoanalytic Quarterly,* no. 75 (1): 197–214

Havens, Leston. 1986. "A Theoretical Basis for the Concepts of Self and Authentic Self." *Journal of the American Psychoanalytic Association,* no. 34 (2), 363–378

Heisler, Mark. 2010. "Cruella Lebron Becomes a Villain." *Los Angeles Times*. June 8th, 2010. https://www.latimes.com/archives/la-xpm-2010-jul-08-la-sp-heisler-lebron-james-20100709-story.html

Helin, Kurt. 2013. "With Two Rings, LeBron's Decision to Go to Miami Vndicated." *NBC Sports*. June 21st, 2013. https://www.nbcsports.com/nba/news/with-two-rings-lebrons-decision-to-go-to-miami-vindicated

Helin, Kurt. 2015. "Report: Jerry West Threatened to Resign if Warriors Traded Klay Thompson for Kevin Love." *NBC Sports*. June 16th, 2015 https://www.nbcsports.com/nba/news/report-jerry-west-threatened-to-resign-if-warriors-traded-klay-thompson-for-kevin-love

Herbert, James. 2020. "Michael Jordan Hits 'The Shot' Over Craig Ehlo: What 'The Last Dance' Doesn't Say About Iconic Bulls Moment." *CBS Sports*. May 17th. 2020. https://www.cbssports.com/nba/news/michael-jordan-hits-the-shot-over-craig-ehlo-what-the-last-dance-doesnt-say-about-iconic-bulls-moment/

Hoffman, B. 2017. "Anthony Bennett, Cut by Nets, Stands Out Among N.B.A. Busts." *New York Times*. January 9th, 2017. https://www.nytimes.com/2017/01/09/sports/basketball/anthony-bennett-nets.html

Hughes, Grant. 2014. "Klay Thompson Not Worth Golden State Warriors Whiffing on Kevin Love Trade." *Bleacher Report*. June 23rd, 2014. https://bleacherreport.com/articles/2107360-klay-thompson-not-worth-golden-state-warriors-whiffing-on-kevin-love-trade

Jackson, Scoop. 2011. "All Hail Lebron James, the Villain." *ESPN*. January 13th. 2011. https://www.espn.com/espn/commentary/news/story?page=jackson/110113

Jung, Carl G. 1981. "The Development of Personality," In *Jung's Collected Works #17* by C.G. Jung. Edited by Gerhard Adler. Translated by R.F.C. Hull. Princeton, New Jersey: Princeton University Press.

Kawakami, Tim. 2012. "Jerry West on Klay Thompson, Trade Possibilities and Whether the Warriors Are Lstening to Him." *The Mercury News*. February 12th, 2012. http://blogs.mercurynews.com/kawakami/2012/02/12/jerry-west-on-klay-thompson-trade-possibilities-and-whether-the-warriors-are-listening-to-him/

Kawakami, Tim. 2017. "Durant's Big Warriors Moment, With the Biggest, Best Step Just Ahead." *East Bay Times*. May 24th, 2017. https://www.eastbaytimes.com/2017/05/24/kawakami-kevin-durant-soaks-in-this-warriors-moment-with-the-biggest-and-best-step-just-ahead/

Klein, M. 1946. "Notes on Some Schizoid Mechanisms." *International Journal of Psycho-Analysis,* no. 27: 99–110.

Lee, M. 2019. "'It Was Worth it': Kevin Durant on Why His Decision to Come to the Bay Has Paid Off in Every Way." *The Athletic*. April 13th, 2019. https://theathletic.com/922020/2019/04/13/it-was-worth-it-kevin-durant-on-why-his-decision-to-come-to-the-bay-has-paid-off-in-every-way/

Loewald, Hans. 1960. "On the Therapeutic Action of Psycho-analysis." *The International Journal of Psychoanalysis*, 41, 16–33.

Lowe, Zack. 2014. "Ready for Love or Time to Klay?" *Grantland*. June 24th. 2014. http://grantland.com/features/kevin-love-klay-thompson-golden-state-warriors/

Mahoney, Brian. 2016. "LeBron James Vindicated as Triple-double Lifts Heat to Title." *Anchorage Daily News*. September 29th, 2016 https://www.adn.com/sports/article/lebron-james-vindicated-triple-double-lifts-heat-title/2012/06/22/

Manning, Chris. 2017. "2016–17 Cleveland Cavaliers Player Review: LeBron James." *SB Nation*. June 29th, 2017. https://www.fearthesword.com/2017/6/29/15891890/lebron-james-2016-17-cleveland-cavaliers-player-review

Mannix, Chris. 2023. "LeBron James Is the Greatest of All Time." *Sports Illustrated*. February 8th, 2023 https://www.si.com/nba/2023/02/08/lebron-james-greatest-basketball-player-all-time-scoring-record

McCauley, Janie. 2017. "Stephen Curry, Kevin Durant Look to Build a Warriors dynasty." *Durango Herald*. June 13th, 2017. https://www.durangoherald.com/articles/stephen-curry-kevin-durant-look-to-build-a-warriors-dynasty/

Meltzer, Donald. 2008. *The Appreciation of Beautify: The Role of Aesthetic Conflict in Development, Art, and Violence*. London: Karnac Books

Mitchell, Stephen. 1993. *Hope and Dread in Psychoanalysis*. Basic Books: New York.

More, Ben. 2021. "Steph Curry: How Golden State Warriors Star 'Revolutionized' the NBA." *CNN*. December 15th, 2021. https://www.cnn.com/2021/12/14/sport/steph-curry-ray-allen-three-point-record-spt-intl/index.html

Moss, Donald. 2001. "On Hating in the First Person Plural: Thinking Psychoanalytically About Racism, Homophobia, and Misogyny." *Journal of the American Psychoanalytic Association*, no 49 (4): 1315–1334.

Murphy, David. 2014. "Tim Duncan, a Case of Substance Over Style." *Deadspin*. February 4th. 2014. https://bleacherreport.com/articles/1948663-tim-duncan-a-case-of-substance-over-style

Nadkarni, R. 2017. "The Case For: Cavs-Warriors Ruining NBA Playoffs." *Sports Illustrated*. May 8th, 2017. https://www.si.com/nba/2017/05/08/nba-playoffs-finals-warriors-cavaliers-lebron-james-stephen-curry-kevin-durant

NBA.com staff. 2013. "Top NBA Finals Moment: Ray Allen's Late 3 Turns Tide for Heat." *NBA.com*. September 14th, 2011. https://www.nba.com/news/history-finals-moments-ray-allen-3-pointer-game-6

Neiman, Ryan. 2011. "NBA Finals Game 2: Was it a Dallas Mavericks Comeback or a Miami Heat Collapse?" *Bleacher Report*. June 2nd, 2011. https://bleacherreport.com/articles/722149-nba-finals-game-2-was-it-a-dallas-mavericks-comeback-or-a-miami-heat-collapse

New York Times. 2017. "Is Russell Westbrook's Season the Best Ever? Some Apples and Oranges to Pick From." *New York Times*. April 12th. 2017. https://www.nytimes.com/2017/04/12/sports/russell-westbrook-greatest-season-sports.html

O'Donnell, Ricky. 2023. "Aaron Gordon Needed the Nuggets As Much As They Needed Him." *SB Nation*. June 4th, 2023. https://www.sbnation.com/nba/2023/6/4/23746391/aaron-gordon-evolution-nba-finals-denver-nuggets-profile-analysis

Pina, Michael. 2023. "Luka Doncic Isn't Just the MVP Favorite, He's the Most Improved Player." *The Ringer*. June 5th, 2023. https://www.theringer.com/nba/2023/1/5/23539424/luka-doncic-most-improved-player-dallas-mavericks

Rafferty, Scott. 2023. "Nikola Jokic, Draymond Green Headline Best Second Round Picks in NBA Draft History." *The Sporting News*. February 9th, 2023. https://www.sportingnews.com/us/nba/news/best-second-round-picks-nba-draft-history/v1wwgb9tnbsiilbeu0dbtlup

Scola, Marco. 2012. "Orlando Magic's Dwight Howard Is the Most Annoying Man in the NBA." *Bleacher Report*. https://bleacherreport.com/articles/1270516-orlando-magics-dwight-howard-is-the-most-annoying-man-in-the-nba

Searles, Harold F. 2017. "The 'dedicated physician' in the field of psychotherapy and Psychoanalysis." Edited by Donnel B. Stern, and Irwin Hirsch *The Interpersonal Perspective in Psychoanalysis, 1960s–1990s*. New York: Routledge.

Sharp, Andrew. 2012. "Deadspin NBA Shit List: Dwight Howard, the Superman of Unfunny." *Deadspin*. November 9th. 2012. https://deadspin.com/deadspin-nba-shit-list-dwight-howard-the-superman-of-5958111

Sherwood Strauss, Ethan. 2016. "Golden State's Draymond Green Problem." *ESPN*. April 1st, 2020. https://www.espn.com/nba/story/_/id/17790252/golden-state-draymond-green-problem

Spears, Marc. 2022. "'Stuff of legends': Warriors' Klay Thompson Caps Long Comeback with NBA Championship." *Andscape*. June 17th, 2022. https://andscape.com/features/stuff-of-legends-warriors-klay-thompson-caps-long-comeback-with-nba-championship/

Stein, Marc, & Shelburne, Ramona. 2014. "Kevin Love Likes Warriors, Bulls." *ESPN*. May 18th, 2014. https://www.espn.com/nba/story/_/id/10949807/kevin-love-tells-minnesota-timberwolves-sign-extension-likes-chicago-bulls-golden-state-warriors

Swartz, Greg. 2013. "Compiling the 'Reasons' Dwight Howard Left Lakers for Houston Rockets." *Bleacher Report*. July 12th, 2013. https://bleacherreport.com/articles/1702189-compiling-the-reasons-dwight-howard-left-lakers-for-houston-rockets

Taylor, Phil. 2014. "Klay Thompson's Rare Transformation Helping Warriors Take the Next Step." *Sports Illustrated*. November 6th, 2014. https://www.si.com/nba/2014/11/06/klay-thompson-golden-state-warriors-evolution-steve-kerr

Thompson, Marcus. 2014. "With Kevin Love Trade Done, Klay Thompson Says 'Warriors Believe In Me.'" *The Mercury News*. August 23rd, 2014. https://www.mercurynews.com/2014/08/23/thompson-with-kevin-love-trade-done-klay-thompson-says-warriors-believe-in-me/

Thompson, Marcus. 2019. "Thompson: The Greatest Defender of All Time? Draymond Green States his Case." *The Athletic*. May 17th. 2019. https://theathletic.com/982490/2019/05/17/thompson-the-greatest-defender-of-all-time-draymond-green-states-his-case/

Thompson, Marcus. 2022. "Andrew Wiggins Found Peace with the Warriors. Now He Wants to Be a Legend." *The Athletic*. October 19th, 2022. https://theathletic.com/3708912/2022/10/19/andrew-wiggins-warriors/

Tinley, Justin. 2017. "Cavs-Warriors III and the Allure of a Sports Trilogy." *Andscape*. May 30th, 2017. https://andscape.com/features/cavaliers-warriors-nba-finals-the-allure-of-a-sports-trilogy/

Toback, Shaun. 2011. "Dwight Howard and the Mystery of Unfulfilled Greatness." *Bleacher Report*. April 11th, 2011. https://bleacherreport.com/articles/661787-dwight-howard-and-the-mystery-of-unfulfilled-greatness

Wallace, Michael. 2012. "James Eyeing Howard's Top Defender Award." *ESPN*. March 13th, 2012. https://www.espn.com/blog/truehoop/miamiheat/post/_/id/12922/james-eyeing-howards-top-defender-award

Washington Post. 2013. "Miami Heat's big three vindicated by second-straight title." *Denver Post*. June 20th, 2013. https://www.denverpost.com/2013/06/20/miami-heats-big-three-vindicated-by-second-straight-title/

Whitebook, J. 2004. "Hans Loewald: A Radical Conservative." *The International Journal of Psychoanalysis*, no. 85 (1), 97–116.

Wilson, Jamie. 2005. "NBA's 'No Bling' Dress Code Prompts Racism Accusations." *The Guardian*. October 30th, 2005. https://www.theguardian.com/world/2005/oct/31/usa.americansports

Windhorst, Brian. 2011. "A Look back at the Tateful 'Decision.'" *ESPN*. July 8th. 2011. https://www.espn.com/nba/truehoop/miamiheat/columns/story?columnist=windhorst_brian&page=jamesdecision-110708

Windhorst, Brian. 2018. "LeBron Changed the Game as a Basketball Prodigy." *ESPN*. March 28, 2018, https://www.espn.com/nba/story/_/id/22924664/lebron-james-changed-game-basketball-prodigy-nba

Windhorst, Brian & McMenamin, Dave. 2017. *Return of the King: LeBron James, the Cleveland Cavaliers and the Greatest Comeback in NBA history.* Grand Central Publishing, New York, NY.

Winnicott, Donald W. 1965. *The Maturational Processes and the Facilitating Environment: Studies in the Theory of Emotional Development.* Madison, CT: International Universities Press.

Winnicott, Donald W. 1974. "Fear of Breakdown." *International Review of Psycho-Analysis,* no 1, (1–2), 103–107.

Wojnarowski, A. 2023. "Sources: Lakers coach, Russell Westbrook Had Heated Exchange." *ESPN*. February 8th, 2023. https://www.espn.com/nba/story/_/id/35616302/sources-lakers-coach-russell-westbrook-had-heated-exchange

Zillgitt, J. 2016. "Draymond Green Suspended for Game 5 of NBA Finals for LeBron James Incident." *USA Today*. June 12th, 2016. https://www.usatoday.com/story/sports/nba/2016/06/12/draymond-green-suspended-game-5-nba-finals/85793294/

Chapter 7

Cheering on Solid Ground

Plotting a Developmental Arc toward Ethical Fandom

Monique S. Bowen

Sports fandom offers a rich terrain for exploring human psychology, offering insights into identity formation, group dynamics, and ethical decision-making. Reciprocal bonds, linking fanhood to fantasy, connect feelings of intense admiration among both individual and group experiences, which can easily venture from the socially sanctioned states of groupthink to more disturbing behaviours like verbal intimidation and physical violence. Psychoanalysts, like anyone, can be ardent sports fans: with a unique understanding of human behaviour and the societal dynamics at play, practitioners can offer perspectives on the experience of sports fandom that both challenge and enrich our practice.

Simply put, our attachments push our development, and our development guides our choice-making over the lifespan. To offer a path forward in working with patients enthralled by their connection to sports as competition, or as an extension of themselves, it is imperative to recognize attachment relatedness as central to telling the stories about our closest emotional bonds. Understanding how individuals use sports as an expressive outlet can inform not only our use of specific, therapeutic interventions, but can also instruct us and our patients on negotiating the delicate balance between loyalty and individuality as well as emphasize the importance of maintaining personal values and critical thinking when faced with our deepest identifications with others. It is these matters that are the essence of an ethical sensibility to sports fandom, a perspective of increasing relevance in our hyper-connected world.

In this chapter, the dual lenses of psychoanalytic and attachment-informed theoretical writing will help frame the account of fan engagement that is presented, addressing the impact of gender and racial polarizations on early fan development, and centering ethical considerations within the realm of sports fandom. As I progress through my thinking on these issues, I will engage fan, gender, and racial and ethnocultural identities in order to highlight the challenges facing the clinician-fan when navigating the knotty relationship between their personal identities and values as well as their engagements with fandom and other fans.

PLAYING THROUGH THE PAIN

For psychoanalysts who identify as sports enthusiasts, understanding the complexities of sports fandom is essential to engaging in critical self-reflection as well as being of use to others who are attempting the same. Being a sport fan as a professional psychologist also requires an exploration of concepts such as blind allegiance, loyalty, as well as feminist and anti-racist perspectives on sports. Blind loyalty and allegiance are terms that speak to an uncritical and unwavering commitment to a team or athlete, regardless of their actions or performances. Such attitudes can have psychological implications, even shaping professional interactions with clients who may harbor differing loyalties. The inclusion of feminist and anti-racist perspectives illuminates the dynamics of power, privilege, and discrimination within sports fan culture that also become factors in the treatment room as another contested space for exploring competitive feelings and desire for closeness or domination. These perspectives can illuminate how social inequalities may be perpetuated within sport's fan communities, and how these can impact the psychologist's behaviour and sense of social identity as it impacts professional practice.

"Hey, you won! I mean that WE won," said my cobbler just a few days following the 2008 U.S. presidential election. His son graduated from my college alma mater, a fact he noted one day when I placed my keys on his counter, and the key fob displayed the name which caught his eye. From that moment on, I was no longer the mother of two brown-skinned children bopping up and down the avenue past his store. Now I was someone he hoped his son would become: a PhD but in history not psychology, someone with a family, and a professional person able to afford life in one of the more expensive neighbourhoods in NYC. To many, I had made it. I had won, right? Meanwhile, my cobbler—a Jewish man of some orthodoxy, wearing a kippah, fiercely grey, probably 10–20 years younger than his appearance—appeared to me now as something more, and differentiated, too. Like me, he listened to the news from our National Public Radio, and he often watched *Family*

Feud on his little colour TV during the evening bustle of shoe repair and dry-cleaning pick-ups. But this slip of the tongue, indicating with unabashed glee that I won—even better, that we won—was not lost on me. We shared a win for the culture(s) we represented and that was not nothing.

In that moment with my cobbler, the thumb of history had been lifted, so I thought I understood what he meant by this rejoinder. Throughout Barack Obama's ascent up the American political food chain, I imagined all the people who first saw Joe Louis, and later Cassius Clay, do battle and meet success in the boxing ring. Or those who were at Ebbets Field in Brooklyn, NY, when Jackie Robinson broke into the Major League Baseball. What of the Olympic teammates of gold medallist Jessie Owens when he tore across the track under the ignominious gaze of Adolf Hitler, or of the spectators watching Althea Gibson receiving the winner's trophy from Queen Elizabeth II at The Wimbledon Championships? The feeling of going from watching other people celebrate year after year the spoils of battle to finally savouring a sort of private, personal victory. Wistful, standing in the winner's circle and holding up that precious, ever-elusive trophy. It must feel heavier than it looks. . . . My cobbler could see that, at first, I didn't know what he meant by "I won." But when he followed with "we won," I knew he meant Obama. We won Obama and with it came the right to party like we had won the World Series or any number of the many World Cups across multiple sports. We had played through pain, limped back onto the court to play the last few crucial minutes of our season, stood on the mound in a blood-soaked sock, landed a round-off handspring off the pommel horse and stuck the landing, only to be carried off the mat by our coach, triumphant. We had all just won, something. And I felt, momentarily, that my cobbler and I understood something about each other's history of pain.

That is how it is for me as a fan of professional sports. Watching, and, in the case of fantasy sports, playing along with the games and athletes I feel deep wells of affection for. It's all there. I have the handwritten letters, voice messages, e-mails, and texts to prove it. Over the past 10 years, I have had running conversations that document the joyous and sorrowful moments with sports. Time, careers, and shifting priorities have made casual in-person chats, fantasy basketball leagues, and viewing games together in local bars nearly impossible to schedule. The 2020 pandemic turned my commitment to maintaining a space for sports, both in the real and in imagination, into a new kind of event where live chatting with close colleagues, who sometimes care more than I do about the players and outcomes, has become the true in-game action.

With gambling a key feature in most sports, how we even talk about games and matchups has changed. Is my friend asking my opinion about a sports team because of my long history following that team, its players, and strategic moves by coaches and managers? Is it curiosity, or because they have bet on the eventual winner, a particular player's final score line, or the over/under? I think about these things now—"is this friend still a fan or is there something at stake?"—and it has altered my enjoyment of watching games. Now that betting is a commercial and ever-present feature of my consumption of sports, I cannot help but reflect on myself as a fan with this additional set of judgements that both connect and separate me from sports, athletes, and other fans.

Gambling will never be the only thing that weighs on me about my consumption of sports or fandom. Wars, interpersonal conflicts, classic narcissism on display, steroid-driven rage, poor conditioning at the start of a season, lack of investment in the city where one plays, money and politics steering amateur and professional competition . . . I could go on. Watching team sports and engaging in the ins and outs of individual competitions, I can experience the decision to devote significant ongoing, diligent attention to be an especially fraught choice. The innocence is gone if there ever was any, leaving fans and the games we love in steady conflict with antiracist and third- and fourth-wave feminist frameworks, which centre empathic concern, equity, and justice across professional and recreational settings alike.

The more established I become in my career, the harder I find it is to muster the same levels of excitement for the games I have always loved. It isn't simply maturity: when in the "right" frame of mind, I'm a pit bull, sweating, gnashing my teeth, swearing at the TV with a bite worse than my bark. I can go there, like all true fans licking their lips in anticipation of total annihilation of the visiting team. I can really go there. And that is what scares me. How blinded, how base, how easily I go to that delicious place of total identification with the aggression that is linked to the soul of sports. And I'm not alone in that feeling, as it is an en masse experience that is part of what it means to be a fan—that you get to share the glory and the pain with others just like you, whether you are together on the couch, in the bleachers, or checking-in via text or social media feed to be sure others are right there with you. Confirming your love for the game, but also your hate and rage against . . . against, you name it: the game, its players, opposing fans, commentators. When raging, nothing and no one is exempted.

LESSONS ABOUT HATRED AND COLOUR BLINDNESS FROM THE GAMES WE LOVE

Football has the enviable reputation as the world's sport. Other than the expansion of the Olympic Games to nearly every corner of the inhabitable world, football (or soccer as it best known in the U.S.) is singular in its persistence as the preferred team sport at the amateur and professional levels. Another of the many games "of inches," it is unlike the other sports for numerous reasons.

Football is not primarily a contact sport. In fact, because the nature of play demands all but one player on each side of the ball can touch it, much of the focus is on maintaining possession through a series of passes to teammates and advancing the ball deftly across the pitch with as little impediment to forward progress as possible. Yes, there is plenty of physical contact and much of it is mediated by referees who must decide how many fouls do run afoul of common sense into sheer theatrics and time-wasting tactics to lengthen periods. In years past, and certainly where decades long rivalries exist, football is Shakespearian, Montague and Capelet style. Neighbour pitted against neighbour, rivals sometimes share more than geographic region but may literally include siblings, cousins, and blood enemies from the same region playing for different local clubs, inspiring legendary animus between teams that has a history so long current fans are no longer sure of their origins.

With the breadth of bloodlust bred long ago between local clubs, between countries of the same region or continent, between former colonialists and colonies, and with the domination of FIFA and the World Cup, oceans may now separate rivals, but the fevered tone of the matches is no less than what one might expect from well-known rivalries, such as that between Manchester United and Arsenal. Fans are fans for life, despite the now common trades and loan agreements between clubs. And the emotions stirred at matches can be as fierce as what one might expect. Except, that is, that the emotions are not what most people would expect. Football is inimitable in that its fans, in some parts of the world, are at their most vile in the expression of their loyalty to their team and at the expense of anything akin to sportsman-like. In the U.S., sports teams' reputations are sometimes cemented by their fans singlemindedness toward disrupting opposing teams' capacities to establish a rhythm. Here, for example, fan voraciousness is extolled by how unruly the cheering is when the opposing team's main play-caller cannot hear the coaching staff from the side lines, leading to miscues and the use of timeouts due to on-field confusion linked to the sheer decibel level. In other areas of the sports world, the disruptive activities may have the same goal, but the levels of disturbance can appear more personal, with targeted arousal of specific players as the goal, including against players on the same team beloved by their raucous fans. Here, displacement, or the act of projecting one's feelings or issues onto others, often becomes the simplest way to avoid dealing with one's own actions and behaviours. In the context of sports, this can manifest in individuals, projecting their own biases and prejudices onto athletes from historically minoritized communities.

At one time in the late aughts, the European football equivalent to the U.S. Major League Baseball player, Derek Jeter, was a striker named Thierry Henry. I am a Jeter fan and for what Henry accomplished in his career, he was undoubtedly the better athlete. A footballer's stamina is at a higher level than most other athletes because they remain on the field of play the entire length of most matches. In Henry's case, his endurance led the Arsenal Gunners to two English Premiere League Championships and three F.A. Cups in the eight-years before his departure from the team in 2007, at which time he increased his stardom in Barcelona by leading the club to UEFA titles and the FIFA Club World Cup, including others. With at least 30 goals scored a year in a five-year period, he could be considered a Bash Brother,[1] alongside former teammate and an all-time best midfielder, Zinedine Zidane. In another striking feat, Michael Jordanesque-endorsement deals abounded for Henry, along with his statue erected outside of the Arsenal stadium in London. Like Jeter, Henry is a caramel-coloured complexion, and, like Jordan, he has been raised to that level of international superstardom where the colour of his skin rarely seems to come up. Sung to *First Noel*, Arsenal fans rained praise on their beloved striker: "Went down the Lane the other night, to tell the scum we got the new Ian Wright. They said to me, how can that be? I said to them we got Thierry Henry, Thierry Henry, Thierry Henry (and three more times)." Football fans have continued to express affection for Thierry Henry and in his birthplace of France, where he was also a hero as the top scorer on France's 1998 FIFA World Cup winning run. That is until France's Kylian Mbappé took international football by storm at the 2018 and 2022 World Cup games, respectively.

Henry has spent the better part of the last 20 years on the international stage actively seeking to combat racism in football. Though he is not alone in the effort to turn the sport's attention to abuses suffered by players at the hands of their teammates, coaches, and club owners, it remains the sport's fans who have gotten the most attention for their hooliganism. Stones and bottles are regularly thrown at players of African descent and to players of mixed-race. Many raised in the towns and cities in which they play, are subject to the common provocation of being faced with insulting chants of "monkey" and ape sounds along with the regular hurled banana. Physical confrontations on the pitch between players and fans is not uncommon and often results from failures on the part of the home team to safeguard visiting teams from raucous fans delivering battle cries, including in the form of race-baiting expletives. Some players of Asian, Latin, and Brazilian descent have been netted into this conflict both in their home countries and with close regional neighbours in similar "not me" circumstances. Having the aura of the other surround them on a team or in a country where individualism and singularity are not of value, looking different continues to levy heavy tolls on many darker-skinned people, including athletes, worldwide.

To summon the literature on hate and rage reactions, threats of annihilation and fantasies of humiliation at the hands of a more powerful other course through the heart of the sport, and the state of competition has been partly driven by attempts to ward off any possible shame and to dominate one's opponent. For Kernberg, "Clinically . . . the analysis of rage reactions—as of other intense affective states—always reveals an underlying conscious or unconscious fantasy that includes a specific relation between an aspect of the self and an aspect of a significant other" (1992, 22). The mechanics of a rage reaction appear to message a disconnection between cognition and affects, both to the victim and onlooker, while the condition itself represents a significant merger of intense feeling and motivation that have a purpose and a structure, with its release and directionality toward an object. In some well-documented instances, players and their families have been routinely targeted with social media threats and for violent acts like armed home invasions (Davis 2022). In some extreme cases, players and coaches have announced their retirements after their homes have been looted or burned by extremists among their own fan bases. In one of the most violent incidents directed at a player, Colombian footballer, Andres Escobar, was murdered after an own goal led to his country's exit from the group stages at the 1994 World Cup (Mercer 1994).

The phrase cultural violence need not only suggest violence between people of different cultures, instead, it can refer to certain forms of aggression that are encouraged through the cultural beliefs and traditions practiced by its own members. Cultural violence, in this sense, includes other kinds of communally sanctioned assaults, which can spring from unexamined assumptions and contradictions within a culture and among its majority members. This can explain how athletes of colour, who represent only a small portion of athletes in particular sports, become the frequent targets for taunting and heckling. Depending on the popularity of the sport and the media attention it receives, fans have gone as far as to demand a trade of all foreign-born players, while others routinely engage in white nationalist allegorics to assure the message is delivered to all non-white contestants on any pitch at their home stadiums. In these cases, despite government and team owner's protestations, there is a place for racism in football as it is sanctioned by the culture of fandom, which is predicated on one's allegiance to a team and on immoral invocations of national pride. Players have cried and yelled while being spit on by hundreds of lewd and drunken men and women; walked off in protest after being taunted for being of mixed-race ancestry; and played in empty stadiums after clubs have barred their own fans from attending matches in order to punish past behaviour toward another club, or to limit disruptions to matches anticipated from the departure of a recently traded player.

And hence, my conundrum about fandom and about my own membership in this community: to call myself a fan means, no matter how much it pains me to do so, that I too remain seated next to all comers, be it the tailgater, the rally cap-wearer, or the entire city of my least preferred teams. And, it also means that I have been among other fans too, including Vladimir Putin, Howard Cosell, and Fidel Castro; as well as Ohioans who burned LeBron James jerseys the night he announced his departure for Miami; or the European football match attendees who have for decades hurled monkey chants and thrown bananas at players of African descent from across the global diaspora, including the "fan-cestors" who did the same to Clyde Best in a long-ago-match between Chelsea and his home club West Ham in 1972. Like these fans, are we not all witnesses to the history and legacy of sports? So, what will we do to demand change within these sports communities? As to the proclivities toward splitting and projection, will we hold up a mirror to ourselves and other members? Or will we, I, continue to shake my head in disgust and proclaim racism, sexism, xenophobia, and hooliganism, rather than own my very elitist and racialized views on fandom, which serve to legitimize my own stereotypes? Is there a developmental path toward becoming an ethically minded sports fan? In the past decade or more, my way back into fanhood has been professionally, where I am compelled to consider players and teams in analytical terms where status, location, culture(s), and social power frame my attention to the action.

As a Black female, psychodynamic psychologist based in North America, I routinely feel confined in a forever-cage match of expectations: racial equanimity versus the unreasoned ferocity of racist animus. When half of the United States' largely segregated electorate voted twice, in 2008 and 2012, to elect a biracial Black academic, turned politician, as its leader, many citizens proclaimed America's race problem no longer relevant. I confess that living in a suddenly and magically post-racial America has often left me contemplating the power of single acts both to confirm and distort our individual and collective relationships to historical records, inviolable truths, and social mores. With a seeming national collective consciousness decrying racial constructs as outdated, inconsequential, and ready for the rubbish heap of memory, familiar exercises in social relegation emerge. Becoming, as opposed to being, irrelevant as a racialized person(s) has remained part of a complicated performance of national pride, where past regret for repeated harms done can be celebrated as wins on behalf of humanity, and the denials of ever having lost any ground since the nineteenth-century emancipation or twentieth-century Civil Rights Movements mark one's allegiance to the majority—a lasting identification with the winning team without much consideration for the lived experiences of history's losers.

More often when it comes to sports, the game-within-the-game holds my interest in ways that the score cannot. The outcomes matter a bit less now, while the journeys impact my engagement. There are times, still, when the thing that keeps me glued to the couch are the saucer-sized eyes of the batter widening ahead of striking the baseball, or when a tennis player indicates at the end of a match that the ball appeared huge as it struck their racket. I recognize those statements as true, especially when I have a simultaneous experience of a slight umami flavour in my mouth. Not bile, nor blood, but a strong taste to savour nonetheless. The heart quickens, my eyes dart back-and-forth, my fingers and shoulders remain tight. I'm present, and I care what happens next more than makes sense.

In his writings on retrospective idealization, Salman Akhtar describes the psychic arcs of optimism and nostalgia as both problematically unhealthy and punctuated by an excessiveness that keeps each in dynamic tension (Akhtar 1996; 1999; 2014). He explores how idealization functions as a part of fantasy that is simultaneously ubiquitous and unremarkable when viewed as a feature of the wordlessness of infancy, to the attempts at cognitive sense-making which are the activities of childhood, and toward the diverse potentialities for meaning-making evidenced across adulthood. In health, optimism (hope) and nostalgia (longing) hold categories of words that imbue the human experience—the ups and downs of lives lived—with affect, meaning and, ultimately, substance. Within treatment settings, Akhtar (1996) marks a key shift away from simple, noble empathy for those stricken by a common affliction, say compromise formation, and towards a recognition of unrealistic optimism as a container for disconnected self-experiences. This broadened perspective captures both the re-experiencing of traumatic impacts from early, unmet needs often expressed as anger and hateful rage, and the activation of defensiveness. Meanwhile, he also notes alternate views which regard this form of idealization as a repeated attempt to problem-solve a known, previously confronted circumstance, despite evidence that one's efforts do not match with reality. Here lies a difficult matchup, but one that, if reorganized on a near-daily or weekly basis on a pitch or a court, presents itself as one of countless, externalized spin-offs whereby serious emotionality and profound externalized conflict are both sanctioned and sanguine.

To be a conscientious sports enthusiast requires some clarity about who you are and are not vis-à-vis your sport(s), and its leagues, organizations, individual players, or teams: addict, aficionado, casual, devotee, die-hard, fair-weather, fantasy, impassioned, obsessed, "Stan." As an aware professional psychologist, I admit to an ambivalence about the language of fandom, and sometimes I feign dismissiveness of the "less kind" labels—adrenaline junkie, aggressive, bandwagoner, crazed, fake, long-suffering, sore loser—that accompany it. As a fan, I am who I am, mostly, and I generally accept any brutish identifications that come along with, or emotional bruising doled out when, rooting for/against my teams/adversaries. However, professionally-speaking, when one understands how deeply our words can wound, and why, despite the win or a loss, some fans carry profound legacies that brand individuals, communities, and nations in distinct ways that are often outsized, it becomes even more difficult to attain and maintain a stable sense of ethical boundedness.

In its healthiest form, sports fandom allows one's individuality and group-mindedness to be expressed through shared devotion to mostly predictable, years-long relationships. When viewed as a positive trait, fan loyalty promotes constancy, social bonds, time-honoured traditions, and a sense of belonging. Yet, as those fidelities slide toward blind allegiances, unquestioned bonds risk negating the healthful elements that represent the best of expressions of connectedness. The essence of fandom, as seen through this lens, is far from being simply a matter of enthusiastic support, but rather, a complex process of identification, where the line between self and other can blur. The ethical responsibilities of the psychologist as a sports fan, therefore, become a nuanced question of managing personal affiliations and biases while maintaining a professionally empathic stance.

Given that the delights and discomforts that accompany even the most mature fan's experience of loss, I consider one task of the psychoanalytically informed psychologist-fan to be paying adequate attention to the developmental, psychological, symbolic, or transformational processes associated with engagement in activities at the nexus of the human mind and body. Here, I include the following case example to illustrate how I positioned sports as a conduit to explore displaced desires, unresolved conflicts, and unmet needs with an emerging adult patient. In an earlier presentation of this case, I discuss themes of identity; self-observation, through connection to others; and wholeness, using my patient's preference for fantasy and heroic figures, his own immigration history and journey, and his knowledge and use of sports as both an athlete and a fan. Looking back on this case has permitted me to revisit fanhood, heroism, and construction of self-image through affiliation in order to broaden conversations on balancing individualism and collective identity with the empathic and relational concerns common to psychoanalytic thought and other depth-oriented theories.

THROUGH THE LOOKING GLASS[2]

In listening to Aden in sessions, I typically had a posture of following him visually on whatever journey he shared with me in each session. As he described his experiences, endeavours, fantasies, and errands, I tried to accompany him as though in the action myself. Equipped with film and literary references from most of our early sessions, I was poised to learn more about the superhero inhabitants with whom Aden most identified. These "grown-ups" figured prominently in his imagination, and I came to believe that understanding their public and private personas might offer insight into his secreted life. I read about these men with whom he connected, sought advice from peer experts about identifications with certain characters and their superhuman strengths, and considered the traits he chose to model based on these *uber*human (and unrealistic) representations.

Three storylines emerged that would serve as helpful guideposts over the course of the treatment: 1) the myth of metamorphosis (Packer 2009), common to superhero stories, provided Aden with a secure, narrative structure from which to assimilate an American identity and to project an emerging masculinity replete with conflicted sexual urges; 2) Aden's most idealized heroes are born of affluence and project self-sufficiency, until they suffer some medical setback that requires a technological intervention to strengthen them physically but that expose their human vulnerabilities; and 3) his heroes have internal demons which they seek to transform by way of chemical or surgical intervention or, in some cases, by entering "recovery"—some form of therapeutic intervention or self-help group—to find answers that have eluded them.

I think because of my receptivity to what at one time was an adaptive response to his childhood and adolescent experience of isolation and rejection, Aden and I were able to discuss the role that fantasy had in maintaining the disconnections he felt from friends, family members and acquaintances. His flights into fantasy had a far-reaching impact, making it difficult for him to tolerate even minimal frustrations without seeking a withdrawal from reality. Modell (1975) writes that these patients have an early experience of their caregivers as not fully capable of fulfilling their needs, and as a result they deny the parent (Modell refers to the mother) as a loving and benevolent object. Though Aden could acknowledge how his fantasy life served him in his daily living, the other associated affect, associated with his parental relationships—chiefly the anger and hatred he felt toward them along with the overwhelming wish he had to feel valued and understood by them—were rejected and powerfully defended against in the real. For example, in the face of disappointments Aden recounted numerous instances of putting himself into trance-like states where he was able to "re-live recent events in my life and put my own spin on them. Control them and have them end the way I want. I can't even tell you—you wouldn't even believe how much time I am there, doing that. It's basically all of the time. I mean like it would have to be 90 percent of the time."

Bollas writes that it is through the reliving of the patient's infant life in the transference, and through the "freely roused emotional sensibility [that the therapist] welcomes news from within himself" (1983, 2) that brings the unconscious derivatives of psychoanalytic work into awareness as the associative material of the countertransference experience. By maintaining access to our internal potential space (Winnicott 1974), Bollas argues, and I agree, that we create a countertransference readiness open to accepting the patient's transference communication, and in turn the patient constructs an environment where the patient and therapist can reside—the therapist in a "not knowing yet an experiencing" state (1983, 4), and the patient in a state of communicating his self- and object-representations, as well as for the unconscious discovering of the therapist's use (as an object).

His fixation with this activity was incredibly gratifying, and so any difficulties that resulted from his passionate devotion to it were acceptable, so long as he got to keep this thing that he so relied upon for sustenance. He derived short bursts of energy from the self-confidence his secret world provided, and the roles (e.g., the leader of a vast army, an arrogant hunk who is indifferent to others but beloved by men and women alike for his confidence and charm) he inhabited there allowed him to feel powerful and special when he often felt insignificant or—even worse for him—ordinary.

In the first year of treatment, Aden approached therapy as though he knew what needed to be done, rendering my presence as largely unnecessary. Not unlike a parent, I was meant to witness his growth and development as he journeyed on his path, both for and by himself. Rather than lean too much into a formulation that pigeonholed us both as limited in our ability to make use of the clinical space, I eventually landed in a quasi-acceptable position as more coach than parental figure. Finding my way as a sort of coach did allow me to join him in the action as opposed to being only a witness. Though he rarely maintained an entrenched stance with me in the treatment around adhering to his rules, he did resort to some fantasy notion about what he wished others would do, what he might coerce others to do for him, and what he could re-create in fantasy such that a given scenario would unfold the way he liked. Aden attempted to thwart the reality of external limitations with the activation of an omnipotent psychic framework that was employed to justify why he was exempt from limits others accepted with greater ease. I interpreted his efforts to control aspects of his real-life interactions, and through his fantasy life, as an attempt to create distance in his relationships, including with me. I suggested that perhaps the day would come when he could shed this frame and welcome one not pre-set, where the outcomes were most welcomed because they were unexpected.

I attempted to illustrate this with Aden by wilfully shifting our fantasy talk to another of Aden's favourite topics, one we shared: basketball. At six feet tall, my love of basketball typically has been misunderstood as a personal longing for my "playing days." My height, combined with knowledge of the sport and a willingness to engage in long conversations about it, has caused men and women alike to make this common, though false, juxtaposition. At first, Aden believed he would have to explain the game to me. Early in the treatment, when I was in a more "blank screen" phase, I said little when he would tell me about pick-up games he was involved in, or on those rare, yet lovely moments, when he would recount highlights from the previous night's matchups . . . except those times, when I would muse about those same plays he described, that I actively processed those unseen coaching decisions that cost one team or the other the win. I appreciated having an opportunity to think about the back-and-forth of Aden's pick-up games—to imagine him on court, managing his self-declared role as the two-guard, shooting from the outside whenever possible. Unfortunately, Aden rarely envisioned the full court game and, therefore, he often missed opportunities to pass the ball to an open teammate, namely the other guard, or to dish the ball to the player in the post, closest to the basket. Though we discussed our mutual disdain for the selfish play by various shooting guards in professional basketball, in truth, Aden aspired to be like them. There was no denying how good it felt for him to identify as a scorer, and to be known by other players as able to make three-pointers with distance between him and the closest defender. I related to him, and to these feelings.

For my part, now that I knew Aden's favourite spot on the court, and that he played his position with little awareness of his teammates and where they were positioned to add to the offense, certain limitations on my role in the treatment room began to make more sense, too. Let me extend this metaphor a bit further: in the beginning of the treatment, I acted more as a coach who thought I could help Aden most if I could extend his playmaking skills, by adding ball-handling to his responsibilities, and by developing his ability to execute plays in the half-court. Later, I was able to acknowledge how restricted I was to the role of either encouraging or discouraging Aden's acquisition of new skills. Instead, I now believed I had to check in to the game as a fellow player. From this vantage point, I was able to share my perspective on the game and to model how to extend his view to include the next several plays rather than maintaining a singular focus on scoring. By becoming more active myself, I also became visible, and my invitations to join me in being curious about the entire, full-court game had greater appeal. Furthermore, a shared space slowly emerged, one where we could leave our present roles behind in favour of exploring what else might be possible for us, as members of the same team.

FANDOM, FIRST AS A RELATIONAL EXPERIENCE

Beyond mere fanhood, engagement in all levels of sports is contingent upon reciprocity. I found my lane in the treatment outlined above once I came to recognize my patient as involved in a unique engagement with me, based in a shared connection and founded on a desire for mutuality to exist between us. Aside from our expressed bonds to our respective teams, I believe I held an appreciation that there was not much more I could personally intuit about Aden's personal fandom. Moreover, any additional felt sense (Gendlin 1970) on my part was not yet connected in my conscious awareness to how I planned to intervene therapeutically.

In Gendlin's (1970, 1996) view, this is modally different from feelings in the sense of emotions; instead, it is at an organized, pre-perceptual, and pre-verbal bodily level, where felt meanings are formed and from which explicit meanings arise. He considered the actualization tendency to be an inborn interaction capacity, which implies that a person has disposal of the capacity to sense implicitly their interaction with the world and others, to sense its implicit meaning, to attend to it, to hold it in their attention, to explicate it, and then to let their behavior be directed by it. This process is also referred to more generally as *experiencing*. Gendlin notes:

> Because there is an inner touchstone that will show the success of any intervention, namely whether a bit of movement comes, a therapist has the option to try interpretations or procedures derived from many methods and theories. If one of these fails to move something in the patient, the therapist can try a technique from another method or theory. With the multitude of theories and methods that exist today it is arbitrary to choose one theory and then impose it on one's patients. Checking for a physical effect happens to be a nonarbitrary touchstone. With it the therapist can make use of what the various approaches have to offer—and swiftly *discard* [author's emphasis] anything that does not have a physical experiential effect. (1996, 10)

What mattered at the time, and in retrospect, is that I moved away from a more transactional arrangement, expecting something in response to my nascent interpretations, and, instead, toward being in a shared, co-created space. This was not so much incidental, as perhaps unintentional. From this stance, making connections at the process level seemed to fit the patient's developmental stage and may have resulted in less defensiveness, and a willingness to tolerate ambiguities. Reciprocity, like fandom, is first and foremost a relational activity.

With a key emphasis on the development of a healthy culture, sowing a morally grounded relationship between fans, athletes, and teams built on communally shared values is much like an effective therapeutic intervention. In longing for the days when watching my usual sports teams evoked a sense of calm and peace, I recognize that I have been suffering from some kind of nostalgia; for those times when the only thing that would get me up from in front of a Yankees game was to shift one of the antennae slightly to the right, with the tip leaning up against the window to improve reception. At night, the location of those bunny ears was not relevant; but during the day, it was always the case that there needed to be some shifting to observe the action, specifically to track the ball. Nowadays, I no longer get up for those reasons. No antennae to shift and often not enough time to fall into the rhythm of a long game. Also, when was it decided that there's nothing more to see when the buzzer sounds at the end of regulation? Have I changed, or have the games changed?

As a fan, postgame coverage has always been important to me. Seeing players congregate on the field, or later in the dugout or clubhouse, mattered a lot, and interviews with media always held a special place because it meant that there would be even more. More time with the athletes for stories that you wouldn't hear elsewhere. Maybe a writer captures a snippet from an interview with a player, basking in the joy of a win or breaking down the box score to make sense of a loss. But the nuances, the pauses, watching players reflect on a question and choose to answer—or to change direction towards subjects of more interest to them in that moment, perhaps saving a little bit of themselves and their pains from public view. This is the inimitable period when time spools like a ball of yarn and many things become possible. Though I am unsure of what shifted more, or first—me and my singular focus and attention on the games I love, or whether the busyness and the interruptions that come with twenty-first-century adulthood, my vice-grip attention to each inning or quarter has turned from a seemingly syrupy pleasure to a guilty indulgence.

A LACANIAN PERSPECTIVE ON ETHICAL FANDOM

I have preferred a framework inclusive of psychoanalytic theories and relational-cultural theory (RCT) to investigate the ways attachment relatedness correspond with the stances we take on competition and in the face of other intense rivalry. Within the realm of sports fandom, ethical considerations often emerge as central concerns with dimensions of fan behaviour, encompassing issues, such as, sportsmanship, loyalty, discrimination, and the impact of fanaticism. Using a Lacanian framework to explore the developmental trajectory of principled engagement with both individual and team sports, encourages an emphasis on the interplay of the imaginary, symbolic, and the Real to offer a unique lens through which to examine the complex dynamics of the sports imagination of fans.

A first developmental stage of ethical fandom corresponds to Lacan's notion of the imaginary order. At this stage (Lacan 1949; 1953), sport fans might typically engage in identification and idealization of athletes or teams, projecting their desires and fantasies onto prominent sport figures, often constructing unrealistic images that can be both exhilarating and fraught. With individual sports, like tennis or golf, fans may come to identify intensely with a single athlete. They may project their own aspirations onto the athlete, living vicariously through their successes and failures. The ethical dilemmas arise when fans become excessively attached to these idealized images, which can lead to irrational behaviour or overlooking the problematic actions of one's favourite players. When collective identification occurs with team sports, fans may be observed aligning themselves with a particular team's character and values, which requires fans to balance their enthusiasm with critical self-awareness. By extension, Lacan's (1953) emphasis on the importance of recognizing the constructed nature of shared identifications can serve as encouragement to fans to acknowledge their own desires as well as their biases.

A Lacanian (1949) symbolic stage parallels the fan's evolving relationship with sports as they move from idealization to a deeper understanding of the symbolic order. At this stage, ethical fandom might involve confronting the complexities and contradictions within sports culture. Here, fans must begin to grapple with their own desires while acknowledging the symbolic significance of sporting events not only as contests of elite, physical prowess but also as cultural phenomena with social and political dimensions. The capacity to embrace a critical perspective, to question prevailing norms, and to remain open to dialogue and change are essential to advancing from symbolism toward a subjective sense of self. In individual sports, this might involve acknowledging the impact of gender and transgender biases or of coaching and doping scandals on all athletes' lives. In team sports, it could entail recognizing the historical and social context of rivalries, as well as the potential for discrimination or violence in fan behaviour. At this stage, a fan might seek a more profound connection with sports that move beyond blind loyalty and toward ethical engagements.

Lacan's Real stage corresponds with a final phase in this arc toward ethical fandom: one's acceptance of conflict and resistance as features of life, as well as the importance of facing complexities in relation to real-world expectations. At this stage, an ethical fan would be expected to move beyond idealization and symbolic recognition to recognize the material aspects of sports, including flaws, controversies, and limitations of leagues, individual players, and teams. Here, one might expect mature fans to engage in critical discourse across all levels of engagement, even advocating for positive change within sports culture while maintaining passions aligned with their own particular interests. Maintaining an adult appreciation and understanding for ethical fandom is an ongoing, reflective process that can position individuals and communities to work actively towards an inclusive, justice-oriented engagement with sports, leagues, and players.

A Lacanian frame offers a valuable perspective, whereby one undergoes a transformative journey and can cultivate a more ethical and reflective relationship with sports, contributing to the betterment of the whole of sports culture. An ethical mindset as a fan does not mean abandoning one's love for sports but rather embracing it from a critical and compassionate perspective. By understanding the interplay of identification, desire and subjectivity, fan behaviours can serve as an anchor for positive changes across all sports.

A RELATIONAL-CULTURAL THEORETICAL PERSPECTIVE THAT SUPPORTS AN ETHICAL SPORT MINDSET

While it can have its own internal ethos, sport helps shape the culture, where its influence extends beyond games, competition, and entertainment value to include passion, identity, and relationship. This allows fan bases: 1) to deepen connections with their favourite athletes and teams; and 2) to observe the ways in which their own behaviours can span from a healthy investment toward maladaptive regard. With respect to empathy and consideration for the role of fan behaviour at the fore, approaching sports and sporting events with an ethical mindset involves a level of engagement with sports that goes deeper than fans simply cheering for a particular team or athlete.

According to Relational-Cultural Theory (RCT), individuals develop their identities and relational patterns through their early interactions (Jordan 2008). RCT emphasizes the significance of relationships in early human development, and it posits that people grow through mutually empathetic and empowering connections. Similar to psychoanalytic theories, RCT stresses the role of early attachment experiences in shaping one's identity and behaviour. Moreover, as a feminist theory that focuses on human connection rather than individualism, RCT considers the impact of power dynamics and sociocultural structures on these relationships. In the context of developing an ethical mindset in relation to fandom, children often form their sports identities through their family members and the communities around them. Parents and caregivers play a crucial role in introducing children to sports, sharing their communal and personal values, and modelling ethical behaviour (Jewett et al. 2014).

As highlighted earlier in this chapter, the paradox of being both a sports enthusiast and a professional psychologist is at the crossroads between fandom and the often-crude labels that describe it. The landscape of sports is rife with deeply entrenched normative behaviours and traditions, often at odds with antiracist and feminist theoretical perspectives. Frameworks centred around empathy, equity, and justice challenge conventional narratives within both professional and recreational sports settings. As a result, fans, and the teams they love, are engaged in oscillating conflicts between matter-of-fact team identity affirmation, and a push for inclusive, fair, and equitable practices that extend the tent under which all can stand. Also essential to this discussion are key concepts such as displacement, projection, and introjection—each important to consider in relation to both individual and collective identities within sports.

So, how can we navigate this complex landscape with a critical lens? How can we use psychological principles to promote antiracism and foster a more inclusive sporting environment for all? These are important questions that require further exploration and contemplation. One way to address racism in sports is by again examining the concept of displacement (Jordan 2008), the projection of one's own feelings onto others to avoid dealing with difficult emotions and mindsets oneself, this time through the lens of RCT. As discussed earlier in this chapter, in sports this can manifest in individuals projecting their own biases and prejudices onto athletes from marginalized communities, leading not only to misunderstandings and ruptures in relationships but also to perpetuating dyadic and group power imbalances. By understanding how displacement works and being aware of our own potential to engage in mislocating our own experiences, we can actively work towards naming the problem, working actively to undo it, and promoting antiracism activities, which involve acknowledging our own biases and taking responsibility for unlearning them, as well as challenging others to join in doing the same.

Another key aspect of this theory is its focus on promoting growth and connection in relationships. RCT advocates for practices such as active listening, empathy, and mutual empowerment that can help to promote understanding and closeness. Additionally, RCT emphasizes the importance of addressing power and inequality in relationships based on race, gender, or class, to name a few. It also explores the concepts of introjection and attachment. Introjection refers to the process of internalizing the values and beliefs of others, which can lead to feelings of disconnection and self-doubt. In contrast, attachment involves emotionally connecting with another person and feeling supported and valued in the relationship. These concepts further emphasize the importance of relationships in shaping our sense of self and well-being. Overall, by promoting practices of mutual growth, empowerment, and addressing systemic inequities, RCT offers a frame for developing more authentic, meaningful connections with others.

EMERGING ADULTHOOD, TEAMS, AND ETHICAL FANDOM: INSIGHTS FROM RCT AND PSYCHOANALYSIS

Team sports have an uncanny ability to evoke intense emotions, forge communal bonds, and cultivate passionate fans who invest not only their time but also their identities into their chosen teams. The realm of sports fandom is not immune to its dilemmas, as excessive partisanship, aggression, and hostility towards opposing teams or fans can serve to disrupt the spirit of the game. Delineating an arc that traces an ethical mindset to fandom from attachment and identity formation, to its mature expression as a source of personal growth and social connection, presents the psychologist-fan with an opportunity to connect RCT with relevant psychoanalytic theories.

RCT emphasizes the significance of relationships in human development and posits that growth occurs through mutually empathetic and empowering connections (Jordan 2008). Similarly, psychoanalytic theories underscore the role of early attachment experiences in shaping one's identity and behaviour. From Freud through Erikson, and toward contemporary theories of Mentalization-Based Treatments for Children (MBT-C), psychoanalytic theorists have argued that childhood experiences continually shape an individual's personality and behaviour throughout their lifetime (Jones 1964). In the context of sports fandom, early experiences, such as, attending games, watching matches with family, and identifying with one's sports heroes can contribute to the development of a child's identity. Thus, positive experiences during this stage can lead to the development of a healthy and ethical attachment to sports.

It follows that for an ethical fandom to come about, it must begin to take root in an individual as influenced by their early relational experiences. This initial attachment can be traced to early childhood experiences where individuals may have watched games with family members or friends. These shared experiences create emotional bonds and imbue a sense of belonging, mirroring the attachment bonds formed with caregivers in infancy. As individuals continue to engage with their chosen team, their identity as a fan starts to emerge. This identity is closely linked to their attachment figures within the fan community, such as family, friends, or online communities. In psychoanalytic terms, this is akin to the formation of a superego, with internalized societal norms and ethical standards serving as a bridge to developing a mature sense of self.

Adolescents often seek validation and connection with their peers (Jordan 2008). In the realm of sports fandom, this may translate into conforming to the behaviours and attitudes of friends and peer groups. Ethical fandom at this stage may be challenged by the desire to fit in or be accepted by one's social circle. Psychoanalytic theorists, including Erikson (1968), whose stages of psychosocial development highlight the importance of identity formation during adolescence, might suggest that adolescents could struggle with their sports identity as they explore their interests and values. Supportive relationships and guidance from mentors can help adolescents navigate this critical phase and develop a strong sense of ethical fandom. Despite the turbulence of adolescence, it is a crucial period of identity exploration and development, and ethical fandom can be both a source of growth and a challenge at this stage. Adolescents often grapple with identity conflicts as they navigate the social pressures of conforming to fan expectations while adhering to societal norms. This internal struggle mirrors the psychoanalytic concept of the ego grappling with the demands of the id (passion for the team) and the superego (ethical considerations) (Freud 1923). Youth may come to experience conflicts when their team's success is achieved through questionable means or when rivalry escalates into hostility. RCT suggests that empathetic connections are essential for healthy development, and these connections become critical in helping adolescent fans navigate identity conflicts. Conversations with peers, mentors, or role models, who model ethical fandom, can guide individuals towards more balanced and empathetic fan behaviour.

As individuals mature, fandom can evolve from a source of identity to a pathway for personal growth and social connection. With age and experience, adolescents and emerging adults gain emotional regulation skills, allowing them to channel their passion for their teams in more constructive ways. With developing engagement in self-reflection, one's capacity for critical self-examination of their behaviours and attitudes as fans also improves. Keeping RCT in mind, an emphasis on the importance of expanding one's empathic connections is a key developmental task. For instance, ethical fans could be expected to extend their empathetic connections beyond their immediate community to include even fans of opposing teams, recognizing the shared love for the sport and the human experiences that stand to unite all fans, eventually fostering a more inclusive and compassionate fan culture.

An ethical mindset in team sports intertwines relational growth, identity formation, and ethical maturation. It binds a profound process at key stages of human development, characterized by the ability to balance passion with empathy, navigate identity conflicts, and foster connections within a diverse fan community. By understanding and nurturing this developmental arc, a fan culture that embodies the ethical principles of respect, empathy, and sportsmanship can be cultivated to enrich both the individual and the broader communities to which one belongs.

ETHICAL FANDOM IN ADULTHOOD

Ethical fandom in individual and team sports is a developmental process that spans from childhood to adulthood. In utilizing both RCT and psychoanalytic perspectives, the role of early relationships, adolescent peer influences, and adult self-reflection highlight approaches to ethical fandom that are not only about fans' support of and identification with athletes on teams, but also emphasises building meaningful and ethical connections with the sports world and fellow fans. Ultimately, these efforts may represent essential contributions to a healthier and more inclusive sports culture, benefiting individuals and society.

Sports fandom can serve as a means of coping with life's stresses and uncertainties from early adolescence and into middle and late adulthood. Fans may utilize defence mechanisms such as displacement and sublimation (Freud 1933), channelling their aggression and anxiety into the emotional rollercoaster of sports events, allowing them to temporarily escape their own psychological conflicts. For Erikson (1968), adulthood represents a key period for individuals to reflect on their values and choices, so it follows that fandom in adulthood would involve a deepened understanding of one's relationship with sports, and its potential impact on personal and social well-being. In adulthood, RCT continues to emphasize the importance of attachment and mutually empathetic growth-fostering relationships (Jordan 2008). As in earlier stages, sports fandom can evolve into a more nuanced and ethical experience. Here, individuals may find a sense of belonging in sports communities, both online and offline, where they can share their passion while respecting diversity of opinions.

By using psychoanalytic frameworks, we can better appreciate, understand, and value the complexities at play when engaging an ethics of sports fandom, challenging traditional norms and practices, and ultimately fostering a more inclusive and equitable environment for all individuals involved in sports. In doing so, we can hope to experience a near future where identities are not merely affirmed but actively celebrated and embraced within the sporting community. Modern sports can retain its platform for promoting empathy, equity, and justice, but not without continuing to challenge fans to think critically, act with compassion, and strive towards a more inclusive future where everyone feels valued, seen, and empowered to foster positive social change.

CONCLUSION

Sports fandom has a long history and has evolved significantly in the past century. With the rise of technology, globalization, and an increased emphasis on ethical practices, being a fan of sports has become more than just rooting for your favourite team or athlete. It now involves critical thinking and consideration of ethical issues within the sports industry. One key aspect that has changed in recent years is the way fans consume sports content. With the advent of social media, fans now have a platform to voice their opinions and engage in discussions with other fans from around the world. This has led to increased awareness about ethical issues within the sports industry, such as, discrimination, abuse, and exploitation of athletes.

Moreover, there has also been an increase in academic research and literature on the topic of sports fandom and ethics. Scholars have examined the developmental arc of ethical sports fandom, tracing its origins back to ancient times where spectators were expected to show respect for athletes and follow certain rules of conduct with differing cultural and societal values influencing fans' attitudes and behaviours towards sports. As fans become more educated about ethical practices in sport, they have a greater responsibility to use their voices and influence to promote positive change. Furthermore, being an ethical sports fan also means holding sports organizations and governing bodies accountable for their actions. Fans have the power to demand transparency and ethical standards from these entities as well as speak out against any wrongdoing.

Ultimately, ethical sports fandom is a continuous journey that requires constant self-reflection and awareness. It also involves actively engaging in discussions and advocating for change, both within our own communities and on a larger scale. With a focus on ethical values and principles, fans can ensure that sport remains a positive and uplifting aspect of our society for years to come. As we continue to evolve and progress, let us strive to be responsible and ethical sports fans who contribute to its betterment. So, being an ethical fan now demands we use our deep and abiding affection for sports players and teams to make a positive impact locally and globally. It is therefore important to continuously re-evaluate our perspectives and behaviours towards sport, rather than blindly adhering to long-held beliefs that fail to consider the role of power and social position.

Ongoing global conflicts and wars have had profound implications not only for politics but also sport. With respect to encounters in contests between tennis players on both the men's and women's tours, beginning in early 2022 and through to this book's publish date, Belarussian and Russian athletes have not been permitted to compete under the flags of their home countries and have had points in tournaments they have won withheld due to sanctions by the sport's governing bodies. Among many instances of regional conflict, the Russian military invasion of Ukraine illuminates the intricate interplay between politics and sport, challenging the neutrality often affiliated with sport. Players from other countries, and fans of individual players representing all countries involved, have been asked about their position and have been drawn into conflagrations, where cordiality is expected after a win or a loss (Bodo 2023). These athletes' experiences can be seen as a journey through a complex emotional and ethical landscape. They must grapple with feelings of animosity, fear, and resentment, potentially impacting their performance and relationships not only with teammates and opponents but also with their fan bases.

By applying our collective expertise, psychoanalytic clinicians and research scholars can contribute to a more ethical culture within sports fandom. Together, we can plumb the intersection of psychology and sport to promote a healthier and more ethical experience for all involved. It is essential to continue writing and researching on this topic to deepen our understanding and provide insights into these crucial aspects of our social behaviours. Through ongoing discussions and critical analysis, we can aim to create a healthier, more inclusive environment for athletes and fans alike. By utilizing psychoanalytic theories and depth therapy concepts, like RCT, we can further our understanding of the underlying dynamics at play in developing frameworks which lead to identifying potential red flags and warning signs for problematic behaviours and may ultimately guide us towards creating effective interventions to address these issues.

In challenging harmful narratives and ideologies, we can agitate for the inclusive sports culture we want to see—one that celebrates and promotes diversity and healthy fan behaviour. This requires continuous effort from all stakeholders involved. As fans, athletes, coaches, media personnel, and governing bodies, it is our responsibility to reflect on our beliefs and ethical positions within the sports world and to work actively towards promoting a more positive and inclusive environment. Only then can we truly harness the power of sports to bring people together, inspire change, and foster personal growth.

NOTES

1. The term Bash Brothers refers to two former baseball players: Jose Canseco and Mark McGwire. Both men were not only famous as home run hitters but also as teammates for seven years of their Major League Baseball (MLB) careers with the Oakland Athletics, even winning the 1989 World Series title together. This period in baseball was part of the now infamous "Steroid Era," which has left many fans disillusioned about these athletes' storied careers and their places in baseball history,

2. The following section is part of a longer journal article that I authored for the *Journal of Infant, Child and Adolescent Psychotherapy*, used with permission from the publishers, Taylor & Francis (Bowen 2013).

BIBLIOGRAPHY

Akhtar, Salman. 1996. "'Someday . . . ' and 'If Only . . . ' Fantasies: Pathological Optimism and Inordinate Nostalgia as Related Forms of Idealization." *Journal of the American Psychoanalytic Association,* 44: 723–753.

Akhtar, Salman. 1999. "The Immigrant, the Exile, and the Experience of Nostalgia." *Journal of Applied Psychoanalytic Studies*, 1 no. 2: 123–130.

Akhtar, Salman. 2014. "The Mental Pain of Minorities." *British Journal of Psychoanalysis*, 30 no. 2: 136–153. https://doi.org/10.1111/bjp.12081

Bodo, Peter. 2023. "Elina Svitolina and the Power of the Handshake." *Tennis Magazine*, July 12, 2023. https://www.tennis.com/news/articles/elina-svitolina-handshake-victoria-azarenka-wimbledon-aryna-sabalenka

Bollas, Christopher. 1983. "Expressive Uses of the Countertransference: Notes to the Patient from Oneself." *Contemporary Psychoanalysis*, 19: 1–33.

Bowen, Monique. 2013. "Through the Looking-Glass: Exploring Identity Development for a Beginning Therapist and Her Late Adolescent Patient." *Journal of Infant, Child and Adolescent Psychotherapy*, 12 no. 4: 286–300.

Davis, Margaret. 2022. "From Joao Cancelo to Raheem Sterling: Football Stars Who Have Been Victims of Break-ins." *The Independent*, December 10, 2022. https://www.independent.co.uk/news/uk/joao-cancelo-raheem-sterling-jesse-lingaard-peter-crouch-b2242842.html. DOI: https://doi.org/10.1080/15289168.2013.850383

Erikson, Eric. 1968. *Identity: Youth and Crisis*. New York: W. W. Norton & Company.

Freud, Sigmund. 1923. "The Ego and the Id." In *The Standard Edition of the Complete Psychological Works of Sigmund Freud, Volume XIX (1923–1925)*, edited by James Strachey, 1–66. London, UK: The Hogarth Press.

Freud, Sigmund. (1933). "New Introductory Lectures on Psychoanalysis." In *The Standard Edition of the Complete Psychological Works of Sigmund Freud, Volume XXII (1932–1936)*, edited by James Strachey, 1–182. London, UK: The Hogarth Press.

Gendlin, Eugene. 1970. "The significance of Felt Meaning." In *Encounter: An Introduction to Philosophy*, edited by Richard Cormier, Ramona Chinn and Ewing Lineback, 561–566. Glenview, IL: Scott, Foresman & Co.

Gendlin, Eugene. 1996. *Focusing-Oriented Psychotherapy: A Manual of the Experiential Method.* New York: Guilford.

Jewett, Rachel et al. 2014. "School Sport Participation During Adolescence and Mental Health in Early Adulthood." *The Journal of Adolescent Health: Official Publication of the Society for Adolescent Medicine*, 55 no. 5: 640–644. https://doi.org/10.1016/j.jadohealth.2014.04.018

Jones, Ernest. 1964. *The Life and Works of Sigmund Freud.* New York: Penguin.

Jordan, Judith. 2008. "Recent Developments in Relational-Cultural Theory." *Women & Therapy,* 31 nos. 2–4, 1–4. https://doi.org/10.1080/02703140802145540

Kernberg, Otto. 1992. *Aggression in Personality Disorders and Perversion.* New Haven, CT: Yale University Press.

Lacan, Jacques. 1949. "The Mirror Stage as Formative af the Function of the I as Revealed in Psychoanalytic Experience." In *Écrits: A Selection*, translated by Alan Sheridan, 1–7. New York: Norton.

Lacan, Jacques. (1953). "The Function and Field of Speech and Language in Psychoanalysis." *In Écrits: A Selection*, translated by Alan Sheridan, 30–113. Norton.

Mercer, Pamela. 1994. "Colombian Who Made World Cup Error is Killed." *The New York Times*, July 3, 1994. https://www.nytimes.com/1994/07/03/world/colombian-who-made-world-cup-error-is-killed.html

Modell, Arnold. 1975. "A Narcissistic Defence Against Affects and the Illusion of Self-Sufficiency." *International Journal of Psychoanalysis*, 56: 275–282.

Packer, Sharon. 2009. *Superheroes and Superegos: Analysing the Minds Behind the Masks*. Santa Barbara, CA: Praeger

Racker, Heinrich. 1953. "A Contribution to the Problem of Countertransference." *International Journal of Psychoanalysis*, 34 no. 4: 313–324.

Racker, Heinrich. 1957. "The Meanings and Uses of Countertransference." *Psychoanalytic Quarterly*, 26 no. 3: 303–357.

Shapiro, Mark. 1987. "Canseco Trade Reunites Bash Brothers." *Chicago Tribune*, January 28, 1997. http://articles.chicagotribune.com/1997-01-28/sports/9701280261_1_bash-brothers-mark-mcgwire-general-manager-sandy-alderson

Winnicott, Donald. 1974. "Fear of Breakdown." *International Review of Psychoanalysis*, 1: 103–107.

PART IV

Identity

Chapter 8

To Know of Manny Pacquiao

The Limits of Identity under Empire

Joseph S. Reynoso

In *Beyond a boundary*, perhaps the greatest work on sport, society, and identity, CLR James asked "What do they know of cricket who only cricket know?" (James 2013, Preface). To begin from a similar but different place, less lofty but still colonized, one may ask "What do they know of Manny Pacquiao who only Manny Pacquiao know?" For James, answering this rhetorical question involved "ideas and facts." Straying a bit from the spirit of James' seminal work on class, empire, and race, one might say, to answer my version of the question (and others I will subsequently pose) will involve facts and fantasies. This chapter is an attempt to think psychoanalysis and sport together through theorizing Filipino boxer Manny Pacquiao.

WHO IS MANNY PACQUIAO?

Emmanuel "Manny" Dapidran Pacquiao was born in 1978 in Kibawe, a municipality on the southern Philippine Island of Mindanao. He boxed professionally from 1995 until 2021. In that 26-year career, Pacquiao racked up 62 wins and 12 world titles in a record eight different weight classes.

To know of Manny Pacquiao is to know of the Philippines. I cannot summarize the history of a land or people better than Carmen Guerrero Nakpil's encapsulation of its Spanish and American colonization as spanning "300 years in the convent and 50 years in Hollywood" (quoted by Jiminez-David 2018). For those interested in learning the textures of Philippine Islands, one should consult the writings of Jose Rizal—especially the fiction. One may riff off Tolstoy to conclude that while all empires are alike, each oppressed people is oppressed in its own way. The Philippines of Pacquiao's time, and my own (though experienced from the distance of American shores), is one of balut and basketball, Marcos's martial law and migrancy, People Power and poverty, remittances and rosaries set with the backdrop of kleptocratic authoritarian rule, state murders, and the precarity of the natural hazards and disasters that accompany being situated on the Pacific ring of fire.

To know of Manny Pacquiao is to know how he boxed. One of the most exciting boxers of this century, Pacquiao combined outstanding raw speed and power with an unpredictable, at times risky, offensive style. Working with his long-time American trainer Freddie Roach, Pacquiao developed tools to devastate his opponents that included a straight left with his dominant hand, a double and sometimes triple left jab, and eventually a counter right hook to match his dangerous southpaw one. A volume puncher who seemed tirelessly active in fights, particularly during the first half of his career, Pacquiao would launch flurries of punches in combinations with frenetic pacing. Supporting this arsenal with unorthodox footwork, showcasing the fighter's incredible agility and athleticism, allowed him to throw blows from unexpected angles.

To know of Manny Pacquiao is to know of his achievements beyond boxing. This includes his philanthropic efforts to aid various communities in the Philippines using portions of his financial riches from boxing.[1] Pacquiao also branched out to other forms of entertainment including film (staring in a woeful superhero movie *Wapakman* in 2009) and television and music (recording songs both in Tagalog and English). He distinguished himself most from past and present sportive comparisons in pursuing a political career while boxing. After a decade's worth (2000–2009) of boxing dominance, Pacquiao continued fighting professionally for twelve more years while also serving first in the congress and then senate of the Philippines. After retiring from boxing in 2021, Pacquiao unsuccessfully ran for president in the Philippines, finishing third.

To know of Manny Pacquiao is to know of his beginnings. Pacquiao origin stories are possibly more well-known than tales of his storied ring encounters with Juan Manuel Marquez (four fights) or Erik Morales (three fights). Though sometimes the details vary—as is the case when a person becomes mythologized—the general story is that he was a child of abject poverty: "Pacquiao was considered poor, even among the poor" (Poole 2010, 20). His father abandoned he and his siblings to be raised by their industrious hard-nosed mother. By his early teens, Pacquiao dropped out of school to sell items like cigarettes and doughnuts on roadsides to help support his family. He turned to boxing at age 14, literally lived on the streets, before eventually making his way to Manila. Legend has it that he either snuck onto the ferry to journey 500 miles from Mindanao to Manila or procured transit by lying about his age.

To know of Manny Pacquiao is to know of Floyd Mayweather. There is no congressman Pacquiao if there is no welterweight champion Pacquiao. He was first and foremost important to the boxing and sporting worlds. Pacquiao was lauded by the bulk of journalists and experts within boxing and widely popular among fight fans and mainstream sport audiences.[2] The positivity for Pacquiao had more to do with his exciting offensive method than the victories it led to. We mustn't forget that Pacquiao's ascendance occurred during a period that was dominated by the best fighter of this past generation, the American welterweight Floyd Mayweather. Mayweather will historically be remembered as the better boxer, and with his undefeated record, should rightfully rank above Pacquiao in any all-time list of pound-for-pound fighters. Much has been said and written (cf. Bonhomme et al. 2020) about the relationship between these two fighters—including their one match in 2015, in which the American won by unanimous decision. Importantly, Pacquiao represented a perfect foil for Mayweather in and outside of the ring. For all the latter's technical superiority, his defensive counterpunching left most experts in reserved awe but many fans in a less than animated state. Mayweather's effective and efficient conservativism in the ring was coupled with a personality outside the ring that was flamboyant and ostentatious. His tendency to demean and race-bait his opponents before fights lay in stark contrast to Pacquiao's personae as a "modest, quiet and deeply religious" family man (Mackay 2015).

But even if one knows all of this, what does one know of Manny Pacquiao? This may seem to be a question of identity, and it is—but whose? For what can be said of they who presume to know anything about Pacquiao?

WHO ARE PACQUIAO FANS?

To know of Manny Pacquiao is to know of his fans. As mentioned above, while Pacquiao (or "Pac man" as he was affectionately referred to) was popular amongst a general sporting audience, no one would deny that his widest and most fervent fan base consisted of those with ties to his home country of the Philippines. Joaquin Jay Gonzalez III and Angelo Michael Merino wrote: "close to a hundred million Filipinos in the Philippines and globally . . . put their lives on hold to watch his fights and beam with pride. During his bouts, there is an unofficial ceasefire between the security forces and rebels in conflict areas. The crime rate also drops to virtually zero" (2012, 115). As Gonzalez and Merino suggest, passion for Pacquiao was felt by those worldwide with ties to the Philippines. For Filipino-Americans, Albert Samaha articulated it this way:

> [Pacquiao] ignited a surge of cultural pride in me and my Filipino American friends. We'd split the pay-per-view TV bill and watch his fights, decked out in shirts and bandannas bearing the sun and stars of the Philippine flag, shouting "Mabuhay!" when his opponents fell to the canvas. Maybe pride naturally spurs curiosity, or maybe I was just self-conscious about so loudly repping a country I hadn't seen since I was six years old, but it was around the time Pacquiao became world welterweight champion that I began to feel a desire to learn more about the place my elders had left. (2021, 307–308)

Some (Horton 2012; Kobayashi and Cho 2019) have emphasized that Pacquiao's appeal reached beyond boxing fans, his home country, and those of Filipino descent worldwide toward a global Asian fanbase. For instance, in a piece entitled, "Finally, an Asian who packs a punch," Thea Lim went further exalting Pacquiao as a Pan-Asian symbol combatting centuries of Anti-Asian stereotypes (2011). Lim asserted, "Pacquiao goes past Filipinoness or Asianness, rousing transracial unity for anyone who has a reason to back the ethnic underdog" (2011).[3]

The former *Time* news editor Howard Chua-Eoan penned this description to accompany Pacquiao's inclusion in *Time* magazine's 100 people of the year in 2009, arguably the zenith of the boxer's career:

> Manny Pacquiao was considered a savior by two groups of people this year: Filipinos and boxing aficionados. For his countrymen, the diminutive (5 ft. 6 in. and change) pugilist once again proved that their archipelago could produce more than tales of violence, poverty and natural disaster—that there was some undefined quality that could produce a fighter of such speed, resiliency and charisma as to be a living legend. For boxing fans, Pacquiao defied physics, rising through six weight classes to win seven world titles—and galvanizing the sport like no other boxer in years. (2009)

Chua-Eoan's naming of two groups who could claim Pacquiao as a savior—like most examples (including the one you are reading) attempting to communicate the boxer's importance—help illustrate why and how Pacquiao's importance depended both individually and collectively on who you were. Was Pacquiao a commercially viable fighter winning back viewers to a failing sport, an inspiring symbol of hope and perseverance to a country perpetually developing in the global economic hierarchy, an activity to bond one familial generation to another, or a response to Anti-Asian stereotypes? One can think of these as questions of identity, and to a certain degree they are. To put this issue in different terms, we might say that to inquire about those who know of Manny Pacquiao is to think why one wants to know of the boxer. A question of identity becomes one of desire.

A DESIRE FOR PACQUIAO

To know of Manny Pacquiao is to know the desire he aroused in his spectators. This is to say that Pacquiao embodied or gave form to the pre-existing desire of his audience. For the psychoanalyst Jacques Lacan, "Desire is a relation of being to lack. This lack is the lack of being properly speaking. It isn't the lack of this or that, but lack of being whereby the being exists" (1988, 223). This lack, developed from a child's socialization into a world of language and symbols that is ultimately other to it, is only related to or experienced in absence. Whatever adult, caregiving, or family configuration the child is born into, it is confronted with a world of limits and incomprehension that desire both springs from and moves towards. It is lack that prompts movement forward, as one Pacquiao associate phrased it for the boxer, "[h]is courage comes from poverty" (Poole 2010, 32).

Mari Ruti summarized the significance of lack for Lacan:

> it's part of the human condition to feel lacking, then it's logical that desire arises as an (optimistic) pursuit of objects, people, ambitions, activities, and modes of life that we hope will compensate for that lack, granting us a sense of wholeness and belonging. But because the lack within our being is constitutive of our subjectivity (the price of being human), it can never be definitively cured. (Ruti 2018, 3–4)

Ruti references the paradox of what we desire in the world of images, language, and symbols to wishfully remedy what within is uncurable. These things, or objects, can, but do not have to be material or tangible. It can be a relationship, a hobby, a role one has, a way of feeling, a vendetta, an idea or anything that serves the unconscious function of restoring a completeness that the subject never had. For Lacan, the temporal aspect here is crucial in the subject's search and retrieval process, as following Freud's teaching, he says: "The object is by nature a refound object. That it was lost is a consequence of that—but after the fact. It is thus refound without our knowing, except through the refinding, that it was ever lost" (1992, 118). Thus, every realized object is unconsciously experienced as a thing regained . . . but not really.

Across his seminars and writings, Lacan theorized the fundamental alienation intrinsic to human subjectivity that characterizes the nature of desire. Building off this, for both Pacquiao and his fans, the desire to achieve or vicariously triumph, must be understood as less about the goal and more the pursuit. Lacan distinguishes the object of one's desire from the "object-cause," which can be thought of as the limit or obstacle that sets desire in motion. Hence, as satisfying as each Pacquiao win was (though some were more than others—Hatton, De La Hoya, Cotto come to mind), it ultimately failed to fulfil, because, as sports showcases, every championship or gold medal earned eventually reveals the ongoing push for more that will never be gratified and in many senses doesn't aim to be.

Retooling Freud's "frontier" concept (the product of but irreducible to either biology or culture) of drive, for Lacan, this unceasing push generates a mode of arousal, *jouissance*, that aims not toward pleasure but beyond it. As Lacan (1992) describes in Seminar VII, enjoyment can come from transgressive acts through boundaries, however they are configured for the subject in society. Associated to this is the aspect of *jouissance's* excess. *Jouissance*, or enjoyment as it gets translated from the French, is related to pain if not more than pleasure. This sustained agitated arousal is not only familiar to Pacquiao fans watching any of his fights but may extend to most sport spectatorship if not participation. The anguished absorption in sport perhaps is the most available public demonstration of Lacan's thought that "*jouissance* is suffering" (1992, 184).[4]

We suffer our enjoyment within webs of unconscious fantasies that are only partially available to us consciously in the language that is available to us in the symbolic context of our time and place. Todd McGowan has discussed the relationship of fantasy and enjoyment this way:

> Whatever the fantasy narrative is, it must represent the great difficulty of accessing the desired object. This difficulty is the source of the enjoyment that the fantasy provides. Even though we consciously identify enjoyment with the object to be obtained, the enjoyment in the fantasy derives from the tortured path to the object, not from the object itself. (McGowan 2022, 178)

Pacquiao stated this within the boxing idiom: "In a fighter's world there is never finality, because no matter what you see or what you do, you know that you have another fight ahead. Until you retire, this thought will always live in your mind. But as a fighter there is a longing for that battle" (Pacquiao 2010, 107). Though, Pacquiao positions retirement as an end, we know that the retirement of professional athletes serves as yet another obstacle to be encountered (Reynoso 2013). Thus, for fans always looking toward the next tournament or season, or athletes themselves, sports highlights how lack and the desire that proceeds from it serve as the subject's origin and motive course. This conversation, however, takes a specific turn when the symbolic world that the speaking subject finds itself is structured to ground the source of its lack in historical theft.

COLONIAL LOSS/LACK

To know of Manny Pacquiao is to know of loss. Sheldon George's work on slavery and race is instructive in thinking through how violence in the name of imperialism shapes the psychic experience of its targets by actualizing constitutive lack as material loss (George 2019). According to George:

> slavery unveiled the psychic condition of alienation that drives subjectivity in its perpetual pursuit of jouissance. The American slave's bondage allowed for a striking manifestation of such subjective alienation, pinning this psychic reality exclusively to the slave while generating race itself as a compensatory source of jouissance, a Lacanian object a. (2019, 109)

Though trans-Atlantic slavery and the Philippines' colonization have immeasurable differences, they both attempt to imprison enslaved and colonized subjects within psychic system that historicizes ontological lack as the imposition of whiteness and empire. In addition to the master gaining from corporal and material theft, there is a reward that is unconsciously enjoyed in the externalization and of a lack onto enslaved/colonized subjects. Enslaved/colonized subjects and their descendants did not only pay with their labor and lives but are conscripted into a symbolic order coded at their detriment that functions intergenerationally (Wapeemukwa 2021).

Though Lacanian theorizing locates the subject as operating from a deficit of perceived loss, which ontological lack expresses itself through, colonization collapses the difference between the two in a fashion similar to how George claims that slavery aimed to expose the enslaved's lack "by making the slave's social positioning mirror his or her psychic reality" (2019, 115). Lack is made concrete for the colonized by violent acts of theft and then future narratives and tellings of these losses across generations. If fantasy uses signifiers of the contextually determined Symbolic order to mask constitutive lack, then the illusions of wholeness the colonized employ are determined within a dialect of loss designed by empire.

Imperialism imprints an inferiority into the national identity of its targets and their descendants through thievery. This was a point the Filipino revolutionary Jose Rizal eloquently voiced across various writings, including in 1889:

> little by little they lost their old traditions, the mementos of their past; they gave up their writing, their songs, their poems, their laws in order to learn by rote other doctrines which they did not understand, another morality, another aesthetics different from those inspired by their climate and their manner of thinking . . . degrading themselves in their own eyes; they became ashamed of what was their own; they began to admire and praise whatever was foreign

> and incomprehensible; their spirit was dismayed and it surrendered to . . . this disgust of themselves. (quoted in Rimonte 1997, 58)

The violence from without can become self-inflicted, as Frantz Fanon (2004) notes. Under the ever-present threat of imperial danger, the colonized subject eventually begins taking the knife to their own cultural histories, rituals, and stories:

> there is a singular loss of interest in these rituals. With his back to the wall, the knife at his throat, or to be more exact the electrode on his genitals, the colonized subject is bound to stop telling stories. After years of unreality, after wallowing in the most extraordinary phantasms, the colonized subject, machine gun at the ready, finally confronts the only force which challenges his very being: colonialism. And the young colonized subject who grows up in an atmosphere of fire and brimstone has no scruples mocking zombie ancestors, two-headed horses, corpses woken from the dead, and djinns who, taking advantage of a yawn, slip inside the body. (Fanon 2004, 20)

Though the subject always endures the signifier's cut, colonization determines a starting position for the colonized that purposes to foreclose the available paths of enjoyment that can be derived from the failure to attain what is missing. The empire leaves the colonized and their descendants in search for objects that have a strangeness to them that accompanies the ache for antiquity or acquiescence to invasion.

Faced with choosing objects of desire coated with ambivalence, betrayal, disdain, and pity, the colonized may become reinvigorated by a figure who activates fantasies of refusal and reversal of loss. Wilfred Bion theorized group dynamics to show that in the interplay between leader and group the latter creates the former (Bion 1961). In other words, a person is placed into the role of leader by a group's collective unconscious fears and wishes.[5] To bring Bion and Lacan together, we can understand that groups become animated around an individual's excellence when achievements are unconsciously linked to, or even name, something felt lacking within the group. The desire that lifts the figure to prominence may point to the lack the group is investing the figure with the responsibility of remedying in fantasy, and in some instances, actuality. For colonized peoples the figure is psychically positioned to fulfill the impossible task of healing or overcoming individual and group trauma that is linked to an admixture of fantasied and "actual" loss(es).

Jose Rizal contemplated what would be needed to galvanize the Philippines, a people divided by the geography of archipelago and language though united by "a common misfortune and a common abasement" even contemplating precolonial mythical Filipino heroes, like Bernardo Carpio, as potential motivational sources against oppression (Scalice 2018). Scholars from various fields have investigated how an athlete's renown can be knitted through a national identity (Black 2016; Black et al. 2021; Galang et al. 2015; Hobsbawm 1992). Conceiving of a celebrity object's fame as embodying the aspirational ideals and traits of the country or its people may be more accurately understood as revealing the anxieties and fears of a nation's history or current predicament. Pacquiao did not become the kind of leader Rizal hoped for. This is not because an athlete is unable to serve a nation's revolutionary needs (think Muhammad Ali), but as I will discuss, the place the boxer occupied in the imaginary limited his emancipatory potential.

LITTLE BROWN BROTHER NO MORE[6]

To know of Manny Pacquiao is to know of excess. After one of the boxer's signature victories against welterweight legend Oscar De La Hoya in 2008, the celebrated commentator Larry Merchant reflected on the spectacle he had just witnessed and said, "We thought Manny Pacquiao was great. He's better than we thought" (quoted in Campbell 2015). For so many of his fans, Pacquiao embodied the fantasy of exception by defying expectations. This of course begins with his achievements in the ring, which were exceptional in themselves but unprecedented for a modern boxer from Asia. Pacquiao steadily climbed in classes to practice his craft at higher weights than Asian boxers customarily apply their trade (flyweight 108 lbs., lightweight 135 lbs.). His signature victories at welterweight (140 to 147 lbs.) were notable in themselves, primarily because this weight division had been dominated historically by white, African American, and Latino boxers.

To the degree that one can say anything about the collective identity of a group, we might think then that following Rizal (2015), to *be* Filipino is a relationship to what has been taken, what is no more, what has been given up, and what one isn't. This negative space swirls with fantasies of what one should be, what one once was, and what one could have been. Though this is certainly the unconscious fantasy process in all sport fandom, to see how this was structured for Filipinos, impacted by centuries of colonization, may particularly be instructive for what it illustrates about identity. For all the qualities—talented, strong, fast, rich, powerful—that may have been involved in the identification with Pacquiao, a dominant fantasy emerges. To be Filipino and watch Pacquiao box in his prime meant seeing oneself as the active agent of one's destiny. As one Filipino journalist said, "[Pacquiao] has indeed helped uplift the Pinoy soul, by making his poor countrymen believe they could themselves be winners" (Poole 2010, 248). No longer the Spanish steppingstone to the East, the little brown brother under the tutelage of the United States, or the sacrificial pawn in the aggressions between America and Japan in World War II. Pacquiao's heroics in the ring inverted the negative space. For many spectators, existing at the margins of many societies, he provided the enjoyment of transgressing existing boundaries.

It cannot be overstated that his popularity was propelled by surpassing what is supposed to be. To identify with Pacquiao's athletic supremacy offered the fantasy of overcoming the racist misogynistic coupling of the Asian man as weak and effeminate. What allowed a figure like Pacquiao to capture/be used in the imagination of so many was the excess of the brutal sport he exceled in. He became a boxing champion hailing from the colonized nation of the Philippines, known for the likability and agreeableness of its people. Gary Poole described it this way in his biography of Pacquiao:

> Talking with Filipinos about Manny Pacquiao can feel like entering a cult. Pacquiao arrived in America when not many Americans could identify a famous Filipino, save Imelda Marcos or Cory Aquino. He might have shared the stereotypical notion of the quiet, sweet, and tireless work ethic of his brethren, an almost anti-celebrity, but instead he became a one-man chamber of commerce. A commonly accepted stereotype was that Filipinos were invisible voices: good in choirs, poor soloists. They didn't really stand up for themselves; they were a gentle, inconsequential tribe. As Pacquiao continued winning and whipping his countrymen into a frenzy, the parades through the streets of Manila grew by the hundreds of thousands. Filipinos started following him with the sort of fanaticism usually reserved for religious idols. Pacquiao's popularity continued to rise exponentially outside the archipelago, which incited Filipinos to become even more Pacquiao crazy. (Poole 2010, 156)

The ascendance of Pacquiao as an Asian athlete might have other sportive comparisons, but it is the excess in the arena of boxing that maximized his potential to subvert stereotypes of Asian docility, passivity, submissiveness, inferiority and subservience. For these fans and many others, to watch Pacquiao knock out Ricky Hatton or pummel De La Hoya into submission offered the possibility to align oneself in fantasy with the possibilities of reversing personal and historical loss, which, while actual, is still a proxy for lack. That Pacquiao's fandom builds on a malignant masculine position, for fans of any gender, to subvert anti-Asian racism reveals the double-edged duality identity offers.

THE COSTS AND LIMITS OF IDENTITY

To know of Manny Pacquiao is to know of the delights of empire. To be a Pacquiao fan means to unconsciously identify with both the fantasy of a non-lacking other as well as the object desired by others. All of us, including

Pacquiao, position ourselves in relation to the regard of some observing other. The other can be in the form of a particular person, institution or a conglomeration of anything serving the function of an exalted arbiter. In the idiom of boxing, a boxer fights an opponent, but performs for three judges' approval, the monied stakeholders (promoters, advertisers, media companies), the audience, and countless others who can more idiosyncratically hold this position. For those whose connection to Pacquiao involved using him as a celebrity object to bolster their Filipino or even Asian identities, the occupier of the position of the other also includes those in the seat of empire.

The thrill of a Pacquiao victory was suffused with the enthralling lure of recognition that had the ability to momentarily, if not longer, override scrutiny of the power invested in such agents of recognition. There is cause to be cautious about projects, individually or collectively, that depend on recognition by the other. As Anne Cheng wrote:

> the promise of acquiring public recognition, while not without its potentials, cannot really grant subjecthood to the disenfranchised since, strictly speaking, to be 'recognized' is still to occupy an object position. To be recognized means that there has to be a recognizing agent, authority and dominant culture in this case. (Cheng 2001, 174)

The fantasy of recognition achieved in the identification with a Pacquiao victory fails to question the authority of any other and the nature of the place one seeks inclusion into.[7] At the extreme, appeals for recognition exalt the other as non-lacking and only requests permission to be considered worthy of desire—to exist.

The Filipinx anthropologist Constancio Arnaldo Jr. has convincingly raised some of the problems Pacquiao's popularity should confront us with. Arnaldo writes that Pacquiao's performance of hypermasculinity and heterosexuality symbolically inverts dominant racialized gendered patterns to represent "a highly masculinized Philippine nation state that locally challenges the U.S. state's emasculating processes" (2020, 666). Doing fieldwork among spectators at Pacquiao fights, Arnaldo discusses sports fandom as a medium for men of color "marked as dangerous and deviant" to "feel a sense of value and self-worth denied them in their everyday existence" (2020, 660). Arnaldo cautions, however, that this is earned "at the cost of denigrating racial, sexual, and gendered 'Others'" (2020, 661). Arnaldo takes aim at a recuperated hegemonic masculinity that still perpetuates hierarchies against "dysselected folks" on the margins, including the poor, working-class, people of color, women, and queer individuals (2020, 671). Though we may agree with this conclusion, and the urging for a process of "imagining differently" (Arnaldo 2020, 669, it may not go far enough to say we need to imagine a new type of, say masculine, identity. It is our relationship to identity itself that requires re-imagining.

Any reversal, alteration, or movement within the structure of identity maintains participation in the possibilities of dominion. McGowan writes, "When I enjoy the identity that I share with others, my enjoyment is tied to the ostracism of those who don't share this identity" (2020, 155). Forbidden from entering a fantasied paradise, one may think the reward lies within the gates. We must consider that once we are admitted to a place we were previously barred from, the enjoyment may be, as much if not more so, from acquiring the privilege of forbidding others entry. Is this not evident in Pacquiao's vitriolic homophobic beliefs and statements?[8] Following Arnaldo, Pacquiao offers a fantasy of phallic enjoyment in a professional athletic world that side-lines women, trans individuals, the queer community, and so many others. As I have discussed elsewhere, though not isolated to professional athletics, sports fans must reckon with the prospect that this marginalization is the unintended cost, a tax if you will, of an entrance ticket to the main attraction that one unconsciously enjoys through disavowal (Reynoso 2021).

MY MINOR FEELINGS

To know of Manny Pacquiao is to know of bad faith. I am a child of immigrants. As a second generation American of Filipino and Spanish lineage, among other things, I am what a history of multiple colonial occupations yields. The poet and writer Cathy Park Hong addressed Asian identities in her book *Minor Feelings* (2020). Hong describes minor feelings as "the racialized range of emotions that are negative, dysphoric, and therefore untelegenic, built from the sediments of everyday racial experience and the irritant of having one's perception of reality constantly questioned or dismissed" (2020, 55). Pacquiao fights summoned the major feelings that drowned out, even momentarily, the minor ones. My experience of Pinoy pride in my identity through Pacquiao, however, cannot cleanly be disentangled from its imposition, exclusion, and subordination of other groups. As Joyce Carol Oates put it: "Boxing is for men and is about men, and is men" (1987, 72). For some Asian-American men, including myself, perhaps what Pacquiao came to represent was the fantasy of lifting what the writer Wesley Yang described as "the peculiar burden of nonrecognition, of invisibility, that is a condition of being an Asian man in America" (2018, xi). This identification with Pacquiao must be thought of in terms of proximities to empire, whiteness, and masculinity. As Yang further asserts "there is no whiteness independent of domination of nonwhites, and there is no masculinity whose constitutive predicate is not the domination of women" (2018, xiv–xv).

I must consider: how my upsurge in Filipino-ness through the dominance of a Pacquiao fight draws from the imperial power that suppressed this presumed identity to begin with? How is this fantasy of identity attainment predicated on the dispossession of others? What portion of my pleasure in watching Pacquiao perform is from viewing him as a commodified body, especially by the position granted me by my Spanish grandfather and my American birth?[9] What do I make of the fact that the excitement that Pacquiao aroused for the audience, including people of color, like myself, was mostly the thrill of a yellow man beating up or being beaten up by brown or black men to fill the pockets of many white men?

In my identification with a victorious Pacquiao, I must consider who the opponents are and what the goal is. Perhaps to distract from the morass of minor feelings, I, like Pacquiao seek victory over my disenfranchised brethren as Fanon outlined:

> Whereas the colonist or police officer can beat the colonized subject day in and day out, insult him and shove him to his knees, it is not uncommon to see the colonized subject draw his knife at the slightest hostile or aggressive look from another colonized subject. For the colonized subject's last resort is to defend his personality against his fellow countryman. Internecine feuds merely perpetuate age-old grudges entrenched in memory. By throwing himself muscle and soul into his blood feuds, the colonized subject endeavors to convince himself that colonialism has never existed, that everything is as it used to be and history marches on. (2004, 17)

In Pacquiao fandom, we see the colonial dynamics elucidated last century in *Wretched of the Earth* not repudiated, only slightly remodeled and replayed with the enjoyment that accompanies the death drive's self-undermining tendencies.

Recent contributions have tried to delineate the political implications of an Asian-American identity that impossibly seeks wholeness at the cost of others. Jay Caspian Kang probed the detrimental political implications of an identity organized around a grievance that seems to ask "'Why aren't we treated like white people?' instead of 'What can we do to liberate ourselves and all other oppressed people?'" (2021, 165). The political scientist Claire Jean Kim has argued that "Asian Americans show bad faith when they insist on 'minority' equivalencies and disavow their relatively advantaged position within an anti-Black order" (2018, 238). Kim and Kang challenge the failings of an Asian-American identity that aims toward an upwardly economically mobile proximity to whiteness and empire. Though, they differ on what, and in many senses, who, is being moved away from. While Kang emphasizes the willful abandonment of other groups who suffer social and economic vulnerability under capitalism, Kim uses Afro- pessimism to frame the triangular dynamics Asians in America participate in as complicit in anti-black violence.

CONCLUSION

Professional sports in general, and boxing may be the exemplar, can help us interrogate how our libidinal political economies are structured through various identity assertions. My euphoric feelings watching a Pacquiao knock out are enabled by identity's illusory promise of continuity and value. When the history of a person, group, or nation includes a trauma imposed by an other or external force, accompanying the damage is a masking of our constitutive lack by providing it tangible recognizable form. Identity's fantasy construction attempts to conceal the contradiction that subjectivity is riddled with, but not without showing its limitations, costs on others, and impossibility. Though, I have used myself, Manny Pacquiao, and Asian identities to discuss these matters, these are just particular iterations of the problems of an over-investment in any identity. I suggested earlier that not just Filipino, but Asian identities are structured around a negative space, but this is universal to all claims to identity.

Organizing around various identity assertions can disrupt hegemonic social orders. As we know, identity assertions can also lead to empire expansion and the invasion of sovereign countries. As seen in efforts to combat anti-Asian violence during COVID, the fantasy object of race can offer protection for, mobilize, and unify communities that are racialized and attacked. Rather than jettisoning identity, transcending it may mean changing our relationship to it and embracing its contradiction rather than trying to overcome it. This was phrased eloquently by the Pulitzer Prize winning novelist, Viet Thanh Nguyen, when he said, "Our challenge is to be both Asian American and to imagine a world beyond it, one in which being Asian American isn't necessary" (2020). In this, and in other places, Nguyen beautifully describes examples of grounding an identity and a social bond in what we lack, what we don't have (George 2016; McGowan 2013).

Another way to embrace the contradictions of identity and its assumptions, has been articulated by the scholar Neferti Tadiar. In her book *Things Fall Away*, she develops a concept of divine sorrow:

> Although the revolutionary community is supposed to transcend older relations of family and kin to become a site of a greater, fulfilling wholeness and love, paradoxically, it is also the site and source of dispossession and loss . . . and consequently the site and source of an abiding sadness. Intensified by recurring

> losses in struggle, including separation from loved ones and the murders and disappearances of comrades and friends, this sadness, as much as militancy, triumphalism, and the exhilaration of radical transformation, is also the very content of revolutionary life. (Tadiar 2009, 359)

Tadiar's paradox of the coincidence of fulfilment and dispossession in any revolution highlights that our lives will always be characterized by an antagonism that is often projected outside ourselves but is inherent to subjectivity itself, no matter what identity we assume.

Rather than, or at least along with, thinking of a group coalescing around what principles, histories, aims, or characteristics unite them, we might want to consider the even stronger bonding potential of the minor and sometimes major feelings that accompany what has given up, lost, or been denied (Copjec 2002). Unconsciously, the trauma of this loss is often disavowed and displaced onto others, even though it maintains its affective source at the site of our divided subjectivity itself. The impossibility of identity is its traumatic source that we seek circumstantial reasons for (Ruti 2018, 170) or have materially imposed on us. But no amount of Pacquiao victories can reverse a country's collective memory being forced to march the 66-miles from Bagac and Mariveles to Camp O'Donnell.[10] Just as no attempt to assert one's identity at the expense of others will steal back the enjoyment that fuels the fantasies of theft that underpin various forms of racism (Hook 2018; Žižek 1992).

Progress, thought of as a world structured by less brutal forms of domination and oppression (Allen 2016), will not come solely with increased inclusion/representation of Asian identities unless it is reimagined. Perhaps, along the line that Tadiar writes about in her injunction to address the "remaindered forms of life-making" as represented by "the intimate, affective interactions of everyday life and forms of social intelligence and imagination that are excessive to existing modes of theorizing social and geopolitical economic relations" (2015, 155–156), I would add, our unconscious imperialistic investment and enjoyment in these exclusions.

Pacquiao's failure to fulfil an emancipatory role more successfully (at least so far) is due to the position he assumed in the imaginary, especially in the Philippines, for those tarrying with impossible loss of a pre-colonial past that never was, and a future of restoration and riches that will never be. To identify with Pacquiao's success primarily allowed for a fantasied separation between excess and lack fuelled by the seductive enticement of the accumulative logics of capital and empire for peoples suffering at the will of others for so long.

NOTES

1. Pacquiao ranked number eight on *Forbes* highest paid athletes for the 2010–2019 decade, with estimated earnings of $435 million (Badenhausen 2019).

2. The Boxing Writers Association of America named Pacquiao their Fighter of the Year in 2006, 2008, and 2009, and was awarded the Fighter of the Decade (2000s) in 2010. In 2009 and 2011, Pacquiao won the Best Fighter ESPY Award, largely considered a popularity measure as it is voted for by fans.

3. A sportive parallel with different dynamics occurring in a briefer period of time was the seemingly meteoric rise of the Taiwanese-American professional basketball player Jeremy Lin with the New York Knicks in 2011.

4. World football fans may hear a familiar note that gets struck by players and managers before playing or even after winning a particular grueling match (Taylor 2017).

5. In other work, I have argued that we can more broadly extend Bion's ideas about groups and leaders to investigate the fame achieved by certain artistic, entertainment and sport figures (Reynoso 2016). The American public's reaction to Tiger Woods, early in his career, can be understood as a function Bion's basic assumption of pairing. Seen this way, Wood's rise to popularity was a mobilization of wishes by the segments of American people to transcend, if not or erase, the country's history of slavery and deliver the United States into a post-racial era.

6. "Little brown brother" was among the racist paternalistic language used by William Taft, who was the first governor of the Philippines (1901–1904), before becoming the President of the United States in 1909.

7. Jasbir Puar's concept of homonationalism (2007) is an example of work arguing for an analysis of what and whom are sacrificed in recognition and inclusion initiatives.

8. As reported by many media outlets, in a 2016 interview Pacquiao claimed that gay people were "worse than animals." His statements were denounced publicly by many people groups and advertising sponsors (for an example of the media coverage see McPhate 2016).

9. See *Feeling in Counterpoint: Complicit Spectatorship and the Filipino Performing Body* (Chow 2018).

10. The three-month Battle of Bataan in the Philippines during World War II ended with approximately 10,000 American and 65,000 Filipino troops surrendering on April 9, 1942. In what has been called the Bataan Death March, the Japanese made these soldiers march the roughly 66 miles from Mariveles to Capas. Then by train and foot these prisoners were forced into their detention at the captured Camp O'Donnell. It is estimated that only 54,000 of the captured survived the route, which aside from the brutal physical toll entailed was also characterized by arbitrary killings and beatings, with some dying at Camp O'Donnell soon after.

BIBLIOGRAPHY

Allen, Amy. 2016. *The End of Progress: Decolonizing the Normative Foundations of Critical Theory*. Columbia University Press.

Arnaldo Jr., Constancio R. 2020. "'Undisputed' Racialised Masculinities: Boxing Fandom, Identity, and the Cultural Politics of Masculinity." *Identities*, 27, no. 6: 655–674.

Badenhausen, Kurt. 2019. "The Highest-Paid Athletes of the Decade: Mayweather, Ronaldo and LeBron Dominate." *Forbes,* Dec 23, 2019. https://www.forbes.com/sites/kurtbadenhausen/2019/12/23/the-highest-paid-athletes-of-the-decade-mayweatherronaldo-lebron-score/?sh=9d1260172d98

Bion, Wilfred Ruprecht. 1961. *Experiences in Groups, and Other Papers*. London: Karnac.

Black, Jack. 2016. "'As British as fish and chips': British Newspaper Representations of Mo Farah during the 2012 London Olympic Games." *Media, Culture & Society* 38, no. 7: 979–996.

Black, Jack, Thomas Fletcher, and Robert J. Lake. 2020. "'Success in Britain comes with an awful lot of small print': Greg Rusedski and the Precarious Performance of National Identity." *Nations and Nationalism* 26, no. 4: 1104–1123.

Bonhomme, Justin, Michelle Seanor, Robert J. Schinke, and Natalia B. Stambulova. 2018. "The Career Trajectories of Two World Champion Boxers: Interpretive Thematic Analysis of Media Stories." *Sport in Society* 23, no. 4: 560–76.

Campbell, Brian. 2015. "Manny Pacquiao's Five Biggest Wins." *ESPN,* Apr 21, 2015. https://www.espn.com/boxing/story/_/id/12662124/manny-pacquiao-top-fights

Cheng, Anne Anlin. 2001. *The Melancholy of Race: Psychoanalysis, Assimilation, and Hidden Grief.* Oxford: Oxford University Press.

Chow, Broderick. 2018. "Feeling in Counterpoint: Complicit Spectatorship and the Filipino Performing Body." *Theatre Journal* 70, no. 3: 327–47.

Chua-Eoan, Howard. 2009. "People Who Mattered: Manny Pacquiao." *Time*, December 16, 2009. https://content.time.com/time/specials/packages/article/0,28804,1946375_1946333_1946328,00.html

Copjec, Joan. 2002. *Imagine There's No Woman: Ethics and Sublimation*. The MIT Press.

Fanon, Frantz. 2004. *The Wretched of the Earth*. Grove/Atlantic.

Galang, Adrianne John R., Diwa Malaya A. Quiñones, Jeremiah Adriano, Paolo Martin G. Portillo, and Michael Erick D. Carvajal. 2015. "The Rise and Fall of the Pacquiao Effect: Contrastive Priming and National Identification." *Asian Journal of Social Psychology* 18, no. 4: 270–87.

George, Sheldon. 2016. *Trauma and Race: A Lacanian Study of African American Racial Identity*. Baylor University Press.

George, Sheldon. 2019. "Jouissance and Discontent: A Meeting of Psychoanalysis, Race, and American Slavery." In *Race, Rage, and Resistance*, edited by David Goodman, Eric R. Severson, and Heather Macdonald, 108–131. Abingdon: Routledge.

Gonzalez III, Joaquin Jay, and Angelo Michael F. Merino. 2012. *From Pancho to Pacquiao: Philippine Boxing in and out of the Ring*. Mill City Press.

Hobsbawm, Eric John. 1992. *Nations and Nationalism since 1780: Programme, Myth, Reality*. Cambridge University Press.

Hong, Cathy Park. 2020. *Minor Feelings: A Reckoning on Race and the Asian Condition*. Profile Books.

Hook, Derek. 2018. "Racism and Jouissance: Evaluating the 'Racism as (the Theft of) Enjoyment' Hypothesis." *Psychoanalysis, Culture and Society* 23, no. 3: 244–66.

Horton, Peter. 2012. "The Asian Impact on the Sportisation Process." *International Journal of the History of Sport* 29, no. 4: 511–34.

James, Cyril Lionel Robert. 2013. *Beyond a Boundary*. Duke University Press.

Jimenez-David, Rina. 2018. "History and Heritage in Her Bones." *Philippine Daily Inquirer*, July 31, 2018. https://opinion.inquirer.net/115006/history-heritage-bones

Kang, Jay Caspian. 2021. *The Loneliest Americans*. Crown.

Kim, Claire Jean. 2018. "Are Asians the New Blacks?" *Du Bois Review* 15, no. 2: 217–44.

Kobayashi, Koji, and Younghan Cho. 2019. "Asian Sport Celebrity: The Nexus of Race, Ethnicity, and Regionality." *International Journal of the History of Sport* 36, no. 7–8: 611–25.

Lim, Thea. 2011. "Finally, an Asian Who Packs a Punch." *Salon*, November 12, 2011. https://www.salon.com/2011/11/12/finally_an_asian_who_packs_a_punch/

Mackay, Hamish. 2015. "Who is Manny Pacquiao? 5 Things You Didn't Know About Floyd Mayweather's Opponent." *The Mirror*, May 2, 2015. https://www.mirror.co.uk/sport/boxing/who-manny-pacquiao-5-things-5607252

McGowan, Todd. 2013. *Enjoying What We Don't Have: The Political Project of Psychoanalysis*. U of Nebraska Press.

McGowan, Todd. 2020. *Universality and Identity Politics*. Columbia University Press.

McGowan, Todd. 2022. "Mainstreaming Fantasy: Politics without Reserve." *Differences* 33, no. 2–3: 177–97.

McPhate, Mike. "Manny Pacquiao Apologizes for Calling Gays 'Worse Than Animals.'" *The New York Times*, February 16, 2016. https://www.nytimes.com/2016/02/17/sports/manny-pacquiao-apologizes-for-calling-gays-worse-than-animals.html

Nguyen, Viet Thanh. 2020. "Asian Americans Are Still Caught in the Trap of the 'Model Minority' Stereotype. And It Creates Inequality for All." *Time*, June 26, 2020. https://time.com/5859206/anti-asian-racism-america/

Oates, Joyce Carol. 1987. *On Boxing*. Doubleday.

Pacquiao, Manny, and Timothy James. 2010. *Pacman: My Story of Hope, Resilience, and Never-Say-Never Determination*. Dunham books.

Poole, Gary. 2010. *PacMan: Behind the Scenes with Manny Pacquiao—the Greatest Pound-for-Pound Fighter in the World*. Da Capo Press.

Puar, Jasbir K. 2007. *Terrorist Assemblages: Homonationalism in Queer Times*. Duke University Press.

Reynoso, Joseph. 2013. "The Professional Athlete: A Conflict in Development." Paper presented at the annual meeting of the Association for the Psychoanalysis of Culture and Society Annual Conference, New Brunswick, NJ, November 1, 2013.

Reynoso, Joseph. 2016. "Dreams of the Father: The Con/destruction of Tiger Woods." Paper presented at the annual meeting of the Association for the Psychoanalysis of Culture and Society Annual Conference, New Brunswick, NJ, October 14, 2016.

Reynoso, Joseph S. 2021. "Boston Sucks! A Psychoanalysis of Sports." *Psychoanalysis, Culture and Society* 26, no. 4: 591–607.

Rimonte, Nilda. 1997. "Colonialism's Legacy: The Inferiorizing of the Filipino." In *Filipino Americans: Transformation and identity,* edited by Maria P. P. Root, 39–61. Thousand Oaks, CA: Sage.

Rizal, Jose. 2015. *The Philippines a Century Hence*. Forgotten Books.

Ruti, Mari. 2018. *Penis Envy and Other Bad Feelings: The Emotional Costs of Everyday Life*. Columbia University Press.

Samaha, Albert. 2022. *Concepcion: Conquest, Colonialism, and an Immigrant Family's Fate*. Penguin.

Scalice, Joseph. 2018. "Pamitinan and Tapusi: Using the Carpio Legend to Reconstruct Lower-Class Consciousness in the Late Spanish Philippines." *Journal of Southeast Asian Studies* 49, no. 2: 250–76.

Tadiar, Neferti X. M. 2009. *Things Fall Away: Philippine Historical Experience and the Makings of Globalization*. Duke University Press.

Tadiar, Neferti X. M. 2015. "Decolonization, 'Race,' And Remaindered Life Under Empire." *Qui Parle: Critical Humanities and Social Sciences* 23, no. 2: 135–60.

Taylor, Daniel. 2017. "Pep Guardiola Says It's Important for Manchester City to Suffer and Still Win." *The Guardian*, November 26, 2017. https://www.theguardian.com/football/2017/nov/26/manchester-city-need-win-games-that-way-pep-guardiola

Wapeemukwa, Wayne. 2021. "Oedipal Empire: Psychoanalysis, Indigenous Peoples, and The Oedipus Complex in Colonial Context." In *Lacan and Race: Racism, Identity and Psychoanalytic Theory*, edited by Sheldon George and Derek Hook, 83–102. Routledge.

Žižek, Slavoj. 1992. *Looking Awry: An Introduction to Jacques Lacan through Popular Culture*. MIT Press.

Chapter 9

Homosexual Football

Perspectives from Lou Andreas-Salomé

Rayyan Dabbous

Any contemporary attempt to understand football and homosexuality through psychoanalysis cannot disregard the striking easiness with which Freudian theories have been abused against the LGBTQ+ community. Is the history of psychoanalysis partially to blame for the lack of openly-gay and -bisexual footballers? Do closeted footballers still live in Sigmund Freud's shadow?

The misunderstanding may have started in 1910, when Freud added a footnote to his *Three Essays on Sexuality* associating homosexuality with narcissism (1986a, 145). He had thus pitted homosexuality against any form of collective development: oedipal family relations, the progressive path of civilization, a team sport, like football. Any growth beyond the individual had become liable to be stunted as a result of homosexuality.

Russian psychoanalyst Lou Andreas-Salomé may have been the first to notice the potential to abuse Freud's thinking on homosexuality. Salomé met Freud in 1911 and worked with him in Vienna during the 1912–1913 winter. At the time, Freud believed repression of homosexuality led to "camaraderie, to *esprit de corps* and to the love of mankind in general" (1986b, 61). Homophobic discourse in sport may take advantage of Freud's remark: if footballers do not repress their homosexual desires, collective spirit would vanish on the pitch. An entry in Salomé's journal in 1912 demonstrated her awareness of potentially abusing Freud's thinking:

> It is Freud's great discovery to have found a link between the seemingly asexual bond among men and homosexuality. Yet I always have the feeling that he grants an unnecessarily large role to "repression" . . . It is going too far to understand kindness as merely a reaction and hence a manifestation of repression and

> to base civilized man on the homosexually repressed savage. The savage, within the smaller circle of his environment, probably shows far more sociability than we do—and animals like bees and ants really do put us to shame in this respect. (Andreas-Salomé 1987, 103)

Salomé did not believe we obtained a higher collective spirit the more we repressed homosexuality. Savages and animals, in whom homosexuality is not repressed, are more cooperative than humans. She also redefined Freud's notion of camaraderie: "in animals and primitives this corresponds to the persistent 'narcissistic identity,' in us it is the ground of our 'sublimation'" (Andreas-Salomé 1987, 103).

Narcissism, according to Salomé, is persistently found in the animal world, not in mankind. Her counter-intuitive remark—isn't narcissism a problem to mankind?—tamed the controversy around Freud's 1910 move of associating homosexuality with narcissism. There was neither selfishness nor a threat to collective identity in Salomé's understanding of narcissism, and by extension, homosexuality.

Moreover, Salomé savvily pairing up narcissism and sublimation in 1912 showed her predating influence on Freud. He had only seriously started working on sublimation in 1910 when he analyzed the artistic and scientific work of Leonardo da Vinci and he was in course to publish *On Narcissism* in 1914. In that transitory period, Salomé may have advised him to more carefully distinguish repression from sublimation. Having had a long and successful career as a creative novelist prior to joining Freud's circle, she was the right brain to pick.

What is sublimation? It is a kind of repression but not every repression leads to sublimation. Sublimation of homosexuality contributes a positive value to the individual and to the collective according to the 1910 Vinci study (1986c, 80). Repression of homosexuality taken to its extreme leads to indifference, antipathy toward others, according to Freud's 1911 Schreber study (1986b, 65). Salomé's 1912 arrival in Vienna was well-timed . . . pointing Freud to the right question implicit in his two case studies: not *why* repress homosexuality, but *how*? To understand the role of homosexuality on a football pitch and assess whether footballers should or shouldn't own up to it, we need to look at how Lou Andreas-Salomé nuanced repression *tout court* from sublimation and better understand her peculiar conception of homosexuality and narcissism.

PRIMARY HOMOSEXUALITY AND PRIMARY NARCISSISM

Lou Andreas-Salomé accepted Freud's association between narcissism and homosexuality. "It struck me further to what an extent the homosexual disposition is in fact equivalent to a purely narcissistic one," she wrote to him (Pfeiffer 1995, 94). Salomé's expansive notion of narcissism—as facilitating collective spirit, rather than inhibiting it—drew from Freud's 1905 claim that children's first love-object is a narcissistic one: themselves (Andreas-Salomé 1986a, 197). Nowadays we tend to think of narcissism as negative and self-love as positive, but Salomé thought it was the other way round. In a 1916 footnote, she wrote:

> We should not forget, however, that all we later understand to be self-love, including a conscious sense of self-contentment or vanity, must be distinguished from a primal form of narcissism that cannot yet distinguish between subject and object, which it perceives as one. (Andreas-Salomé 2022, 23)

In 1914, Freud distinguished narcissism between primary and secondary, likely after Salomé's advocacy in 1912–1913. Primary narcissism is connected to a self-world union, where love of self and love of world coincide together. Secondary narcissism, a later development, is related to a calculating ego mediating between self and world. Freud's and Salomé's diligence shall not pay off: narcissism *tout court* would survive them, denoting the secondary type Freud outlined and which Salomé warned as connected to conscious experience rather than the unconscious.

Our dismissal of primary narcissism shaped much scholarly research about sport including football which exclusively interrogated secondary narcissism (Cin & Yasar 2022; Elman & McKelvie 2003; Welch 1997). Researchers employing self-report narcissism inventories would be collecting data on what Salomé regarded as self-contentment or vanity. Salomé would agree with the conclusion of such studies—a high level of narcissism is present among athletes—but she would classify these attempts as social rather than psychological analyses.

What about homosexuality? Do we also deal with primary and secondary homosexualities, unconscious, and conscious? Salomé thought we did:

> I felt strengthened in my opinion by the lecture on homosexuality that followed, by Adler himself (primarily a case history). The homosexual whom he portrayed is basically not that at all; he does not construct his homosexual fiction out of the real facts of life, but on the contrary he is alienated from reality and shuns the facts exactly as a neurotic likes to do. He is not neurotic in that he is

> homosexual, but he is homosexual in that he is neurotic and needs precisely this fiction. An instinctually organized homosexual will perhaps even construct a quite different, contrary fiction in opposition to his real desire in order to protect himself against it (Andreas-Salomé 1987, 53).

Salomé's view of a neurotic homosexual desire may ring as problematic nowadays, but her reasoning is sound. Like narcissism, she was postulating a primary homosexuality involving an unconscious choice, removed from social context, and a secondary homosexuality involving a conscious choice and mediated by society and language.

What Salomé regarded as "true homosexuality"—primary homosexuality—is "not so much a disinclination toward woman as a search for pleasure in oneself and a consequent self-affirmation through the person of the same sex" (Andreas-Salomé 1987, 77). This *instinctually organized homosexual* can develop neurosis if his unconscious choice for himself is spurned once entering a social context. Because primary homosexuality is a cause bearing an effect, a primary homosexual can still form a visible heterosexual attachment because "a search for pleasure in oneself" can have heterosexuality as its consequence.

Secondary homosexuality, the one Alfred Adler, the psychoanalyst of the ~~unconscious~~, highlighted in his lecture, is a socially-and language-mediated effect rather than a cause. It cannot lead to a visible heterosexual pairing since it is itself the desired effect. It is a conscious choice: one is drawn to the same-sex as a direct and tangible sexual object rather than a symbolic representative of oneself or of sameness.

It is important to note that Salomé is not describing two rigid types of homosexuals, but homosexual attitudes. Thus, in the same person one can detect a homosexual love-object due to neurosis (a neurotically–motivated insecurity that makes one desire *this specific* person of the same-sex) and a homosexual love-object that may produce neurosis (a longing for oneself that makes one desire *this specific* person of the same-sex whose eventual markers of distinctions cause neurosis).

Since we have now distinguished primary narcissism and primary homosexuality from their opposites and more commonly understood conscious namesakes, we can begin to analyze how footballers, by sublimating, preserve these unconscious forces.

FOOTBALLERS SUBLIMATE

An analysis of sublimation in sport cannot omit the concepts of homosexuality and narcissism. Salomé believed an inherent bisexuality and an elimination of the self-world divide are the motor of any properly sublimated activity. One cannot *consciously sublimate*. Freud's notorious comments to Salvador Dalí said as much: classical art devoid of wild motifs—rather than wild surrealism—is the mirror to the wild unconscious (Dalí 1961, 397).

Thus, sport, especially football, is an ideal candidate for evaluating the sublimation of homosexuality precisely because we regard it as devoid of homosexuals. I insist on football's privileged position because a sport with substantial same-sex contact, like boxing, rugby, or American football, defeat the purpose of sublimation. A sport like football, and, to a lesser extent baseball, where close contact is dangerous to its enterprise and long-balls welcome, is a perfect environment for a sublimation which requires a carefully followed prohibition against conscious expressions of homosexuality.

Contact in hockey and basketball is also mediated by the ball and yet their area of play is significantly smaller than a football pitch. Therefore, among the most known contact sport, football, *in involving the least body contact*, is the most fertile ground for primary homosexuality and primary narcissism to be *properly* sublimated. Here, Salomé did see a relationship between narcissism and *diminished contact*: "The erotic defect of the narcissistic person lies precisely in that his own love's outburst nearly suffices for him. It is contact enough for him with the world that he expresses his love" (Andreas-Salomé 1987, 109). Passing the ball is an "outburst" that "nearly suffices" to the passer. Even a long ball is "contact enough" for a footballer whose primal narcissism is momentarily satisfied. Salomé understood narcissism as operating on a short-period: not 90 minutes, but precisely the time it takes to pass or shoot a ball.

Football's fans can recall the frustrating effect of Tiki-Taka, the style of play popularized by the Spanish national team in and around 2010, which emphasized possession of the ball and endless slow passing over dangerous and quicker movement toward the opposite box. What is really frustrated about that style of play is our narcissism—both as players and, to a lesser extent, as spectators—because the opponent no longer gets to suffice with the outburst or diminished contact.

Narcissism in Salomé's understanding is not the opposite of selfless devotion: the footballer seeks to be self-serving, but only in small doses, in outbursts. Leave the ball entirely under his control and he will be as unsatisfied as he had been without it. This narcissistically inflexible desire for just enough contact must therefore be sublimated: rather than restrict his vision to his own need for contact, the footballer becomes satisfied with its collective transformation. Since narcissism is expansive and relies on the fluidity between self and world, one is content not getting the ball so long as his teammate—and thus himself—gets it. Narcissism paradoxically calms the egoism of footballers, their personal need for the ball.

Homosexuality must also be sublimated but for a more critical reason. Salomé depicted in her journal the problem of the instinctually organized homosexual:

> If on the other hand the invert [i.e. the homosexual] should be afraid of his instinctual drive it might be not only on account of its prohibited nature but also because in his case sexuality might exercise a destructive influence on the ego instinct . . . Sexuality thrusts on him a form of sexual life which is unadapted to his primitive ego since it is derived from a later developmental period, fully directed toward objects. (Andreas-Salomé 1987, 102)

There is a disconnect between primary homosexuality and reality. We have said it is unfazed by social relations and language and cannot distinguish between self and world. It is precisely that childlike naivety which clashes with a world full of clearly-defined objects. Salomé interpreted Narcissus in Ovid as worshipping the world, not himself, through the river: his self-destruction began only when he realized he had been contemplating an object, i.e., him/self (Andreas-Salomé 1962, 9). Homosexuality proceeds like narcissism: it must be sublimated, otherwise the weight of reality and rationality would remind it of its incompatibility with a world of objects, of others.

To better understand primary homosexuality on the pitch, one need only compare Cristiano Ronaldo and Lionel Messi. Every other year gay rumors are sparked about the Portuguese footballer, not the Argentine. Yet if we follow Salomé carefully, the true homosexual would be precisely the seemingly asexualized Messi, not Ronaldo and his (homo)sexual appeal. Ronaldo is to Messi what American football is to football or surrealism to classical art: homosexual or wilder *only superficially* or *consciously*.

Thus, Messi clothed in a traditional black robe and lifting the World Cup trophy in Qatar was thus the greatest geopolitical irony: what triumphed with him was true homosexuality. For Messi's victory, more so than could have Ronaldo's, represented the victory of childhood. "She specifically needed the child-attitude," Salomé wrote to Freud about her analysand, "because that is the one where one feels in both a homosexual and a heterosexual way, and is able to love both father and mother without distinction" (Pfeiffer 1995, 37). Footballers are allowed to *play* as children do. Ronaldo, however, is adult-like because his strong physical attributes and robust runs break apart the Other, mark a schism in the self-world unity.

Messi, on the other hand, is precisely immune to that adult "disappointment which sometimes comes from no longer having enough space to maintain a creative, poetic, 'playful' relation" with others (Andreas-Salomé 2012, 67). Ronaldo has hardly ever been the embodiment of a team player: his own boundaries are too sharp, and he is dangerous precisely on that account.

Yet Messi, historically in partnership with Xavi and Iniesta but especially in Qatar, as veteran captain, has blended so well with the whole team that he truly has embodied athletically Salomé's conception of the "persistent feeling of identification with the totality" manifest in narcissism (Andreas-Salomé 1962, 5). Creative, poetic, playful . . . how can we further lend footballers qualities usually ascribed to artists? Now that we have established the role of sublimation in football, let us move onto reckoning with footballers as *creators*.

FOOTBALLERS AS CREATORS

We have said footballers are carrying with them two unconscious forces—primary homosexuality and primary narcissism—which must imperatively be sublimated. In 1910, a year before her formal initiation to psychoanalysis, Salomé was already wondering how that inner conflict is resolved:

> It is only because this interior urgency that forces us to raise all things to a higher power, to idealize them, means, in the most primitive sense of the term, "to behave as a creator," that we find this same urgency at all the high points of human activity, and everywhere, finally encountering death at the pinnacles of lived experience. (Andreas-Salomé 2012, 72–73)

Footballers must *behave as creators*: they oscillate between creating opportunities and seeing opportunities die. "For this same reason, our highest creativity shows the strange characteristic of being experienced almost as a conception, the subtlest peak of our activity as autonomous beings," Salomé continued, "so that our extreme achievements involve a giving of ourselves at levels that lie beyond us" (Andreas-Salomé 2012, 73). This oscillation between autonomy and mechanical reproduction is present in football and it is "when we are masters of life, as at no other time, do we feel ourselves nearest to an atmosphere of initiatory fervor" (Andreas-Salomé 2012, 73). Each footballer is an initiator of a new process whenever he passes and moves around the pitch, "as if, in the quest for evermore fertile freedoms, for evermore creative being, our Self would remain sterile if it did not feel, at the heights of its being, once again mysteriously split, rediscovering the original duality of its beginnings, the sole guarantee of its unity" (Andreas-Salomé 2012, 73).

What is that original duality which sends off footballers on a chase for evermore freedom and creative opportunity? Salomé's thinking on duality became clearer around fifteen years later: "surely all creativity is only another name for the clash of a dual sexuality within us" (Andreas-Salomé 2003,

55). We have said an inherent bisexuality is constitutive of sublimation: this bisexuality involves not gender but a dual split between sameness/difference, unity/schism. For, according to Salomé, it is precisely "the property of sexuality to dissolve boundaries": each sexual striving aims to patch divided parts into form, into a larger whole (Andreas-Salomé 1987, 102). "The productive force, the will to form," she thought, "arises in its might out of the undifferentiated unity of passive and active" (Andreas-Salomé 1962, 28–29). Notice how footballers are ideal candidates in Salomé's dynamic process of sexuality: neither purely active nor passive, neither purely whole team nor purely part player, footballers thrive precisely on that clash of a dual orientation within them.

I may have unfairly cast-off Messi and Ronaldo as mutually-exclusive: it may be truer to contend that a Messi and a Ronaldo exists in each player. It may be less the product of chance than the powerful rules of probability that we were left battling about these two superstars: our dual sexuality demands that the best of the best would produce two opposite models, one repatching unity, the other breaking it. The same goes with football's oscillation between favoring strength or sleekness: that Luka Modriç and his smaller frame represents the ideal midfielder where more robust players like Michael Ballack once found similar praise in the same position only confirms the bisexuality at play everywhere in football.

Is this dynamic oscillation not exhausting to footballers? "To become form means to endure to the end structurally unalterable in being and presence," Salomé thought (Andreas-Salomé 1962, 28–29). Not only do footballers create form and opportunities—they become form and the opportunity. They create themselves. "We frequently find in men the wish to give birth to themselves," Salomé wrote (Andreas-Salomé 1962, 12), arguing that sublimated narcissism makes its appearance precisely "as a double, with a fate supplementary" to our own (Andreas-Salomé 1962, 6). A footballer has ten other doubles with him on the pitch.

It is worth mentioning that against conventional wisdom, the sublimation of homosexuality is more critical in a sport like football than art. Salomé hinted at the difference in a marginal note in her Vienna journal:

> It is only those slightly homosexual men who see the universally human qualities in woman and are erotically disposed toward them. (MARGINAL note: Except for artists, who need their bisexuality all for themselves.) Men with no homosexual tendency whatever remain even in their most powerful and most genuine passion inclined toward the purely female—plus friendship and the like, excluding erotic rapture. (Andreas-Salomé 1987, 188–189)

Artists, free to be more isolated, and, thus, more egoistic than athletes, need their bisexuality all for themselves. It is not a stretch to align those *slightly homosexual men* with footballers. Their slight homosexuality would bring them an athletic advantage absent among men with *no homosexual tendency whatever*. The capacity to see universally human qualities, not only in women but in our racially-mixed teammates, is crucial to a collective sport like football. An English footballer cannot regard his Senegalese or Korean teammate as fundamentally other: primary homosexuality here does its magic. Is it the dazzling bow of Cupid? Now that we have established footballers as creators of a united front, it is time to assess whether they are lovers.

FOOTBALLERS AS PLATONIC LOVERS

Salomé thought "homosexuals show a much greater inclination toward 'platonic' love, and all varieties of romantic enthusiasm" (Andreas-Salomé 1987, 102–103). The meaning of platonic love has historically wavered between designating homosexual love and asexualized love; the latter meaning triumphing nowadays. In either case, Plato survives, especially his metaphysics, wherein the magnificence of an object lies in the idea behind it. Thus, platonic love, properly speaking, is a metaphysical love . . . whether it is sexualized or asexualized, homosexual or heterosexual, is secondary. We have said distance is an essential quality in football particularly: footballers can only love each other metaphysically for their respective positions effectively places them in long-distance relationships.

The intimacy we see footballers engaged in during goal celebrations is intense all the more because it marks the rupture of that long-distance, a goal line threshold finally crossed, metaphysical lovers who may have been mere chimeras all of a sudden parachuted from the skies onto the earth. These moments in themselves are not particularly moving—no one ever shed a tear watching footballers huddle together except in trophy-winning cases—for they draw their intensities precisely on account of what came before them. What is being celebrated is never the actual moment, nor the reunion at last of bodies, but the fact that these bodies had been deprived of each other for too long. Goal celebrations are testaments to the hardness of platonic love, its deprivation not of sexual intimacy but of a material existence, a physical basis to relationships.

For this deprivation according to Salomé "is the psychological price one has to pay for the arrogant ambition to be all mind and almost no body" (Andreas-Salomé 2022, 32). Football is mind exercised everywhere . . . not through the disregard of bodies but in their metaphysical existence. "These are the true cases of 'sublimation'," Salomé continued, "men and women who direct the entire fecundity of their warmth toward asexual aims (including a conceptual rather than personal love of their fellows)" (Andreas-Salomé 2022, 32). This platonic love binds footballers who see each other as concepts and who therefore "leave the root of their sexuality behind in the sunless depths of the unconscious from which it can never blossom into a joyous affirmation of the ego and where it can never unite the forces of earth and light within itself" (Andreas-Salomé 2022, 32). We regard athletes as capable of great physical sacrifice and yet accepting to lead a metaphysical existence is the ultimate sacrifice. No joyous affirmation of the ego until a goal is scored.

It is important to recall that primary narcissism does not distinguish between objects: it is thus incapable of thinking, whose chief function is to discriminate. Surely a great level of thinking is required of footballers yet our tendency attributes their clever feats to the dim concept of instinct. Instinct may, however, only be another name for narcissism and acts of narcissism could be nothing else but acts of love. What makes a winger so sure the striker would be in the right place? He takes a leap of faith . . . and Salomé (Andreas-Salomé 1885, 55–117), in her first novel, explored how being full of faith and full of love was the same thing.

Freud discovered the relationship between love and thinking, defining repression—the fruit of calculated thinking—as "an incapacity for loving" (1986a, 267). Yet, he rightly posited that sublimation unlike extreme forms of repression has as one of its main tasks to preserve love—certainly a love too intense to bear consciously—but a love which man rightly senses to be worth preserving. If we return to the Schreber case, hate is the most premature stage of repression (Freud 1986d, 63). It is therefore a matter of course that football has its homophobes as much as its silent bystanders: the homophobic footballer and his queer-friendly teammate, who only sublimates, both fight off the tomorrow of repression, its development into mere indifference. What enables that delay is a continued relationship with homosexual love—a distorted relationship in either cases—and yet a relationship nonetheless.

Platonic love is a love of ideas and it may be only incidental that the metaphysical rapture in question involves a genuinely concrete same-sex attachment. Fears that gay desire would ruin a collective sport would be unfounded due to a lack of direct path from metaphysical to physical love in the course of sublimation. "There is no direct path from 'sublimation' to 'sublimation' or from peak to peak; we must pass through the valleys between" Salomé thought (Andreas-Salomé 2022, 32). What homosexual desire necessarily meets in the rapture of creative practice is its death. The valley returns us to point zero: restart, repeat. This set of repetition, and whether the outcome will always mimic what preceded it, make our investigation turn to seeing footballers as free agents in a game of probability.

PROBABILITY OF THE GAME

Desire is a matter of probability: either it arises, or it doesn't, and whether it would or wouldn't one may well bet on it. Betting found an almost unassailable role in the world of sport. The way the English Football Association recently reduced Ivan Toney's suspension after correlating his betting breaches to a formal gambling addiction diagnosis is indicative of its unquestioned faith in the general fair nature of betting and the incorruptibility of footballers (Olley 2023, 1).

The well-chronicled history of betting in sport (Huggins 2017), accompanied by the rise and use of statistics in and outside training and pundit studios, show our steadfast reliance on numbers. James Clerk Maxwell in the nineteenth century spoke of "*statistical* certainty": there was a firm wall between statistics and the real world (Knott 1911, 215). We nowadays speak of statistical *certainty*: hundreds of millions of dollars are forked out on account of a player's stats alone.

Primary homosexuality and primary narcissism are responsible for that sliding from statistics to reality. We have said neither of them are concerned with social relations and language. They are thus immune to *confounding variables*: arbitrary social codes and linguistic categories are to be barred from influencing predictions. A footballer is meant to be a dice sharpened to perfect balance: neither side ought to be heavier than (or influenced by) the rest, otherwise foul play and failed statistics. Perhaps we are increasingly weary of homosexuality in sport for betting reasons, as though an unpredictable desire or a new identity with its own emerging set of inputs would shift the odds which we treasure and find difficult to maintain even in ideal—that is, asexualized—conditions.

But that prohibition actually owes its success to the statistics-proof nature of platonic love. "Detached from the goal of sexual possession," Salomé thought, "everything imaginable seems attainable to the libido thus elaborated" (Andreas-Salomé 1962, 13). Everything imaginable now attainable is a statistically-relevant neutral zone with data that may now be processed and organized without conditionals or strenuous clauses. Thus, because footballers seek to possess the ball, not each other, the ball may well be that "tertium quid," Salomé continued, "this 'third,' which is able to forge bonds stronger than those of personal erotism" (Andreas-Salomé 1962, 13). Salomé's concern was the freedom one found in platonic or non-possessive love and this freedom is no doubt necessary, not only for footballers alone, but for the very scientific apparatus evaluating their choices and fitting them into a numerical shape.

"In exchange for the narrow scope imposed by the genital love of a particular person," Salomé continued, "the broadest compass is permitted to narcissism that has successfully developed outside the range of genitality" (Andreas-Salomé 1962, 13–14). The broadest compass is not only the wide range of possibilities which footballers must recognize on the pitch, but also the probabilities attributed to their successes or failures. Footballers and fans alike "strive relentlessly toward conviction through faith, that faith for which 'nothing is impossible'" (Andreas-Salomé 1962, 14–15). The unpredictability inherent to football is not only necessary for our faith in the *anything goes* motto of the game, but it is primarily the symptom of a narcissism and a homosexuality truly at home, which have successfully developed outside the constricted range of social contexts normally assigned to them.

Of course, neither the sanctity of statistics nor the moods of footballers are infallible. One need not accept a bribe to tilt the odds: footballers naturally feel a range of emotions on the pitch, and anger, as much as vanity, may still conspire to meddle with expectations. There was, however, one emotion which Salomé thought did not stunt the probabilistic engine of narcissism: hope. "The optimist will always be right in his intoxication with life," she wrote, "an intoxication fostered at the source by narcissism" (Andreas-Salomé 1962, 15).

Footballers can only be optimists, seeking to defy the odds weighing against them. Optimism is also the key to the broadest sexual compass: all sorts of sexual objects—heterosexual and homosexual—may arise as desirable with an excessively hopeful attitude in life and in people. Only "the pessimist, presumably judging without benefit of this inner 'unrealistic' attitude, judging without libido and without love," would not entertain the possibility of scoring in improbable places (Andreas-Salomé 1962, 15). An athletic attitude, he who "is pushed by his all too confident assurance, his abundant vitality into painful collisions with reality" is indispensable in sex and sport (Andreas-Salomé 1962, 16). One must be agile enough to follow the whims of narcissism and homosexuality and their unpredictable secondary manifestations.

It is precisely this volatility among objects and opportunities which makes sublimation necessary, and with it comes the greater-than-life narratives we attribute to athletes. "It is of extraordinary interest with respect to narcissism that not only the object but also the subject may ascend to a 'higher' position in the scale of values," Salomé continued (Andreas- Salomé 1962, 16). Football becomes more than a game and the footballer more than man. Values—the neutrality of which the statisticians of football begin with—are elevated to the point of the extraordinary, that which cannot be predicted in advance.

But the fact that we will always look at football statistically has to do with the terminus of narcissism: "If at the start it expresses its fervent conviction, 'Life is itself value!'—ultimately its mature judgment rings out: 'The only true life is value!'" (Andreas- Salomé 1962, 17). The alliance between capitalism and sport—in its ever-growing channels of monetization in the entertainment sector—can be thus explained by this inversion, signaled by Salomé. If the footballer makes the growth of his own venture, of his own success, the ultimate value, its realization brings about an overestimation of value itself. The plethora of valuation in football—transfer market worth and salaries, goal and assist tallies, strength markers in card and video games—corroborate the motto "the only true life is value!"

Primary *hetero*sexuality, if we may call it that, makes it first appearance here . . . upon the deathbed of primary homosexuality. Homosexuality had shouted "life is the only value!" in its quest for freedom: within the first hour of liberation, heterosexuality took over and made valuation, the ability to distinguish, its new mantra. But the birth of heterosexuality from homosexuality's self-immolation must be regularly repeated from scratch. It becomes a matter of probability whether the phoenix would rise from the ashes, whether a heterosexual love-object can arise from a homosexuality that primarily dealt with no objects. A miracle, as it were, is needed here: creation, declaring *let there be another!* not once but each and every time a heterosexual attraction *may be* formed. Since we have vested homosexuality, narcissism, and footballers with divine qualities, it is worth mentioning the connection between sport/sexuality and religion.

RELIGIOUSLY COMMITTED

In a statement that would embarrass a few homophobic priests and sheikhs, Salomé thought gay men specifically have a "proclivity to religious faith" (Andreas-Salomé 1987, 221). What matters in such cases is "a substitute for male superiority, whose role is to punish or reward," which "represents an idea congenial to all homosexuals" (Andreas-Salomé 1987, 221). A connection among homosexuality, football, and religion, cannot only be on account of being rewarded with 3-points or punished with none. Let us follow more closely Salomé's theory of narcissism: "In the religious experience of the man disposed to piety, object libido originally directed to the parents flows into the narcissistic stream, so producing narcissism's most brilliant performance: the two energies unite to the glory of God, ruler of all, and at the same time nearest and dearest of all" (Andreas-Salomé 1962, 18–19). We earlier saw Salomé qualifying the playtime of childhood as the only arena where homosexuality and heterosexuality, father and mother, were still accessible. She now went farther and claimed it was precisely this dual orientation of narcissism which created a God encompassing both "respect [of] the father" and the "promise of the mother's warm embrace" (Andreas-Salomé 1962, 18). Footballers and religious people are not alone in needing to maintain their own bisexuality: their God, too, must be dual. If heterosexuality—or even secondary homosexuality—completely took over the reins of a primary homosexuality that had built God in its reflection, both homosexuality and God must collapse. Once again, we meet a geopolitical irony: religiously motivated homophobia persecutes its own saviour.

It is important to recall we are not dealing with rigid types of people, straight or gay, but attitudes. It is not a heterosexual man who cannot be devout but a heterosexual attitude: what strives to distinguish a fundamental difference precisely to reap pleasure from such schism can no longer worship "the ruler of all," whose totality only primary homosexuality in its naivety can apprehend. It may be that Christianity's formula of a personal God sought to remedy precisely that problem: God became a product of difference, an Other. Yet, however inherently homophobic we may make of the Christian God—and ironically however homophile Islam's Allah, who sought to retake over the seas and the skies—there remains his omnipresence in either case, which restores the self-world unity inherent to both primary homosexuality and primary narcissism.

Since only a platonic love reigns on the pitch, the only heresy emerges when a footballer becomes God himself. We have said football must remain statistically neutral, with the broadest compass. The sudden appearance of God on the pitch, in the form of a player who evokes his own might to influence the outcome of the game, is bound to tilt the needle of that compass. We see this phenomenon most sharply in Major League Soccer, where clubs fork out on Designated Players from Europe, whose superstar status, when left untamed, brings a damaging effect on the pitch. In the sublimation of homosexuality on the pitch, and its starving off of heterosexuality, there can be no designation for footballers who obey Salomé's ideal of love: worshipping not one another but becoming fellow worshippers (1969, 25–39).

Do footballers become crusaders, fighting for faith and love? "Our narcissism in its struggle to sublimate and idealize turns us into those legendary Toggenburgers,"[1] Salomé thought, "who are supposed to adore their beloved the more as the possibility of actual union with them recedes" (Andreas-Salomé 1962, 18). Narcissism dies fighting for a lost cause precisely to furnish whatever comfort the ego—not itself—will later enjoy. The faith to which footballers so dearly clung during playing time, by the final whistle, will have receded into the mists of what seemed like nothing but a beautiful dream.

NIETZSCHE, RILKE, FREUD: BAD FOOTBALLERS?

Early researchers working on Salomé, too obsessed with her muse-like relationship to Nietzsche, Rilke, and Freud, would have attributed our application of her clever observations upon sport to such male influences. Yet, a closer analysis would bring about the opposite view: it is due to her compatibility with sport, not Nietzsche's, Rilke's, or even Freud's.

We have said footballers cannot be heretical. To start with Nietzsche, readers only familiar with his claim that God is dead could guess his unsuitability for the game. Nevertheless, according to Salomé it was precisely his over-religiosity that constituted a problem:

> His various philosophies are for him just so many surrogates for God . . . time and again, we come upon his impassioned battle against religion, belief in God, and the need for salvation because he came precariously close to them. Here Nietzsche reveals a hatred of fear and love, with which he wishes to convince himself of his own godly strength and riddance of human helplessness. (Andreas-Salomé 1988, 88–89)

Nietzsche may have been no different than a Designated Player in the MLS, convinced of his own godly strength and riddance of human helplessness.

In Rainer Maria Rilke, Salomé met Nietzsche's opposite. If the philosopher was all player and no team, the poet was all team and no player. Rilke, to whom "the work always was more important for him than the man," often complained to Salomé that he felt his individuality wither away (2003, 55). Salomé's response to him would encourage footballers who create more assists than goals:

> Nothing in the world could persuade me that even the smallest piece of you has in the interim crumbled away, for you are fully preserved in it . . . How make available to you this strange capacity of yours, for which it makes almost cruelly no difference whether it comes from the bliss of feeling yourself given over to all things, or from the horror of being mixed up with everything isolated and unclaimed? (Pfeiffer 1952, 291)

The focal point of individuality in football cannot be oneself as in Nietzsche or nowhere as in Rilke; it is mirrored along wherever the ball is going.

Salomé met Freud last. Loyal to him in spite of his split with Adler and Jung, Salomé still harbored the dream of a united team at the height of the mutiny:

> Gentlemen . . . I can thank psychoanalysis that it demands more than the work of isolated scholars at their desks and hence admitted me here to a kind of

> fraternity. The source of its vitality does not lie in any hazy mixture of science and sectarianism, but in having adopted as a fundamental principle that which is the highest principle of all scientific activity. I mean honesty . . . It is for this very reason that cleavages and conflicts are more likely to come to be in this group and beyond it than elsewhere. (Andreas-Salomé 1987, 130)

A speech well worth a locker room during half time! Salomé embodied in early psychoanalytic history a uniting force. She was only substituted into the game too late: the secessions were due, and neither Adler, nor Jung, nor later Rank, would respect Freud's captain armband. In times of *division*, the most nefarious phenomenon in a team sport, it was Salomé rather than Freud who resisted despair. These opposing attitudes ring poignantly in his letter to her during the divisive period of World War I:

> I do not doubt that mankind will survive even this war, but I know for certain that for me and my contemporaries the world will never be a happy place. It is too hideous. And the saddest thing about it is that it is exactly the way we should have expected people to behave from our knowledge of psychoanalysis. Because of this attitude to mankind I have never been able to agree with your blithe optimism. (Pfeiffer 1995, 21)

We showed earlier the necessary role of optimism in football. Despair is already defeat. It is precisely the carefree attitude Freud reproached Salomé which hands her a score over him.

Nietzsche, Rilke, Freud—no, after all, the heroic athlete in her life had been herself. What matters here is the extreme potential of women's football, where empowering the attributes that Salomé found missing in the men around her may well lead us to discover the *dark continent* [of football] as Freud prophesied about studies on woman.

TO COME OUT, OR NOT TO COME OUT?

I hope the premise of this chapter was not proving homosexuality existed in football. Any thorough psychoanalysis would reveal it: disappearance does not mean inexistence, but transformation. The problem which this chapter wishes to arrive to is not whether or not there are homosexual footballers—a redundant phrase, not an oxymoron, we conclude—but whether any footballer with sufficient homosexuality, primary and secondary, should or should not come out.

Coming out may well be a helpful political statement. It may well affect a chain reaction, encourage others, and yet the transpiring domino effect is bound to remain limited, person to person, rather than succeed to fundamentally change the larger system. Both the fears of conservatives and the hopes of progressives are unfounded. No, the first few footballers to come out will not mark the beginning of the end for the current masculinity in sport—these singular acts will not liberate everyone else.

The reason for the vein effect of coming out upon the larger strata of any collective is due to its conscious status. We have said Salomé insisted on primary homosexuality and primary narcissism, unconscious desires rather than their secondary spin-offs, which are wholly conscious, calculated, the mechanisms of socially-inscribed thinking. The wall dividing conscious and unconscious is not as porous as we wish: what we consciously experience only rarely re-configures the content of the unconscious, desires that cannot be in themselves expressed socially or linguistically. Primary homosexuality never shrieks: "I am gay"—it would already consider that phrase part of a confusing heterosexual matrix.

The heroism expected of gay footballers is thus slightly unfounded, even dangerous. Any progressive narrative championing homosexuality through social convention and language is bound to be hypocritical: if we follow Freud's and Salomé's analysis to the end, progress is the chief culprit in the persecution of primary homosexuality. It is a disservice to history to champion the victim in the name of its executioner. Even the pride so commonly associated with coming out and LGBTQ+ representation would be dangerous: where conscious pride is, primary narcissism had been. Likewise, where conscious homosexuality is, primary homosexuality had been.

May the slave use the master's tool? Can we return the repressed by that which repressed it? Since we have hit a dead-end on whether or not gay footballers should come out, it is time to test out the strength of our overall argument. To settle the draw, one must go into penalty shootouts.

CONCLUSION

Team captain, Lou Andreas-Salomé, is about to take the final kick against her adoptive Germany. Scoring would earn her native Russia their first World Cup, a victory set to send world politics into mayhem. Salomé has spoken against the Kremlin's imperial ambitions, but she did not cede to calls pressuring her to boycott the Russian national team. In the pre-game press conference, she had described her decision to play in the World Cup as a call of duty: "Because my real goal no longer belongs to me: I belong to it" (Michaud 2000, 205). Her participation amid LGBTQ+ persecution in Chechnya has also been questioned amid her own rumored lesbian relationship (Michaud 2000, 143). Hold on, Salomé is getting set to shoot . . . she rushes up to the ball . . . and she—

What do you think? Did she get the ball into the back of the net, or miss on purpose? Where precisely did Salomé's duty end: merely representing her motherland, or bringing the trophy back home?

Our fictional dilemma is not unlike what is at stake when it comes to football and homosexuality. The obvious reticence of footballers toward the homosexual question has to do with their notion of duty. Does a footballer represent his team, or himself? I am not as inflexible as UEFA who have barred footballers from showing solidarity with the LGBTQ+ community (Evans 2021, 1). Rather, I find their reasoning—defining rainbow flags as a political symbol—(which they later denied) as highly instructive. I have said coming out can have a political function, but homosexuality itself is a private concern, not a public one. Perhaps allyship, like Manuel Neuer wearing a rainbow captain armband during the Euro 2020 (Skysports 2021, 1), ought to be banned if what we fear is sectarianism, otherness within a pile of sameness. But a *true* homosexual footballer in Salomé's understanding blends with his team since primary homosexuality is aversive to differentiation.

Secondary homosexuality as we saw is no different than heterosexuality: both are secondary processes that come with social contexts. It is hard to make a science, let alone an ethics, out of secondary processes. Not only are they always haunted by that which precedes them, but they also enter social and linguistic configurations that make truth hard to ascertain or difficult to protect from the hypocritical gap between motivation and speech and arbitrary relativism. But the problem of our chapter lies precisely in a sacrifice of truth. Recollect Salomé's half-time pep talk, added to it the sentence I had originally omitted, which I now italicize: "[We] adopted as a fundamental principle that which is the highest principle of all scientific activity. I mean honesty. *It turns to this principle over and over again even in the most individual reality, and in so doing it subjects life to knowledge*" (Andreas-Salomé 1987, 130). While honesty may seem divisive at first, it ultimately aims at making out of life an object of study. Without honesty, no knowledge—only unrooted blabber. Salomé clung onto primary narcissism and primary homosexuality because they could constitute knowledge; they had a logic a psychoanalyst could properly map out. Because the unconscious alone is honest. Fighting about secondary processes bound to social conventions is not only divisive, but beside questions on truth. The limitedness of science, and ultimately serious discussion, is stretched too thin when we generously entertain conscious and socially-inscribed aspects of mental life, like representations of gender. What we end up with is not only a shadow over primary processes like narcissism and homosexuality but also the death of the psychoanalytic movement whose chief innovation had been a description of unconscious, not conscious, life.

What is the duty of footballers? Truth. Salomé would have taken and scored that penalty in spite of Russia's politics in the same way Socrates stayed in Athens and took the poison. "It does not matter what fate one has," the Russian psychoanalyst once told Anna Freud, "if one only really lives it" (Young-Bruehl 2008, 230). The answer to our hypothetical enigma has been scattered throughout the chapter. A homosexuality and narcissism that are sublimated to shield themselves from untruth. Footballers as creators hung up on the genuine existence of dual drives. Footballers as platonic lovers protecting the truth of their ideas. A probability of the game necessarily free from arbitrary confounding variables. A religious ideal which would collapse when a member bears false witness. Footballers end up being no different than philosophers: their homosexual and narcissistic beginnings in Socrates and Plato must endure the egoistic triumph of Descartes, the homophobia of Rousseau and Kant.

It is every football fan's nightmare: to be told the drama we have just witnessed is untrue, victim of bribery, or rehearsed beforehand. Truth must be defended in football . . . and with regards to homosexuality, acknowledging its genuine presence everywhere in the game is the first step toward building a conscious reality from the catacomb of the unconscious. Not only footballers, but coaches, commentators, television pundits, journalists, spectators, bystanders—all of us need to re-devote ourselves to truth and ascertain what is or isn't real, there or not there, actual or potential, primary or secondary. In that ideal society, we may have as many homosexual as heterosexual footballers due to the bisexual nature of the game and its need for perfect balance and the broadest compass. But only the landscapes of press conferences or post-game celebrations with significant others would change and thus reflect the genuine plurality of sexuality. On the pitch none of that would matter because sexuality will have been sublimated into epic proportions.

NOTE

1. Allusion to Friedrich Schiller's "Ritter Toggenburg," a poem on the unfulfilled love of a Swiss knight. The Toggenburgers were originally valley dwellers in the modern-day canton of St. Gallen whom eighteenth century historian Edward Gibbon described as "25,000 to 30,000 men, good soldiers and determined to defend until the last drop of blood what they regard as their most sacred privileges," (Gibbon, 1952).

BIBLIOGRAPHY

Andreas-Salomé, Lou. 1885. *Im Kampf um Gott.* Leipzig: W. Friedrich.

Andreas-Salomé, Lou. 1962. "The Dual Orientation of Narcissism." *The Psychoanalytic Quarterly* 31, no. 1: 1–30.

Andreas-Salomé. Lou. 1987. *The Freud Journal*. London: Quartet Books.

Andreas-Salomé, Lou. 2003. *You Alone Are Real to Me*. Rochester: BOA Editions.

Andreas-Salomé, Lou. 2012. *The Erotic*. Translated by John Crisp. New Brunswick, NJ: Transaction Publishers.

Andreas-Salomé, Lou. 2022. "Anal and Sexual." *Psychoanalysis and History* 24, no. 1: 19–40.

Cin, Hülya, and Onur Mutlu Yaşar. 2022. "The Relationship among Narcissism, Machiavellianism and Happiness of Female Football Players." *Viref revista de educación física* 11, no. 4: 144–157.

Dalí, Salvador. 1961. *The Secret Life of Salvador Dalí*. New York: The Dial Press.

Elman, Willie F., and Stuart J. McKelvie. 2003. "Narcissism in Football Players: Stereotype or Reality?" *Athletic Insight: The Online Journal of Sport Psychology* 5, no. 1: 1–9.

Evans, Simon. 2021. "UEFA Prohibits 'Rainbow' Protest at Germany vs Hungary Game." *Reuters*. June 23, 2021. https://www.reuters.com/lifestyle/sports/uefa-turn-down-request-rainbow-lights-munich-2021-06-22/#:~:text=MANCHESTER%2C%20England%2C%20June%2022%20(,at%20an%20anti%2DLGBTQ%20law.

Freud, Sigmund. 1986a. *The Standard Edition of the Complete Psychological Works of Sigmund Freud Volume 7*. London: Hogarth Press.

Freud, Sigmund. 1986b. *The Standard Edition of the Complete Psychological Works of Sigmund Freud Volume 12*. London: Hogarth Press.

Freud, Sigmund. 1986c. *The Standard Edition of the Complete Psychological Works of Sigmund Freud Volume 11*. London: Hogarth Press.

Gibbon, Edward. 1952. *Journal de mon voyage dans quelques endroits de la Suisse*. Lausanne: F. Rouge & Cie.

Huggins, Mike. 2007. "Betting, Sport and the British, 1918–1939." *Journal of Social History* 41, no. 2: 283–306.

Knott, Cargill Gilston. 1911. *Life and Scientific Work of Peter Guthrie Tait*. Cambridge: Cambridge University Press.

Michaud, Stephane. 2000. *Lou Andreas-Salomé: L'alliée de la vie*. Paris: Seuil.

Olley, James. 2023. "FA Reduced Ivan Toney's Suspension Ddue to Gambling Addiction Diagnosis." *ESPN*. May 26, 2023. https://www.espn.co.uk/football/story/_/id/37732597/fa-reduced-ivan-toney-suspension-due-gambling-addiction-diagnosis

Pfeiffer, Ernst. 1952. *Rainer Maria Rilke, Lou Andreas-Salomé: Briefwechsel*. Zurich: Max Niehans.

Pfeiffer, Ernst. 1985. *Sigmund Freud and Lou Andreas-Salomé: Letters*. New York: W. W. Norton.

Sky Sports. 2021. "Manuel Neuer: UEFA Drops Review of Rainbow Armband Worn by Germany Captain at Euro 2020 During Pride Month." June 21, 2021. https://www.skysports.com/football/news/19692/12337162/manuel-neuer-uefa-drops

-review-of-rainbow-armband-worn-by-germany-captain-at-euro-2020-during-pride-month

Welch, Michael. 1997. "Violence against Women by Professional Football Players: A Gender Analysis of Hypermasculinity, Positional Status, Narcissism, and Entitlement." *Journal of Sport and Social Issues 21*, no. 4: 392–411.

Young-Bruehl, Elizabeth. 2008. *Anna Freud: A Biography*. New Haven: Yale University Press.

PART V

Play

Chapter 10

Turning Two

Psychoanalysis and the Poetics of Pivoting; Or, Initial Thoughts for a Topology

Patrick Scanlon

For Michael Mallozzi

"I tell ya what . . . It's a great game!"

PREFACE: WHAT FEATURES IN THE FEAT

Given his terrible performance days earlier against the University of South Alabama—striking out four times, and his lackluster batting performance thus far in the season—Jim Lafountain was once again at the batting cage hitting off the tee for another set of hours. In major college baseball programs like the University of Louisville, there are at any moment two or three players vying for your position. According to Lafountain, in a conversation with me slated last February (Jim Lafountain pers. comm.), his assistant coach Stan Prager then approached him with a bit of quick advice: "Jim, never take batting practice (BP) after a bad game; you'll only solidify bad habits." This tip is but one of the many baseball proverbs that one has on hand to affect their mental performance—a touch counter intuitive, or at least difficult to execute in light of that sort of failure for which no remedy appears to exist. Paradoxically, the game of baseball necessitates a certain feel regarding one's body, bat, glove and ball, yet within a temporal situation whose scarcity of action elicits a great bounty of thought. Fortunately for Lafountain, as Kevin Czerwinski notes in the article "Lafountain L'Grande" (2022), Stan Prager was not only Coach Prager, but a psychologist at the University of Louisville, and his advisor for the minor in psychology he was pursuing. Prager then told him to put the bat down, grab his glove, and walk with him around the infield. "Jim, pick up some dirt" (Jim Lafountain pers. comm.). Jim complied, though not without suspicion. "Smell the dirt" (Jim Lafountain pers. comm.). This one took some convincing. "Smell your glove, the leather of your glove . . . " (Jim Lafountain pers. comm.). While these instructions are a bit more conventional today, in 1976 they were not, especially for Lafountain, a successful bodybuilder and self-styled gym rat.

Prager insisted, "The feel and smell of the dirt, the green of the grass, the shape of the glove . . . These were the things that made you love the game as a kid. Now, it's about something else" (Jim Lafountain pers. comm.). Lafountain admits, "He was right. I was focused on getting a pro contract. I was pressing too much; I couldn't relax" (Czerwinski 2022). This teaching moment was not simply good advice, or inspirational cliché to get one back on track. It engendered the payoff of all payoffs: The very next game, March 24th, Lafountain hit four homeruns, three of them grand slams, and two of those in one inning, all which gave him fourteen Runs Batted In. There actually could have been more, as the game was cut short because of the "mercy rule," a courtesy that ends a game prematurely due to the large disparity in runs. Even without a perfect understanding of what the terminology entails, it is possible to conceive that his performance remains one of the most incredible of any hitter in the history of baseball.

In taking Lafountain back to Little League, to his youthful experience with what ailed him at present, Prager puts us in the sort of generalized realm of psychoanalysis. Adding the sensuous element with the grass, glove and dirt, and we have something less typical, though there is certainly precedent in several psychoanalytic lineages for emphasizing the corporeal. Is it not in fact the staging of the body's ineluctability as it confronts the intensity of psychic zeal that makes psychoanalysis and sports such a compelling topic? Somewhat regardless of the rules that constitute this particular field of play or that court of contest, one is apt to hear language that invokes the bifurcation of body and mind, however simplistic the premise: "You are thinking too much"; "Get out of your head"; "I have no feel today"; "Center yourself"; "Let your emotions go"; "You're dead out there"; "Concentrate"; "Relax"; "Put your head in the game"; "Pull your head out of your ass;" etc. While in no way comprehensive or even unique to baseball for that matter, these examples—and the fundamental enigma they reestablish, in seeking to abolish—provide insight to the obsessive, if not at times maniacal, fidelity to preparation: the training, the drills, the aphorisms, the analysis.

It is perhaps this paradox of the mental or psychic as they contend with the sensual or corporeal that elicits a fortune of speech acts, and somewhat in concert with the psychoanalytic scene. In baseball, the great necessity for the proverb, will nevertheless give way to the poetic—in the form of poem, song, quip or well-placed pun, to say nothing of the on-hand proliferation of nicknames. The intense utility and repetition of circumstance from which the adage is born must at some point encounter that space-time largesse which is more explicitly baseball's domain. It is not so much that poetry opposes necessity or utility, but finds its requisite impulse arising from within the syntax and grammar of ordinary language usage. Its necessity is composed from the exigencies of words themselves, it seems, rather than from what is imposed externally. Such a structure and movement can provide us special access to the function of language and speech within the psychoanalytic scene, because the relation is formal, and concerns how figures are positioned spatially. Therefore, I shall have recourse to the crucial topological work that has been done in psychoanalysis, primarily by Jacques Lacan.

PART I. TURNING TO: WHEN THE TENSILE SETS RITUAL

To be seated more comfortably within baseball's domain, however, to sense with greater acuity its atmosphere, it is necessary to revisit Lafountain's situation one last time. In doing so, the necessity and efficacy of his coach's intervention will be displayed appropriately, but also, to be revealed, is the feat by which baseball accrues its singular status: hitting a baseball is the most difficult act in sports. Stating a claim with such confidence that is for all intents and purposes unprovable, is risky to any fair-weather fans, to say nothing of those nonfans for whom *America's pastime* is already intolerable to consider. Beyond the veracity of this status, are the details through which such a feat is realized. These notes are what delineates the otherwise vague anxieties the hitter must contend with at any given at-bat, and sets a tone that warbles into all facets of the game.

Geometrically speaking, the act itself requires that one contact a round ball by using a round bat. This doubling of roundness means that the notion of contact is, at a base level, more uncertain than not. Firstly, a batter is trying to make a very specific type of contact, and must put the ball in play between the two flanked foul lines or *within* the baseball diamond. The sheer velocity of the pitch is the primary source of difficulty. Sean Quinton, of the *Seattle Times*, presents some of the schematics, which are stated plainly enough:

> Say a 100-mph fastball takes 375 milliseconds after the pitcher releases the ball to reach the plate. After lopping off the first 75–100 milliseconds in "processing lag time," and 100–150 milliseconds needed to swing, the hitter is left with almost no time to decide what kind of pitch it is, where it's going, and whether or not they will attempt a swing. (2017)

Ultimately, the time allotted for the round bat to hit the round ball in the right place amounts to 5–7 milliseconds. It takes only a tenth of a second, or one-hundred milliseconds to blink, which is time spent trying to see the ball, quite literally. But the ball itself is not the only thing to observe: In addition to whether it is going to be a strike, of which the hitter gets three or where it will cross the hitting zone, there is also the spin of the ball. Certain pitches curve, and in several possible directions: breaking from up to down; breaking away from the batter; away from the batter and down; toward the batter; toward the batter and down; or rise up and running in. There is the cutter, the slider, the slurve, the knuckleball and the forkball. Even a fastball can be made to move, as the seams on the ball, set differently in the hand and subject to small amounts of pressure or changes in speed can cause the hitter to miss or make an unsound connection.

With a specificity and utility that matches the positivity of data listed above, Quincy Troupe (1996)—poet, journalist, jazz scholar and son of professional baseball catcher Quincy T. Trouppe Sr.—expresses the chaotic mess of challenges facing the hitter in his "Poem for my Father (for Quincy T. Trouppe Sr.)." The first stanza, which begins with "the glory of great black men swinging their lives, as bats, at tiny white balls," proceeds through a description of the variety of movements that a pitch employs with a precision that only poetry can manage. The ball comes "burning in at unbelievable speeds, riding up & in & out / a curve breaking down wicked, like a ball falling off a table" (1996, 80). It is worth noting briefly that the typical danger a hitter feels with the great velocity is here doubled by Trouppe's reference to race. The stark challenge of hitting, for whoever digs in the batter's box, is given perfectly here as the ball can both almost hit the player, and also sink without warning. Once the batter is brushed back from the plate, perhaps appropriately fearful of getting hit, the pitcher can then, as Trouppe continues, have the ball "moving away, snaking down, screwing its stitched magic / into chitlin circuit air, its comma seams spinning" (1996, 80). What is especially astute in these lines is the subtle difference between the ball "dropping off the table" and it "snaking down," a motion that entails sinking, but with a curving tract. And the method for such a repertoire of movements? The seams of the ball, which resemble the comma, and deliver that "stitched magic."

The verbs used in the following lines compound the speed of the ball which clips time, with its direction of transit—the breakdown; the dipping; the wrist curling—gesticulations that Trouppe can liken perhaps, only to the play of the ecstatic music and dance: "like a hipster bebopping a kneed-dip stride, in the charlie parker forties" (1996, 80). Eric Rynston-Lobel, in his article, "Hitting a baseball is the hardest skill to pull off in sports. Here's why," adds something vital to the spatial domain of hitting. He notes that a well hit ball comes down to a contact point that is "half the width of SIM-card in your Iphone" (2020). Perhaps the most salient points of data for the difficulty of hitting is the fact that a professional player whose succeeds three out of every ten times, over their career, will be a candidate for the Hall of Fame. Hitting a baseball is, to quote Paul Sajda, Professor of Engineering at Columbia University, like hitting a bullet with a bullet.

Beyond litigating the acute challenges of a sport's activities, the set of facts above allows us to understand an important reason for which baseball remains an excellent target for analysis. The extreme intensity of the bout, and the absolute necessity of maintaining some notion of neutrality in the nervous system, for which there are a variety of physical ritualistic acts, personal axioms to repeat, breathing techniques, etc. With even a cursory glance at a batter inside the batter's box readying for the pitcher's delivery, or in the on-deck-circle, where the hitter next in line waits, there are a flurry of tiny recursive stunts—loosening one's jersey off their shoulders, ripping open and closed the Velcro strap to one's batting gloves, retightening one's belt, or discharging gobs of practice swings whose odd form bears little resemblance to the actual game time version. One is readied with whatever methods are on hand, and according to how current feel touches past tendency.

What are these transgressive acts that relegate baseball to the sphere of the religious or judicial domains? Generally speaking, they mostly concern a regulation of exuberance that vacillates between sacrificing the release of tension which celebration implies, the sacrifice of utility and conservation, and the righteousness of formality, a conference of the just. With the most dominate offensive act, a homerun—in which the ball sails over the fence in the air, a batter must never run around the bases too slowly, nor too fast, or in any type of gate that might seem flashy or ornamental. Often one knows as soon as they hit the ball that it is a homerun, and yet they must never stand there and watch it fly, or flip their bat in too ostentatious manner. Any of these flamboyant gestures will most likely get the next batter hit with a fastball right in the back, or get a pitch up and in, toward their helmet.

This regulation of behavior need not be interpreted cynically or pathologically; it results instead, I would argue, from a formalness that is inherent to all sports, but which finds its consummate shape within baseball. The uniform one dons is another dignifying gesture supportive of structure and ceremony: there are the long pants, belt, special socks, gloves, a button-down shirt and a cap, which is increasingly maintained in a very crisp manner—unbent and unsullied. In fact, while baseball caps have been worn by children and adults alike for decades, it is only recently that the impeccable care for the baseball cap has infiltrated the world on nonplayers. What is more, the almost courtly treatment of the hat is no longer relegated to baseball fandom, as a variety of other sports, business ventures, and fashion startups utilize the baseball cap.

It is perhaps no surprise that—considering the intensity with which the physical and psychic are fastened together during an at-bat, and paired with the great formalness in costume and conduct—the atmosphere of significance borders on the sacred, and is supported by fan and player alike. The exquisitely manicured field is nonetheless verdant with superstitions maintained by prohibition and intervention alike: at times certain things must be said; at others, they can never be mentioned; players touch specific objects and spots on their uniforms; keep unique objects in their lockers; mutter to themselves custom phrases; add clothing items under their unis; reverse clothing items; eat specific meals; watch pregame routines; hide from ceremonial acts.

Naming. Wearing. Seeing. Doing. Or their obverse. Some are private. Some require an audience. There is, without a doubt, favor to be found in this florid economy of blessings and curses. Ira Stone, in his review, "Well, It's a Game, No? A Meditation on Baseball and Poetry" (1987) articulates well how baseball stages the monotony of routine as its tethered to the glory of destiny. He writes:

> In the routines of life we see the inexorable working out of our fate, and the fate of each of us is ultimately the same. Baseball moves us because we see in it both the futility and the grandeur of questing after perfection. In it, every detail of physical movement reveals both that quest and its impossibility. The routine becomes the sacred for what else is available for sanctification? (Stone 1987)

How tightly expectation, neurosis, and fantasy tie into notions of perfection, but in such a manner that one is rarely able to experiment with the boundaries of their capture confidently. The field of play, as it were, is of course everywhere, and thus never quite in session. What is extra special here, it seems, is the fairly rigid parameters of the field itself, and within the playing of this game. One must confront the cleanliness of order, as it is sort of hoisted above, some big Other perhaps, retractable dome or ballpark domicile, and negotiate their own encounter through which they contribute personally to order's maintenance and its illusion.

Any of these behaviors, whether personally employed, or in collaboration with the specifics of the game itself are worthy themes to pursue under the auspices of "sports and the psychoanalytic," as is the limited but emblematic intervention in the life of player that began this essay. And yet, is it possible for sport to be in relation to the psychoanalytic through a proximity that is not so much analogic, but topologic in nature? Are there elements of nearness with this sport—as it already expresses so much of the material magnetized by the psychoanalytic, those objects that still so willfully under its gaze—for which the setting and structure can model something of how language can function within the psychoanalytic scene?

There is of course precedent for placing psychoanalysis within the topological: we have the Copernican, or Keplerian revolution, that refigured not only the position of the sun, but the course of planetary movement—circle into ellipse—which helped Freud frame the unconscious as humanity's third narcissistic wound. Additionally there, are the innovative applications of knot theory available through Jacques Lacan's study of the Borromean link, torus and other curved surfaces. No doubt psychoanalysis has benefited from pursuing topology in addition to the analogical comparisons more akin to other disciplines in the humanities. So while I answer the question of geometric relevance and efficacy in the affirmative, it must also be stated that any topological study requires not simply the space and time to present the necessary elements in a suitable manner, but there must also be corroboration through collaborating with the liveliness of the analytical situation.

I shall proceed then, but through what can be deemed more appropriately—initial thoughts on a topological study. Nevertheless, this change in frame will allow—in the looseness of *this* term or the hastiness of *that* example—enough space to play with and through the poetic as it associates, repeats, sounds and doubles up meaning. The one scene in baseball that proximates the analytic situation, fulfilling that topological quality of nearness is the double play. This event—half nave, have navel—is fashioned by the necessary twists and turns, angles of intent and bodily risk to resemble something of a speech that seeks the analyst and, simultaneously, establishes the subject's position.

PART II. TURNING TWO: WHERE DUBIETY DUPES THE DOUBLE

While there are a variety of ways for the defense to record two outs during one continuous play—an offensive act or an at-bat—the most complex and impressive example of the double play (DP), and the one for which this term and others of note have been generated, involves the Second Baseman and the Shortstop pivoting around second base. Known collectively as "middle infielders," as they exist in the geometrical center of the baseball diamond, these two players presuppose the potential for completing this play by positioning themselves closer to second base and the batter before the ball is pitched. This gesture, which limits their range and reach, expresses openly a desire for that distinctive edge, and as a consequence, the fields' attention sharpens and the stakes are raised. Once the ball is hit the fielder must—whether the ground ball is caught by the shortstop or second baseman—toss it to the other who will then, in one single move: catch it; touch the base; reorient the body; and throw the ball to the First Basemen—all before the offensive runner on first base reaches second base, and before the hitter reaches first base.

William Curran, in his *Mitts: A Celebration of the Art of Fielding* (1985), describes the double play somewhat in kind with its spectacular fashion. His description includes a runner, not only on first, but on second and third base as well, which is put forth a situation where the bases are fully loaded. This scenario highlights the power of the double play to change the tide of the game and ruin momentum, and also suggests why it is affectionally called, "the pitcher's best friend":

> Bases loaded, tying run on third, one out. The batter hits a hard smash to the right of second [base]. The wiry little second basemen, in motion before the crack of the bat, reaches across his body to spear the grounder just as it's about to escape into center field. Without straightening, he flips a waist-high throw over the bag. The rangy shortstop takes the throw in full stride, leaps lightly over the sliding baserunner, twists his upper body to the right, and at the height of his leap fires the ball to the first baseman, whose gloved hand is stretched toward second as far as his tall frame will permit. Double play. Elapsed time: under four seconds. Magnificent. In fact, I don't believe you will see it topped at Lincoln Center. (Curran 1985, 69)

This defensive triumph depends on the fielder's capacity to "turn it" or "roll it," a movement designed to diminish the velocity of the received ball, while repositioning the fielder's body for the next throw. Technically, the ball is not caught in the glove and stopped, but rounded or redirected, an essential conversion of momentum given the unfavorable set of angles to be negotiated. The immediacy at stake here is augmented by the fact that the pivot point, where the fielder performs this delicate transmutation, is the very destination of an advancing runner, a circumstance that makes collision almost inevitable. Thus, the DP has generated some of baseball's most remarkable plays: acrobatic feats, daring leaps, and at times, unfortunate season ending injuries.[1]

It is fair to expect that the specifics of baseball, especially "inside baseball," a phrase that denotes discussing the esoteric elements of any subject, may escape those unfamiliar with its tenets, if not also those who claim to be fans. Providing a suitable amount of information is no doubt then a tricky affair, for one also risks confusing the reader, or boring them to sleep.

Baseball is notorious for inducing the deepest of sleeps. More important than not inundating the reader with a written account of its web of rules and exceptions is the possibility that the sonic and semantic repetition in terminology might evince something of the topological closeness to come. The most obvious example of this is supplied by the following triad, which comes from the colloquial phrase that describes the double play: *turning two*, signifying the acquisition of two outs during one offensive play. Within this term can be heard, *turning to*, as in positioning oneself toward another person or thing—a direction, an orientation. Finally, there is *turning too*, or turning also, like in addition to another movement. Obviously, even with the official designation, *a double play*, there are several crucial associations to that psychoanalytic theme, The Double. And further, we have the sense of double playing, in regards to language's capacity, if not the unconscious' tendency for polysemy—all awash in the play of signifiers.

The relevance of language extends beyond the ultimate designation of this play, and into other elements that concern the movement of the players. There are also semantic allusions to the smaller repetitive skills, the sort of phonemic structures, involved in the middle infielder's training. It is thus not simply that terms are shared, but also their manner of operations. Suggesting that the reader take pleasure in the prosody when listening to the rhyme and rhythm of language, in addition to what is given in the prose, is an orientation familiar to psychoanalysis. Besides, as psychoanalysis reminds us, information is not knowledge, and knowledge is not truth. This middle term, knowledge—what seems a reasonable thing to put forth in an essay on a special topic—remains, paradoxically, of less worth in psychoanalysis than is typical of other professions; it is often, in fact, rendered as impotent if not characteristic of the very thing that defers the cure. Likewise, poetry, or language in which the poetic functions, is also not in the business of giving information, at least not primarily. This notion, along with the emphasis on reading, writing and speech as constitutive acts—all relatively contingent and thus capable of that sort of saying which signals the unconscious, is what puts the poetic and the psychoanalytic in such tight rhythm.

The cadence is one in which emphasis is placed on the precariousness and sovereignty of the signifier, rather than on the indelibility of the signified. A word is of course related to its respective thing, but like the line that does not touch the curve, there is not any symmetry or fusion. For Lyn Hejinian, poet, theorist and scholar of Gertrude Stein, "the language of poetry is a language of inquiry, not the language of a genre. It is that language in which a writer (or a reader) or both perceives and is conscious of the perception" (2000, 3). Language in which the poetic functions has the capacity to present phenomena in their infancy, as they manifest to and through our perception. She states, "Poetry comes to know that things are. But this is not knowledge in the strictest sense; it is, rather, acknowledgement—and that constitutes a sort of unknowing. To know *that* things are is not to know *what* they are, and to know *that* without *what* is to know otherness (i.e., the unknown and perhaps the unknowable)" (Hejinian 2000, 3). While the purposes of poetic inquiry and psychoanalytic inquiry are not completely in concert, their methods can, and often do, intertwine. In a moment of haste, one might designate the poetic as concerned with the objects of the world, though in a manner that paradoxically includes the perceiver. And the psychoanalytic, though directed to the subject, whether caught in the statement of speech, or lurking within the enunciator of speech, nevertheless must attend to those things of the world, no matter how furtive their advent.

Quite infamously, Lacan suggested that the analyst might be sanctioned not simply from obtaining a Doctor of Psychiatry, but rather through a devotion to the variety of language's forms through which the analysand speaks. Befittingly,, he arrived on the scene in part through his remarkable reading of Edgar Allan Poe's short story "The Purloined Letter," a tale written by a poet about a poet detective, however amateurish, who solves the crime precisely through recognizing that the thief was not only a mathematician, but also a poet. We might take Lacan's own words on the import of poetry, which he presents in *Seminar XI: The Four Fundamental Concepts of Psychoanalysis*: "What hierarchy could confirm him as an analyst, give him the rubber-stamp? A certificate tells me that I was born. I repudiate this certificate: I am not a poet, but a poem. A poem that is being written, even if it looks like a subject" (1981, viii). It is this notion of being written that binds us even closer to the type of poetry that might allow us to utilize with some measure of worth, the double play as a topological model for the function of language in the psychoanalytic scene.

Posited in a rather general fashion, the Lacanian is the one for whom language—linguistics, semiotics, semantics, grammar, literature—is the material of note for the analytics scene; thus they maintain a rigor and vigor regarding language's variety of forms, regardless of how they meet, make and breach the limits of logic. Although this was and remains a radical position within the larger psychological, psychiatric and even psychoanalytic communities, it is easier to concede of this linguistically ground to poets, though Stein, Hejinian and their like are now and have always been in that similar rarefied company. In the game of baseball, the middle infielders are the ones whose skill with the very materials of the game—glove and ball, hand and foot—surpass the rest of the field, which is not just a matter of talent.[2] There is a theoretical disposition that warrants a certain modicum of pleasure and play, given the extreme nature of their encounter within the game. No doubt these qualities are motivated by succeeding at one's profession, though there is, in kind with the two other figures, a devotion to the materials themselves. Middle infielders can hide the ball, flip it, throw it underhand, sideways, behind their back, while spinning, while blind to the target etc. What's more is that most of these acts of transferring the ball can be performed with their gloves as well—a fact which means this device is not something only, or even mostly to catch, enclose and hold the ball.

In one of the most famous baseball poems ever, "Baseball's Sad Lexicon," by Franklin Pierce Adams (1910), we see the efficacy of the double play, and how its unique vocabulary convenes on the sufferer through a speech act echoing all about the park. The author, a fan of the NY Giants is lamenting the phrase that is repeated by the announcer again and again, broadcasted throughout the stadium: "Tinkers to Evers to Chance." The poem posits a groundball that has been hit to the Chicago Cubs' shortstop Joe Tinker, which is then flipped to the second baseman Johnny Evers, and then flung to the first baseman Frank Chance. In the games parlance this is routinely stated by the number associated with their positions, 6-4-3, or by their names as presented in the poem.

> These are the saddest of possible words:
> "Tinker to Evers to Chance."
> Trio of bear cubs, and fleeter than birds,
> Tinker and Evers and Chance.
> Ruthlessly pricking our gonfalon bubble,
> Making a Giant hit into a double—
> Words that are heavy with nothing but trouble:
> "Tinker to Evers to Chance."
> —*Baseball's Sad Lexicon* (Franklin Pierce Adams, 1910)

Admittedly, baseball players often have fantastic names—sonic *and* semantic. Or maybe the game itself, as it bounces around engendering culture, is the agent provocateur, granting to their privileged pairing, the tonal glory of grass staining and sun burns

The agility and preparation, this fleet-footedness, in kind with the siblings of the poetic field, that quick-wittedness, necessitates that one not only play *with* their respective objects, ball and word, but abide *in* the play of ball and word as the game, whether baseball or language, engages a field that is, in and of itself volatile. In other words, the poet, psychoanalyst and middle are expert with the elements of their game, a certain play of signifiers on one hand, and the whirling pivot of glove and limb on the other. Lest one categorize this mingling of methods as fanciful, we might be assured by the verb use of Hejinian's description of the poetic and its field. For her, the poetic "is a process in and of language, whose most complex, swift, and subtle forms are to be found in poetry—which is to say poetic language." She writes:

> In the course of the experiencing of experience, poetic language puts into play the widest possible array of logics, and especially it takes advantage of the numerous logics operative in language, some of which take shape as grammar, some as sonic chains, some as metaphors, metonyms, ironies, etc. There are also logics or irrationality, impossibility, and a logic of infinite speed. All these logics make connections and forge linkages. That, indeed, is the function of logics; they motivate the moves from one place to another. But the emphasis in poetry is on the moving rather than on the places. (Hejinian 2000, 3)

While the psychoanalytic scene has its unique design, its scope has stretched following Lacan who, according to Jane Gallop, "has generalized it into a way of receiving all discourse, not just the analysand's" (1985, 22). As a result the nimble nature of the psychoanalyst—who "learns to listen not so much to her patient's main point as to odd marginal moments, slips of the tongue, unintended disclosures"—refigures the limits at stake within the analytic office (Gallop 1985, 22).

It is therefore through the effects on the patient and, if traced more broadly still—by virtue of scholarship and public facing enterprise—that all the dimensions of culture constituted from the signifier are transfigured. Sport, in turn, exceeds the specificities of contest, imprinting its mark likewise in domains that share no point of contact, nor any resemblance to its charter. Impressed nonetheless, it appears here—in the semiotics of fashion, repeats there—as misplaced ritual; gathering the indices of childhood, dispersing the scars of utility—already resonant, ever variegated, always specious, this world what spins into speech.

PART III. TURNING TWO: HOW SHAPE STIRS MOTION

Before the interview officially starts, the former NY Yankees pitcher Mariano Rivera, one of baseball's recent legends, says to the interviewer, sports media figure Brandon Steiner, "It's cardboard . . . it has to be a carton, or cardboard" (Rivera and Steiner 2011). From off camera Rivera is handed a piece of cardboard. He continues, "I need the knife . . . let me have the knife . . ." (Rivera and Steiner 2011). Within a few moments, Rivera cuts around the edges reducing its size, makes a slit toward the bottom, sticks his hand through and squeezes in from the backside, so that the flat surface is now slightly curved from within his palm. He grabs a baseball and tosses it into this device, squeezing around it: "OK. Now you got a new glove . . . This is your glove. That was my glove . . . (Tossing the ball into it). Now it's a good glove . . . Perfect" (Rivera and Steiner 2011). When growing up in Panama, Rivera explains, this procedure was the most common method of making a glove among the majority children who lived in poverty.[3]

There is much to be said about this anecdote, and perhaps nothing is more consequential ultimately than emphasizing the terrible discrepancy in wealth that exists across continent and country. There is some truth to the unfortunate societal conditions that make destitution an exceptional motivating factor in the world of sports, and Rivera suggests as much in the interview. And yet, if this case of the homemade glove is conceived more narrowly still, it can introduce us to the final section of the essay, where the game's geometry, if not its topological potential, will help to analyze the paradoxical manner in which the subject is composed through language—gathered, dispersed, sustained. It is not irrelevant that this knowledge from Rivera is given through a speech that cannot be proffered in anything but the present, while it nonetheless glosses over scenes of the past. And ultimately what is made is made from the cut.

Although the cardboard works well enough as a glove in the general sense, to stop and hold the ball, and to protect the hand, it is, structurally speaking more of a surface or plane, and not a net or contraption. For the majority of baseball situations that require a glove, the superficiality or absence of depth represents a design flaw. Yes, for just about all of the defensive scenarios except one of course: the double play. The success of this special feat rests largely on how rapidly one can receive the thrown ball and transfer it to another player, a situation in which the ball is not caught and held, but has its linearity redirected, "turned" or "rolled" and through a shape that is toroidal, spiraled, torus-like. With a surface, or when the glove's depth is foreclosed, the elliptical movement comes from the arms and hips, which are first set up first by the feet.

The record holder for the most professional DP's turned, Bill Mazeroski, addressed the secret to this advantageous play by emphasizing the importance of communicating one's desire to the other: "the only thing that the second basement needs to agree on with his partner [the shortstop] is where he wants the ball thrown" (Curran 1985, 137), a simplistic answer that belies the intricacies therein. As the second baseman approaches second base to receive the throw, toss, or flip—depending on the angle and distance from the shortstop—he would show his hands as a target. Some prefer the ball chest high, others at the waist. More importantly though, is where one wants it in relation to the bag: Mazeroski names the options, "in front of the bag, over the bag, or behind the bag" (Curran 1985, 137). The differences here require one to step on and across the base, or straddle the bag, left foot in front and right foot behind, or one can step on the bag for the catch and then step back, or rock back, for the throw. While these are preferences, ultimately, the position is determined by the throw, which is often rushed and given from quirky inclines—to say nothing of the runner coming from first base, and fast, with the express need to intimidate the fielder, as he is sliding into this same bag. In other cases, the runner will slide into the bag with feet up, or slide directly into the fielder with only a faux gesture at touching the bag. As middle infielders, we are taught to ask for the ball in specific place, to show our hands in front as a target, emphasizing that spot, but that we must also, always expect an errant throw.

Paula Murphy (2005), in her review of Bruce Fink's text, *Lacan to the Letter: Reading Écrits Closely* (2004) notes the remarkable dexterity in how Lacan's utilizes "double and triple entendres, his frequent, often bilingual jokes, and the repletion of references to prominent thinkers from all disciplines" (Murphy 2005). This deft facility with language, which Lacan has designated as *linguistricks*,[4] is essential for working with the subject who speaks, as it is not only linguistics at stake, or what he associates with the subject of the statement or the enunciation. There is also however, the one who is speaking in the moment of speech; there is an enunciator, and this figure, Fink states, implies "a bodily component that is introduced: breathing and all of the movements of the jaw, tongue, and so on required for the production of speech" (2004, 144). The enunciating subject, Fink continues, "is the one who may take pleasure in speaking, who may find it painful to speak, or who may make a slip while speaking. The enunciating subject is the one who may let slip something that is revealing of his or her feelings, desires, or pleasures" (2004, 145).

One sensible way to conceive of the double play then is through the dual nature of the subject who appears in, or somewhat as, the dual nature of language. Before looking at how Lacan does this, and through topological figures that bear some relation to the kinetic action of the DP, it seems useful to double down, as it were, on how this split is otherwise conceived in evenemential terms, and as such, contingent on time and space. Of course, we can expect only some distorted picture sketched in haste, and yet, if it regards language with the requisite complexity, which is to say, it is not only about language but given through language, our attempt can proceed confidently. There is undoubtedly no one who does portraiture with such grand acuity as Gertrude Stein, whose "Portraits and Repetitions" (1998) and "Tender Buttons" (1998) gave rise to her most enduring concept, *the continuous present*. Astrid Lorange, in her fantastic study, *How Reading Is Written: A Brief Index to Gertrude Stein*, characterizes this notion as "a mode of composing that retained the constant repetitions, recursions, and disruptions of linguistic construction" and not something employed for "signifying a smooth continuum of time" (2014, 60). Here we have a description that again mimics the verbing of Lacan and the middle, all suspicious of the idealistic or imaginary purity of abstraction.

What is more, Stein references speech as that which informed her pursuits: "I began then to consciously listen to what anybody was saying and what they did say while they were saying what they were saying. This was not yet the beginning of writing but it was the beginning of knowing what there was that made there be no repetition" (1998, 305–306). There is no repetition because even if the same words are spoken, each utterance cannot help but carry a distinct emphasis. In the psychoanalytic scene, there are countless instances where some trite term in the analysand's repertoire is suddenly and without warning imbued with emotional significance. The fact that Stein is here discussing her attempt to conceive of an other places her closer to the position of an analyst, and in fact, as it was revealed to Freud, she notes later in the piece that her own doubleness is activated when listening. She writes:

> In other words the making of a portrait of any one is as they are existing and as they are existing has nothing to do with remembering and one or anything. Do you see my point, but of course yes you do. You do see that there are two things and not one and if one wants to make one portrait of some one and not two you can see that one can be bothered completely bothered by this thing. . . . Then we have insistence insistence that in its emphasis can never be repeating, because insistence is always alive and if it is alive it is never saying anything in the same way because emphasis can never be the same not even when it is most the same that is when it has been taught. (Stein 1998, 290–291)

The *continuous present* can be felt as one reads her passage due to the special attention one must employ to read what is actually written, not what is to be read. She describes this pursuit of "the two," which also takes the form of inside/outside and clarity/confusion, as a bother as it persists without any final or total resolution.

To situate this study closer to Lacan, in terms of discipline at least, we might invoke Maurice Merleau-Ponty's (1964) *reversibility*, for which he uses the curvature of a glove to illustrate the doubling of being toward and the subsequent *double representation*. There is, as David Morris (2010) details, the seer as the flip side of the seen, which represents, nonetheless, a divergence that is unrecouped. These doublings, taken up in his *The Visible and the Invisible* (1964) and "Eye and Mind" (1964), may be most applicable to the DP when discussing the complexity of touch, which is in some ways the instance of note for Merleau-Ponty, and us, as each figure of the middle is not the mirror image of the other, and so might be framed structurally through his notion of chiral enantiomorphs. In using the hand and glove for the pairing of non-mirror objects, Merleau-Ponty calls attention, inadvertently for sure, to the element most at stake for turning two. The middle is always considered by their hands—how soft, how quick. One might also conceive of the feet, during the double play, as chiral to the hands. In the confusion of infield dirt and baserunners, the enantiomorphic nature of the middle—which is to say, the coupling of objects that are similar but not symmetrical—means that the players must rely heavily on their points of embodiment: the feel and press of the cleated foot, and the soft curling of the glove, which both orient one toward a target that is not visible, given the oblique angles involved.

Closer still, is the stunning work of Giorgio Agamben (1993), whose notion of *infancy* is not simply complimentary with Lacan's derivation of the subject through the distinction of linguistics and speech, but it is also additive. In fact, like Lacan, Agamben finds special favor with Roman Jakobson and Ferdinand Saussure, even if ultimately it is difference that compels the former pairing from the latter. The special figure for Agamben's *Infancy and History: On the Destruction of Experience* (1993), is the structural linguist, semiotician and cultural anthropologist, Émile Benveniste, who Lacan also encountered. Although dubbed by some as the "theoretician of the enunciation," the influence on Lacan remains murky, for the arrow may point the other direction. Agamben hones in on his *On the Nature of Pronouns* (1971) and specifically, the singular and strange effects of the "I." For Benveniste, it is not the *langue* and *parole of Saussure,* but the *double signification* of the *semiotic* (linguistic sign) and the *semantic* (discourse)—a division in language that is "distinct and contrasting" (1993, 61).

Agamben combines this *double signification* with a *double inheritance*, comprised of the *endosomatic* (genetic heritage) and the *esosomatic* (cultural heritage), and figures Jakobson's *phonemes* as resonating in the gap between the respective pairs, and thus has cause to consider topology. Of the phonemes he writes: "they are located in the correspondence-difference . . . between the two regions, in a 'site' which can perhaps be described only in its topology and which coincides with that historico-transcendental region—before the subject of language and without somatic substance—which we have defined above as human *infancy*" (Agamben 1993, 61). The momentary transfer from one region to the other is a suitable description for the movement of the double play as well, and with the recognition of topology, we might speculate on what other points of each figure retain a relation. As we approach the end of this exploration, it is fair to say that there are a few candidates for a more thorough topological study. Or maybe instead of separate topological sites, we could take the repetition—Lacan, Stein, Merleau-Ponty, Agamben—as a sign of that vital psychoanalytic notion of Freud's: overdetermination.

There is no doubt that a serviceable topology based around the double play, as it models something of the role of language in the psychoanalytic scene, would locate its primary foci in the work of Jacques Lacan. A more concentrated study, therefore, would take up his labyrinthic texts and talks in which he sought—in the words of Will Greenshields exhaustive study, *Writing the Structures of the Subject: Lacan and Topology*—"not to present [the insubstantial subject] but to demonstrate it with topology" (2017, 43). And while Lacan's initial shape, the sphere, was fairly useless for his demonstrations, given "its imperforated surface acting as a clean boundary between inside and outside," we might simply note, with a touch of snark that the baseball has seams that protrude on it, complicating it, making it not so perfect to handle (Greenshields 2017, 38). Or maybe it retains some of its imaginariness, it remaining vulnerable to wear and tear, to the smear of sweat and soil, to the vagaries of the game.

The figure next from the sphere, the interior eight—which sort of intends a circle but misses the starting point thus making an extra loop on its return—can well enough *describe* the acute turn of the double play, and like the next terms, the Möbius strip and torus, can inspire the question of what other points of the DP may engender the requisite nearness of structure. With the former we have a situation in which a source of the unconscious—"The signifiers that originally determined the subject are lost to him and yet they will continue to obliquely haunt his speech" (Greenshields 2017, 47)—might be modeled in the shifting, slipping, missing activity inherent to the double play, if not the game at large. These gestures can lead to a flash of the subject or a palpable sign of the unconscious, in a manner that epitomizes the hitter's struggle to first make contact and then to reach first base safely. There is the runner who is already on first that must, with their own set of risks, break up the doubling, slow the process, interrupt it. We have the ball and vectors of force, intent, meaning that are nonetheless rolled up-in-with the other like the tori of desire and demand.

Are these concerted efforts to contact and reach base safely, or with sliding and dividing, which revel in the reveal, an alienation already slated and set at home plate or sooner, when circled on deck? But here the batter lifts of the shoulder with one last shudder, pinched jersey tug for the sticky skin in warming weather. Through swipe or swing, the ball touches and downed, by dint of dented grass, cleats forage, dig dry sand sounds and scrape. Quickly a glance is had toward second showing the shortstop sifting into crescent step with ball pressed against leather layer for to flip at squish square base or straddled, rounding one line into another. What flings at first such some stretch and scoup is determined at last lunge the double.

Not all that slips falls however; and even miss hits score runs. With the potential for give, there is loss yes, but the risk of a fleet foot, a fleeced feed, a slowness that is smooth and thus quick. We are, regardless of sport or team, already captured in the cut, always coerced in the cull. Along with a language that rounds, there is a subject to roll and spin, turning lines of meaning that intend over and under barreling a speech that bends. And the others, crowded and costumed as friends, applaud timely for a space upending an ideal symmetry, putting into play therefore, the glory of sacrificed utility, the measure of speech unbound, the probable impossibility of a game that never quite quits.

NOTES

1. If this essay is of a special interest to the reader, I recommend looking up a video—something to the effect of "Spectacular Double Plays." These videos will include mostly the DP under examination here, what is called 6-4-3 or 4-6-3.

2. An exception to this rule would be the catcher who, in a similar way that the goalie is considered the best skater on the ice, puts forth an incredible display of the games most coveted attributes.

3. They could not afford a baseball or tennis ball either, and so were forced to make them out of tape and string.

4. See Seminar XX. It is worth mentioning that Danny Nobus, in "Lacan's science of the subject: between linguistics and topology," makes a good case for translating this as *linguisteria*, which is, he writes, "a combination of linguistics and hysteria or, even better, a hysterical transformation of linguistics" (2003, 68n.29).

BIBLIOGRAGHY

Adams, Franklin Pierce. 1910. "Baseball's Sad Lexicon." *New York Evening Mail*, July 12, 1910.

Agamben, G. 1993. *Infancy and history: The destruction of experience*. London: Verso.

Curran, William. 1985. *Mitts: A Celebration of the Art of Fielding.* New York: William Morrow and Co.

Czerwinski, Kevin. 2022."LaFountain L'Grande." *BallNine*, January 22, 2022. https://ballnine.com/2022/01/22/lafountain-lgrande/

Fink, B. 2004. *Lacan to the Letter: Reading Ecrits Closely*. Minneapolis, MN: U of Minnesota.

Greenshields, Will. 2017. *Writing the Structures of the Subject.* New York: Palgrave Macmillan.

Hejinian, L. 2000. *The Language of Inquiry*. Berkeley: U. of California Press.

Lacan, Jacques. 1998. *Seminar XI: The Four Fundamental Concepts of Psychoanalysis.* Revised Ed. W. W. Norton & Company.

Lorange, A. 2014. *How Reading is Written: A Brief Index to Gertrude Stein.* Middletown, CT: Wesleyan University Press.

Morris, D. 2010. "The Enigma of Reversibility and the Genesis of Sense in Merleau-Ponty." *Cont Philos Rev* 43: 141–165.

Murphy, Paula. 2005. "Linguistricks: Reading Lacan to the Letter. Review of *Lacan to the Letter: Reading Écrits Closely*, by Bruce Fink." *International Journal of Baudrillard Studies* 2, no. 2. https://baudrillardstudies.ubishops.ca/linguistricks-reading-lacan-to-the-letter/

Nobus, Danny. 2003. "Lacan's science of the subject: between linguistics and topology." In *The Cambridge Companion to Lacan,* edited by Jean-Michel Rabate, 50–68. New York: Cambridge University Press.

Quinton, Sean. 2017. "Don't Blink: The Science of a 100 MPH Fastball." *Seattle Times*, March 31, 2017.

Rivera, Mariano, and Brandon Steiner. 2011. "Mariano Rivera Talks About His First Glove," YouTube video, 6:17, September 21, 2011. https://libanswers.snhu.edu/faq/48007.

Rynston-Lobel, Eric. 2020. "Hitting a Baseball is the Hardest Skill to Pull Off in Sports. Here's Why." *Popular Science.* August 6, 2020.

Stein, Gertrude. 1998. "Portraits and Repetition." In *Writings, 1932–1946*, 290–291. New York: Library of America.

Stone, Ira. 1987. "Well, It's a Game, No? A Meditation on Baseball and Poetry." *The SABR Review of Books* 2: 64–70.

Troupe, Quincy.1996. *Avalanche: Poems*. Minneapolis, MN: Coffee House Press.

Chapter 11

Becoming-ball

A Schizo-soma Ball Movement

Shani Samai-Moskovich

While the body is well discussed in psychoanalytic theory, a lacuna still remains regarding the development of the athletic aspect, which includes elements such as integrating body image into the self, practicing motor acts, controlling the body in space, and experiencing competence and pleasure through the acquisition of athletic skills (Sherick 2012). One way of exploring the athletic aspect in psychoanalytic theory and practice is via Deleuze and Guattari's concept of "becoming." "Becoming" is easily understood as a symbiotic process, an ongoing metamorphosis in which participants lose their boundaries, becoming-other. It is a continuous process of "subjectification." Accordingly, in the below, I demonstrate working with "becoming" using the notion of becoming-ball. Through a close reading of the prologue to Don DeLillo's *Underworld, The Triumph of Death* (first published as the novella *Pafko at the Wall* (1992)), and a discussion of a clinical vignette, I demonstrate this "becoming-ball" by referring to the relationship between the athletic body and it's connection to mental transformation.

BALL-GAMES: MINORITY IN THE PSYCHOANALYTIC CONTEXT

Though rarely discussed in the psychotherapeutic context, ball games have both developmental and clinical relevance. Typically coming with a clear set of rules and a concretely staked out site of action (the playing field), they nevertheless include many creative elements.[1] Ball games moreover also resonate in the media, the audience, and the political contexts they reflect and produce as a result of their national and international significance.[2]

Freud introduced the concept of the *body ego,* and later theories have elaborated how mental and physical development interact (e.g., Hartmann 1952; Meissner 1997; Nagera 1968; Spitz 1953). Even though talking therapy relies on a physiological theory of drives and many theoreticians have attributed a key role to the somatic body as inseparably part of mental development (e.g., Ferenczi 1930; Klein 1952; Winnicott 1954; Milner 1987), the athletic, movement-related aspect of human mental and social development has been neglected. Sherick (2012), a psychoanalyst, adds the athletic body as a major factor in the development of the self, constituting a primary source of pleasure, competence, and contributing to ego development.

The role of the body as a nonverbal source of communication in the therapeutic encounter has been noted by contemporary authors (Alvarez 1992; Amir 2014; Anzieu 1989; Davies 1994; Ferrari 2004; McDougall 1989; Ogden 2001; Tustin 1992). Ball games offer another layer of observation and experience of the body in psychoanalytic thinking: this plane includes athletic motion in space and interactions with inert objects—ball, goal, net, basket, or line markings on the playing field—as well as human interactions.

Sherick (2012) has argued that body image evolves from an initial narcissistic investment in the body, including libidinal pleasure. Successful efforts at meeting internal as well as external bodily challenges support the development of a sense of competence. Gradually, infants perceive their body parts as distinct from other objects in their surroundings, and on this basis, a spatial experience of the ego emerges. Toddlers, as a result of experiences of frustration, gradually learn that hunger and thirst originate inside themselves. The gratification of needs yields physical pleasure, which, in turn supports attachment patterns.[3] Later, the comforting feeling of a finger sucked in the mouth or contact with auto-erotogenic zones are a source of pleasure and competence and produce a connection between the body and early emotional experiences. Motor activity during the development of hand-eye coordination is associated with feelings of potency. Lightness and speed of pace develop at nursery school age, while, by age six, children will have become skilled at jumping, running, and climbing. Ego-driven body movement is accompanied by a sense of pride, and children with well-developed motor skills will enjoy popularity which confirms their self-confidence (Sherick 2012).

Sport games take a central place in our culture, as can be gathered from the sport related metaphors prolifically used in politics, business, and everyday conversations. Sports have a powerful and lasting effect on supporters. Group games moreover allow people to realize certain social, group related needs, such as, group membership and physical contact (Sherick 2012). In the lives of toddlers and children, balls have a strong presence. And even though ball games feature prominently in university life in the western world (in the form of scholarships, status, etc.), the presence of sports inside the actual lecture halls and in the theories taught is negligible (Le Mahieu 1990).

Moreover, the experience of fanhood has a great personal and collective psychological impact. The social-psychological concept of "doing fandom" describes a prolonged process of acquisition of practices of support on the way to becoming a proper supporter. These practices once acquired have their physical correlates: jumping, hand and arm movement, song, and verbal and emotional expressions. A "feel for the game" consists of ostensibly automatic, embodied knowledge, which helps supporters situate themselves and act at the playing field (Friedman 2020; Friedman and Rapaport 2020). The experience is a physical one which is naturally acquired in the course of development; it does not constitute a conscious state or mode of obedience (Bourdieu 1990). To a child who is leaping up and down among sweating adult bodies in the stands—surrounded by sights and sounds, chanting and drumming—the experience is an entire choreography: the intense atmosphere is internalized, producing a sense of physical solidarity based in a collective experience of power and belonging. During the game, when cultural restraint drops momentarily, the body can be celebrated spontaneously (Friedman 2020; Friedman and Rapaport 2020).

Since the athletic aspect is developmentally significant, ball games are culturally important, and given the emotional drama they involve, psychoanalytical thinking would do well to give attention to these matters. The strength of the ball game on both individual and crowd will be explored through reading DeLillo's novella, which takes place at a baseball game. The mental, physical, and social implications of the experience will be elaborated, helping to reveal new aspects of psychoanalytic thought and practice.

THE NOVELLA: *THE TRIUMPH OF DEATH*

Don DeLillo was born in 1936 to parents who were Italian immigrants, and he was raised in the north Bronx. He first started publishing short stories in the 1960s, followed by novels in the 1970s. Only with hindsight, DeLillo has told, did he realize that the narrative of *Underworld* (1997) was influenced by the story of his parents' immigration to the U.S. and his childhood in the Italian-American Bronx (Duvall 2002). *The Triumph of Death* was initially published as a novella, *Pafko at the Wall,* in 1992, and then reappeared as the prologue to DeLillo's *Underworld* (1997). The story centres on a major event in the history of baseball, when Bobby Thomson scored a home run during the third and final playoff between the Dodgers and the Giants in the National League Championship, at the Polo Grounds in New York City on

3 October, 1951. Duvall (2002) describes the novel as following the spread of paranoia in the American mindset during the Cold War, recounting the United States' triumph through its powerful military actions overseas, and the flourishing development of consumer culture. The novel dwells on the idea of capitalism, which, by wielding its political power through the media (radio, TV, advertising), steers the public discourse (for instance, by normalizing the environmental dangers of nuclear waste disposal).

The Triumph of Death is narrated through three perspectives. The first originates in the private box shared by a group of four cultural icons: Jackie Gleason, Frank Sinatra, Toots Shor, and Edgar J. Hoover.[4] The second perspective is provided by Cotter Martin, a 14-year-old Afro-American boy, who, having gate-crashed the game, finds a seat in the left part of the stands. And the third point of view is located in Russ Hodges' radio commentator's box. For Duvall (2002) these angles combine to make up an aesthetic domain affording an experience of elevation, of being in a timeless and universal sphere, a type of ideal order.

In the first of these perspectives, an agent arrives to inform Hoover, in the middle of the game, that the USSR has just conducted a nuclear test. The Soviet nuclear experiment will enable Hoover to ramp up his anti-communist campaign. At the level of the second perspective, DeLillo uses the white baseball to reflect the dominance of white people in sports in 1951—a state of affairs that was soon to change. The black boy, Cotter, and Bill, a white architect, become friendly because they both support the Giants. For a while, their shared love of the game causes class and racial identity to recede into the background, but division flares up again as soon as the ball comes their way, and they struggle to get hold of it. Russ Hodges, the radio reporter, illustrates the centrality of the media at this place and time and its formative role in shaping reality: any event that fails to make the media will not enter history.

The reading of the Novella below will focus on Cotter's actions, demonstrating how to find the bodily movements and state of mind of Cotter's "becoming-ball." We will follow Cotter's process of becoming and reveal its' connection to the political atmosphere and the composition between individual and society.

READING THROUGH THE PRISM OF BECOMING-BALL

Cotter and the Ball—Becoming-ball

Cotter and another fifteen or so boys are trying to slip through the turnstiles to the historic baseball game in the middle of a regular school day: Cotter is "fourteen and you know he's flat broke by the edgy leaning look he hangs on his body" (DeLillo 1997, 12). Aware that his chances of getting into the game are slim, Cotter undergoes a metamorphosis of mind and body, and we witness Cotter's becoming-ball:

> Cotter thinks he sees a path to the turnstile on the right. He drains himself of everything he does not need to make the jump. . . . A couple of stadium cops are rumbling down the ramp. Cotter sheds these elements as they appear, sheds a thousand waves of information hitting on his skin. His gaze is trained on the iron bars projected from the post. (DeLillo 1997, 13)

"Drain[ing] himself of everything he does not need," Cotter clears his mind, leaving his ball-like movement the only relevant reality. Next, he loses all particular marks of adolescence, opening himself to new ways of experiencing the world:

> He picks up speed and seems to lose his gangliness, the slouchy funk of hormones and unbelonging and all the stammering things that seal his adolescence. He is just a running boy, a half-seen figure from the streets, but the way running reveals some clue to being, the way a runner bares himself to consciousness, this is how the dark-skinned kid seems to open to the world, how the bloodrush of a dozen strides brings him into eloquence. (1997, 13)

Like the ball in motion, he is half-seen. The ball's motion communicates itself eloquently to his and our consciousness, leaving his adolescence behind. In the space thus created, Cotter reaches the bars, with his body unconsciously attuned to the ball:

> Then he leaves his feet and is in the air . . . His head is tucked, his left leg is clearing the bars. And in one prolonged and aloof and discontinuous instant he sees precisely where he'll land and which way he'll run . . . there is less fear in him now. . . . he feels the knowledge start to hammer in his runner's heart—that he is uncatchable. (DeLillo 1997, 13–14)

He knows precisely where he'll land, and which way he'll run conveying the precise vector of the ball's movement. The movement gives him confidence: there is less fear in him, he is no longer a gangly boy, he is uncatchable, like the moving ball.

The awkwardness of the adolescent boy, his insecurity, fear, and raging hormones all of a sudden make way for the sharp focus of the bouncing ball's motion. DeLillo makes eloquent the motion of the thrown ball, half-seen because it is so fast; the boy's consciousness of movement, a new experience of openness to the world. These are the motions and energies of becoming-other, of metamorphosis. A new, sharp, and clear knowledge suddenly becomes available, and Cotter no longer is an awkward gangly teenager. His head tucked, his whole trunk hunched and rounded, becoming-ball leaps and bounds between the bars and evades the ticket taker. When, towards the end of the game, Thomson scores the winning homerun, the ball shoots towards the spectators' stands. With all his being Cotter strains to grab hold of the ball:

> It is a small tight conflict of fingers and inches, a lifetime of effort compressed into seconds. He gets his hands around the rival's arm just above the wrist. He is working fast, thinking fast—too much time and people take sides. The rival, the foe, the ofay, veins stretched and bulged between white knuckles. If people take sides, does Cotter have a chance? (DeLillo 1997, 47–48)

The story raises the question whether Cotter stands a chance in the major, hegemonic world once people around him "take sides." He may have an opportunity though in the minor mode of becoming-ball.[5] This zooming into the soma is mediated through the human hand grabbing hold of the baseball and its seams:

> And Cotter's hands around the rival's arm, twisting in opposite directions, burning the skin . . . And Cotter holds the rival's arm with one hand and goes for the ball with the other. He sees it begin to roll past the seat leg, wobbling on the textured surface. He sort of traps it with his eye and sends out a ladling hand. The ball rolls in a minutely crooked path into the open. The action of his hand is as old as he is. It seems he has been sending out this hand for one thing or another since the minute he shot out of infancy. Everything he knows is contained in the splayed fingers of this one bent hand.
>
> Heart, my heart.
>
> The whole business under the seat has taken only seconds. Now he's backing out, moving posthaste—he's got the ball, he feels it hot and buzzy in his hand. . . . The ball is damp with the heat and sweat of the rival's hand. Cotter's arm hangs lank at his side and he empties out his face. . . . The raised seams of the ball are pulsing in his hand. (DeLillo 1997, 48–49)

Buchanan (2010) argues that according to Deleuze and Guattari, the objects with which children play rather than being symbolic (representing the phallus) are what they call *machinic*. They supply the means by which desire expresses itself (like a desiring machine) while at the same time producing something constructive.

A desiring machine, according to Bogue (2003) is a system of fragmentations which Deleuze and Guattari name *cut-flows* or *schizo-flows*.[6] These are the flow cycles of all matter which keep getting interrupted and cut by messages and processing stations dispersed along the flow. They can be streams of energy, of information, or signs. This is how the paradoxical function of connection-by-cutting comes about, the formation of continuity through disconnection (Bogue, 2003). The desiring machine we are looking at here lifts the ball out of its arc and the hand from the rest of the body. This movement, this desiring machine, is essential in Cotter's life: "The action of his hand is as old as he is" (DeLillo 1997, 48). The hand and the seams of the ball, joined, pound heart-like, animate and inanimate, and fuse as the entire body transforms into a becoming-ball. We can of course refer to physiology to explain Cotter's great excitement, so that he senses his racing heart all the way in his hands, but DeLillo decidedly writes about the pounding seams of the ball: "The raised seams of the ball are pulsing in his hand" (DeLillo 1997, 49)—not Cotter's body. The passage shows us the emergence of a desiring machine, not a subject.

The raised seams create rifts and a pattern of cuts on the white baseball and they make it possible; at the same time, the schizo-flows attach themselves to the pounding hand.[7] In these movements, human motility blends with the movement of a ball: fingers spread, the handpalm rounds, and the body accelerates, flies, and skips. The movement vector is obvious and the becoming-ball machine comes into action.

The Rules of the Game Change

> And the man catches his eye. This is not what Cotter wants, this is damage to the cause. He made a mistake looking back. He allowed himself a glance, a sidewise flash, and now he's caught in the man's hard glare. The raised seams of the ball are pulsing in his hand. Their eyes meet in the spaces between rocking bodies, between faces that jut and the broad backs of shouting fans. Celebration all around him. But he is caught in the man's gaze and they look at each other over the crowd and through the crowd and it is Bill Waterson with his shirt stained and his hair all punished and sprung—good neighbor Bill flashing a cutthroat smile. (DeLillo 1997, 49)

One sharp thrusting movement shakes whatever has occurred between the black boy and the white man, Cotter and Bill. Cotter, having gotten hold of the ball, manages to get out of the stadium. Still in a state of becoming-ball, his steps bouncing, making him rise and fall: "Cotter walks at a normal pace in the afterschool light. He goes past rows of tenements down Eighth Avenue with a small solemn hop in his stride, a kind of endless levered up-and-down, and Bill is positioned off his shoulder maybe thirty yards back" (DeLillo 1997, 51). For a while, the movements of becoming-ball ("a small solemn hop") enable him to ignore Bill's calls. Major hegemony however is taking hold of reality: Bill attempts a softer approach ("Now tell me what it's going to take to separate you from that baseball, son") (DeLillo 1997, 54) in order to get what he wants. But Cotter insists: "'You can talk all you want,' Cotter says. 'The ball's not yours, it's mine. I'm not selling it or trading it'" (DeLillo 1997, 56).

Bill assumes that the baseball establishes the status quo in terms of class and property, missing out on the understanding that by keeping boys off the streets and teaching them valuable attributes, like courage, independence, and risk-taking, the ball allows black boys to challenge the white man's claims on property (Duvall 2002). While Bill does all he can to restore hegemonic relations, becoming subverts his efforts. Cotter draws resilience in the face of hegemonic power from becoming-ball. Social power relations are undone and the rules of the game change. The movements of becoming-ball enable Cotter to elude Bill:

> Cotter stands there for one long beat. He wastes a head-fake, then starts to run down the empty side street with Bill right on his neck and reaching. He cuts sharp and ducks away, skidding to his knees and wheeling on his right hand, the ball hand, pressing the ball hard in the tar and using it to pivot. Bill goes past him in a drone of dense breath, a formal hum that is close to speech. Cotter sees him stop and turn. He is skewed with rage, face bloated and quirked. (DeLillo 1997, 56)

Approaching Harlem, Cotter begins to feel safer, teasing Bill, as if to say—we're on my patch now:

> They are past the ballpark crowd, this is unmixed Harlem here—all he has to do is get to the corner, to people and lights. . . . Cotter goes south on the avenue and runs half a block and then he turns and does a caper, he does a physical jape—running backwards for a stretch, high-stepping, mocking, showing Bill the baseball. He's a cutup in a sour state. He holds the ball chest-high and turns it in his fingers, which isn't easy when you're running—he rotates the ball on its axis, spins it slowly over and around, showing the two hundred and sixteen raised red cotton stitches. Don't tell me you don't love this move. (DeLillo 1997, 56–57)

Only now, after Cotter's teasing, does Bill understand where he is:

> The maneuver makes Bill slow down. Because the maneuver makes him realize where he is. The fact that Cotter's not scared. The fact that he's parading the baseball. Bill stops completely but is too smart to look around. Best to limit your purview to straight ahead. Because you don't know who might be looking back at you. And the more enlightened he becomes, the more open grows the space for Cotter's anger. He doesn't really know how to show it. . . . he spins the ball up and over the back of his hand and catches it skipping off his wrist

> with a dip and twist of the same hand, like fuck you mister who you messing with. (DeLillo 1997, 57)

When they reach Harlem, these movements ebb and dwindle: Bill now is the exception, weak, scared of exchanging glances with passers-by, lest he lock gazes with the wrong person. Cotter now allows himself to feel anger. Here Harlem is the name of the game, hegemonic rules or even those of baseball don't obtain.[8]

Alongside the movements of the ball and the changed rules of the game, the story indicates another two features that characterize becoming-ball: the schizo aspect, and the link to becoming-child. The ball, as an inanimate object, refers to the schizo mode of experience. However, here, this mode of experience, commonly perceived as troubled emotional and social coping, is now experienced as neither necessarily disturbance nor defense, but rather as part of a creative manoeuvre. What occurs in becoming-ball allows to escape hegemony major social categories, breaking through the obvious social power relations, and shaping them differently. This allows Cotter to enter the Polo Grounds, to chase after the ball and enter becoming-ball. It is through detachment from the human-social that a creative realization of a line-of-flight emerges, consisting of energies simultaneously human and non-human, as life encompasses both the human and non-human: human beings are inseparable from rocks, seedlings, or light.

Becoming-ball also includes becoming-child (children's universal love for balls suggests this): playfulness, childlike movements, the usual prohibitions that fall by the wayside, the legitimacy of playfulness and disinhibition—all these are integral to becoming-ball and are responsible for its emotional and physical intensities.[9]

Ball and Wave Are Deeply Embedded in the Mass Spirit

DeLillo creates a connection between the baseball game and the Cold War, by referring both to Edgar J. Hoover and the respective geographic locations in which ostensibly unrelated events occur—one in the full glare of the game and the other secretly. New York's Polo Grounds situate us near where the Manhattan Project was conducted—the U.S. secret nuclear project.

Loeffler (2014) points out that the collective experience of longing rendered by the narrative becomes the bridging element between the dramatic course of the game and the American-Soviet arms race. As the narrator states at the beginning of the prologue: "Longing on a large scale is what makes history" (DeLillo 1997, 11). In addition, *The New York Times'* front page featured both "blasts" ("The shot heard around the world," and the nuclear experiment) side by side and in the same size and font (Loeffler 2014, 96).

The notion of "superposition" from quantum mechanics can help us gain a broader understanding of becoming-ball. The famous "double-slit experiment" and its elaborations showed that matter and energy may simultaneously carry particle and wave-like traits, i.e., "wave-particle duality" (Davisson and Germer 1928). Superposition, in quantum theory, refers to all multiple states existing at once and the same time.[10] The point when this uncertainty is resolved is the moment of measurement or "collapse"—now the superposition collapses into one of its possibilities with the other possibilities vanishing.

Becoming is a state of collapse: the observation of the author (or experiencing subject) is the moment of measurement. It is generally accepted in the field of physics that quantum mechanics obtains in the smallest order of observation. Similarly, we could think of processes of becoming as more likely to occur in minor reality. We may borrow the concept of superposition to discuss becoming by looking at the individual simultaneously as a singular entity as well as a multiplicity enfolding the entire mass.[11]

Throughout DeLillo's novella, oscillations between wave and particle-based movement are felt through the relations between individual and mass, private and public. One instance of that is the way Cotter is described: "He speaks in your voice, American" (DeLillo 1997, 11). And subsequently:

> He cuts into an aisle in section 35 and walks down into the heat and smell of the massed fans, he walks into the smoke that hangs from the underside of the second deck, he hears the talk, he enters the deep buzz, he hears the warm-up pitches crack into the catcher's mitt, a series of reports that carry a comet's tail of secondary sound.
>
> Then you lose him in the crowd. . . .
>
> In the radio booth they're talking about the crowd. Looks like thirtyfive thousand and how do you figure it. When you think about the textured histories of the teams and the faith and passion of the fans and the way these forces are entwined citywide, and when you think about the game itself, live-or-die. (DeLillo 1997, 14)

You cannot detach Cotter from the buzz of the masses—this is the wave itself. By definition, this wave can simultaneously be in different locations and the condition of particles (individuals) is determined by it. In our case, the wave function is contained within the confines of the stadium, but it ripples out beyond it through sounds and into people's homes carried by radio waves. The sense of walking in the streets during an important game when shouts of joy, disappointment, and encouragement issue from the windows is a very good illustration of the forceful wave the ball game produces. This wave brings together the energies of ball, supporters, reporters, the audience at home, passers-by in the street—individual and mass (the actual "wave like" motion of the supporters seated and standing in the stadium further bears this out, physically).

Becoming-ball also enfolds the mass psyche:

> Russ hears the soul of the crowd repeat the sorry arc of the baseball, a moaned vowel falling softly to earth. . . . Now the rhythmic applause starts, tentative at first, then spreading densely through the stands. This is how the crowd enters the game. The repeated three-beat has the force of some abject faith, a desperate kind of will toward magic and accident. . . . The crowd is up, heads weaving for better views. Men running through a slide of noise that comes heaving down on them. . . . The hit obliterates the beat of the crowd's rhythmic clapping. They're coming into open roar, making a noise that keeps enlarging itself in breadth and range. This is the crowd made over, the crowd renewed. (DeLillo 1997, 35–37)

While Cotter's becoming-ball shows us its particle traits (e.g., focus, flexibility, form), the spectators embody the wave-like nature of becoming-ball: "the soul of the crowd repeats the sorry arc of the baseball" (DeLillo 1997, 35), the entire mass of people is swept up in becoming-ball. We will now turn to a clinical vignette that demonstrates working with this concept of becoming-ball.

BECOMING-BALL—A VIGNETTE

At age 26, Noam sought therapy on the advice of a psychiatrist: he had been on a turbulent, unstable course of living. In his own words, he went through phases of feeling "one with the world"—which made it hard for him to think clearly and subjected him to mood swings and fluctuations in his "ideology of life," setting him on an ongoing search after sublime meaning.[12] Feeling confused and upset, Noam tried to get himself organized around one proper structure, a clear meaning.[13] Our meetings shifted between us looking at his childhood and his relations with parents and siblings, and trying to understand how these were tied up with his schizoid coping mechanisms, which had also included slippages into psychosis. Another focal point in the therapy was our relationship, which stood in the sign of the great ambivalence of his wish and ability to develop a relationship with me or place trust in the therapeutic process.

Following a long spell (starting before the inception of therapy) of feeling remote and disconnected from the world, he entered the clinic stating: "I am getting out of my home a little more often. On Thursday I went to play soccer, but that completely finished me off. I throw up, when I'm done, I have a headache, my body isn't used to it." There's excitement in the air because this is the third week running that Noam, with an incredible effort, manages to get out of his home, meet people, and play soccer. It leaves physical traces too, the effort: his body aches and expels waste, and his cramped muscles give him constant trouble. Noam entered the clinic—about nine months into therapy—with different energies, reflected in his voice, his body tonus (often tense and tight), and his expression. The emotional and concrete energy he brought into the room, along with the physical intensities he described when talking about his soccer games, brought into being a different space between us too. Alongside my great concern for his condition, I allowed myself to play along with the ball that was thrown my way.

"If this is what people feel when they go to work every day, the way I feel when I play soccer, then I understand why they work. Somehow that's the only place where I feel motivated, only there I feel I am good," says Noam—the first time he tells me he feels he is good at what he's doing. Excited, I tried to clarify his experience: "Don't know. I go into a different mood, just me and the ball. Don't care about anything else." This was the first time I came across becoming-ball. As the session continued, Noam described in detail what becoming-ball involved for him: "You know, on Thursday this ball hit my head like never before. I crashed. This is the only place where that can happen, and me just taking it as it comes. Without wondering why and what did I do wrong. It was simply what it was and you just go on." I was stunned: these words were in total clash with how Noam usually conducted himself, how he experienced the world, his tendency to stop and analyze everything that happened to him, find reasons, be extremely judgmental with himself. Like Cotter, becoming-ball released leaps, agility, falling and rising, previously unknown to body and mind: like a ball hitting the ground, he fell and immediately got up. He wasn't overthinking or (negatively) analyzing, just moving. The material body left behind all thoughts, concepts, and logic, in surrender to the intensive movements of becoming-ball which unfolded seemingly unprompted.

Once, I too, following Noam, entered the state of mind of becoming, loosening my organizing theoretical thoughts, imagining what it must be like on the soccer field, entering a different mode of experiencing—I began to be and think differently.[14] Noam's change was far-reaching. Now he experienced the soccer games, which had initially caused him to throw up, suffer from headaches and insomnia, as a profound shift expressing itself in his body, which had forgotten to move, to be supple, and active. Like Gleason in DeLillo's story, who vomited after drinking too much alcohol, Noam too threw up in the wake of a long athletic and mental effort. Stretching themselves to their very limit they reach a point where control vanishes, and the physical body reacts. Noam had been there in the past, taking himself to the limit, but though he feared the threatening abyss, something felt different this time.

In subsequent meetings, Noam told how rare this state of mind he had entered during the soccer game was for him, but then, with some surprise, he added: "And even though it hardly ever happens to me that I move along so easily with the people around me, it doesn't actually happen only there, but also with my nieces and nephews." Becoming-ball, in other words, comes under one of Deleuze and Guattari's cardinal modes of becoming: becoming-child. Zehavi (2018; 2019) comments that though children are subject to adult hegemony on the molar level, on the molecular level, children suggest to adults the possibility of shedding their biological age and its attendant social conventions. Since children are a minority in the major political domain, becoming-child is a political praxis enabling adult people to remove, for instance, their social-cultural shackles.

Becoming-child also implies non-verbal modes of communication. Shifting away from meaning, communication involves sounds, gestures, expressions. This takes it out of the social-symbolical order, in which the expectation of meaning is dominant, and which often resists other modes of communication, like a yell, wail, "acting out," hurling, or screaming. Becoming-ball allows these restrictions to slacken, even if briefly, for moments, and via certain routes. The event, as we have seen, is carried by the body (the hands struggling to get hold of the ball; the bouncing movements) and sound patterns that have a wave-like quality (like the spectators' hum, howl, "the soul of the crowd repeats the sorry arc of the baseball" (DeLillo 1997, 35)).

In addition, as DeLillo's story bears out, the rules of the game change in the course of becoming-ball. With power relations being undermined, attitudes to class and property alter too. Becoming has unsettled the law of the father and subverted the social-symbolic order. In Noam's case, the latter was bound up with a relentless search after meaning, which grew rigid and obsessive, and had the paradoxical effect of annihilating meaning and blocking self-acceptance. When he felt "at one with the world," he was prompted to look for one, organizing meaning. It was a false support, this meaning, because not only was it not to be found, but the constant search after it left Noam feeling deeply frustrated and stuck. Once Noam stopped looking for meaning, the ball hit him. Even though he made a big fall—something very unusual for him—Noam did not stop to consider what the event might mean. Under normal circumstances, Noam knew very well, he would have made meaning which would then have led him to a sense of guilt: "Probably it was my own fault." But the rules shifted in becoming-ball and falling led to elevation rather than a deep descent: "This is the only place where that can happen, and me just taking it as it comes. Without wondering why and what did I do wrong. It was simply what it was and you just go on."

Our conversation, verbal and nonverbal, opened new worlds:

> I wasn't always open to the ball in the past. It felt too much like a war. I'd get angry, annoyed. But now it's different. Now I am wholly into the fun of it, into the game. The ball, nowadays, connects me in a different way. In the presence of the ball, something in me opens up. I can't explain . . . It takes me way back, suddenly I'm . . . I'm like a child. I always felt I was good at soccer. At night—I feel something stirring, I think about strategies, how to win. When I'm on the field, I know what to do.

Physically, socially, mentally . . . unlike in ordinary life, when he's on the soccer field, Noam knows what to do. Like Cotter in DeLillo's story, Noam discovers the new mobility of becoming-ball: both conduct themselves with untold confidence, uncharacteristic of them normally. They find a line of flight that allows them to elude the conventional rules of the game, subverting the power relations between adults and children, between verbal and nonverbal communication.

Our joint look at these modes of action, experience, and nonverbal communication, offered Noam mobility beyond the soccer field. A choice of rules of the game appeared in different situations, and here and there, alongside more familiar patterns, new experiences occurred—whether he was alone, with his family, or with friends.

In our clinical work, schizoid speech, conceptualization, and mechanisms may indicate the presence of a becoming-inanimate or a nature-related becoming. Becoming invites us to steer clear of the human-inanimate dichotomy, that between human and nature, and, instead, prioritize their link. In our case, this would be the link between a person and a ball, but many other connections are possible like becoming-tree branch, becoming-bug, becoming-dial. The *ball-shaped schizo-soma movement* that emerges in becoming-ball is both a turning inwards/convergence and an appearance of new vectors of movement. These new vectors of movement in turn produce an experience of competence that questions the hegemony as well as the dichotomy between health and illness.

Identifying becoming-ball, in the therapeutic container, allowed for a significantly different encounter. For both Noam and I, the rigidity of social constructions stood out more clearly—the way they manifest themselves out there in the world, and the way he experienced them mentally—and we witnessed the line of flight he had unwittingly generated for himself. Something about Noam's earlier ambivalence regarding therapeutic attachment and possibility changed essentially. My entering the playing field, and the fact that I could move along with Noam in his becoming-ball, greatly deepened our connection, helping me to understand him and be close to him in critical, new ways, that would not have emerged otherwise. I felt I was able, for the first time, to think and feel in schizo-language and join Noam's experience in a manner I would not have believed possible before. In these moments, I did not offer interpretations, make past experiences "meaningful" or "help him revert to reality." All we did was move together within this becoming-ball. Noam, from his side, was amazed and surprised how differently he now could look at himself and what he had been doing—he grew more flexible, less judgmental, and more curious.

Acknowledgment of the schizo-soma ball movement made a difference. Therefore, in addition to the classical interpretations, in terms of schizoid defences or flight into the infantile, we should also pay attention to these moments when becoming emerges. Patients, like authors, create a grammar of their own, and therapists must pay great attention in order to enter the unique world of the person facing us, so as to avoid binary thinking with the judgement and hierarchy it may imply. This might help us discover new rules of the game, reaching new dimensions and allowing patients' transformation on psychotherapy's playing field.

NOTES

1. For further reading on structured and ball games during middle childhood, please see Maroudas, Wiseman & Harel (2023).
2. FIFA's World Cup in Qatar, 2022, is one obvious example.
3. There is a similarity between the process I describe here and Bion's (1967) description of the development of thinking. Thought emerges in the encounter between preconception and the experience of frustration. The frustration of having to endure a physically unpleasant experience enables thought about the body and its association with self-experience. Bion also refers to intuitive experience and soothing experiences with a caring figure as constitutive of the personality, a realization of ourselves as anchored in our bodies. Winnicott (1954) mentions that reason, under functional circumstances, does not overtake the role of the environment but rather enables understanding, and eventually use of, its relative failure.
4. Jackie Gleason was a Tony Award winning actor, comedian and musician. Frank Sinatra, singer and actor, was one of the most influential singers of the twentieth century. Toots Shor was a successful restaurateur and owner of a saloon, who moved among New York's in-crowd. J. Edgar Hoover was director of the FBI whose methods of examination were controversial, including blackmail and victimization of political opponents.

5. For Deleuze & Guattari (1980/2007), the minor undermines the balance of power and the rigid structures of the major hegemony.

6. The infant's mouth and the mother's breast are a desiring machine which produces a flow of its own while blocking the flow of air and voice.

7. "There's a crack in everything, that's how the light gets in," sings Leonard Cohen in "Anthem," illustrating how schizo-flows act. The crack in a desiring machine ("in everything") is exactly what allows the rays of light to flow in: the crack itself constitutes the possibility for a new desiring machine to come into being.

8. Anderson (2010) in an article on the TV serial, *The Wire*, distinguishes different layers of meaning in expressions like "the game is the game" and "it's all in the game," reflecting the complexities of the "rules of the game" of Baltimore gangs and organized crime. The rules of the game in Baltimore, like in "The Triumph of Death," are "do or die": "The game doesn't change the way you sleep or wash your face or chew your food. It changes nothing but your life" (Anderson 2010, 32).

9. Kidron (2006) claims that Play requires the de-construction of existing structures so that an infinite variety of possibilities can emerge. In our context, the ball game is the substrate that enables the becoming.

10. Schrödinger's cat thought experiment illustrates this paradox: a cat is sealed in a box, with a poison and a Geiger counter. His fate is linked to a random subatomic event that may or may not occur. As long as the cat is in the closed box, out of our range of observation, the cat is in superposition, and we must consider it simultaneously dead and alive. Only the opening of the box will collapse this superposition and at this moment of collapse the cat will appear either dead or alive.

11. Deleuze and Guattari employ the concept of multiplicity in order to avoid the one-multiple dichotomy. Multiplicity does not consist of the fragments of a lost or desired whole, or parts that make up a whole. It exists in its own right and we must experience it as such (Deleuze and Guattari 1980/2007, 32).

12. The experience of wholeness may suggest psychotic collapse, with psychoanalytic terminology suggesting a blockage of multiplicity collapsing into dichotomy—the experience of self going to pieces, yearning for unity (with god or nature)—as a result of difficulty experienced in tolerating multiplicity as such.

13. Winnicott refers to "excessive integration" when external persecutory factors are not neutralized by the caring figure. This failure may be the outcome of failed care whether physical (holding) or psychological (empathy or understanding), possibly leading to the fixation of primary isolation and a paranoid psychotic structure.

14. This state of mind relates to the minor which, as said, undermines rigid hegemonic structures (characteristic of the major).

BIBLIOGRAPHY

Alvarez, Anne. 1992. *Live Company: Psychotherapy with Autistic, Borderline, Deprived and Abused Children*. London: Routledge.

Amir, Dana. 2014. *Cleft Tongue: The Language of Psychic Structures*. London: Routledge.

Anderson, Paul Allen. 2010. "'The Game Is the Game': Tautology and Allegory in 'The Wire.'" *Criticism* 52 (3–4): 373–398.

Anzieu, Didier. 1989. *The Skin Ego.* (C. Turner, Trans.). Yale University Press.

Bion, Wilfred Ruprecht. 1967. *Second Thoughts*. London: Routledge.

Bogue, Ronald. 2003. *Deleuze on Literature*. New York: Routledge.

Bourdieu, Pierre. 1990. *The Logic of Practice* (Trans. Richard Nice). Cambridge: Polity press.

Boxall, Peter. 2006. *Don DeLillo: The Possibility of Fiction*. New York: Routledge.

Buchanan, Ian. 2010. *A Dictionary of Critical Theory.* Oxford University Press.

Cowart, David. 2003. *Don DeLillo: The Physics of Language*. Athens and London: University of Georgia Press.

Davies, Jody Messler. 1994. "Love in the Afternoon: A Relational Reconsideration of Desire and Dread in the Countertransference." *Psychoanalytic Dialogues* 4(2): 153–170.

Davisson, Clinton Joseph, and Lester H. Germer. 1928. "Reflections of Electrons by a Crystal of Nickel." *Proceedings of the National Academy of Sciences of the United States of America* 14 (4): 317–322.

Deleuze, Gilles, and Felix Guattari. 1972 [2005]. *Anti-Oedipus: Capitalism and Schizophrenia* (Trans. R. Hurley, M. Seem & H.R. Lane). Minneapolis: University of Minnesota Press.

Deleuze, Gilles, and Felix Guattari. 1980 [2007]. *A Thousand Plateaus: Capitalism and Schizophrenia* (Trans. Brian Massumi). Minneapolis: University of Minnesota Press.

DeLillo, Don. 1997. *Underworld.* New York: Scribner.

Duvall, John. 2002. *Don DeLillo's Underworld.* New York: Continuum.

Ferenczi, Sandor. 1930. "The Principle of Relaxation and Neo-Catharsis." In *Final Contributions to the Problems and Methods of Psycho-Analysis*: Vol. III, pp. 108–125. London: Routledge.

Ferrari, Armando B. 2004. *From the Eclipse of the Body to the Dawn of Thought*. London: Karnac Books.

Friedman, Tali. 2020. "A Fan's Emotional Pendulum," in Tamar Rapaport (editor), *Doing Fandom: Lessons from football in Gender, Emotion, Space*. Palgrave Macmillan, pp. 59–80.

Friedman, Tali, and Tamar Rapaport. 2020. "How Children Become Fans Learning fandom via the Cody," in Tamar Rapaport (editor), *Doing Fandom: Lessons from football in Gender, Emotion, Space*. Palgrave Macmillan, pp. 35–38

Hartmann, Heinz. 1952. "The Mutual Influence in the Development of Ego and Id." *The Psychoanalytic Study of the Child* 7: 9–30.

Kidron, Carol A. 2006. "The Homeric Hymn to Hermes: A Journey Across the Continuum of Paradox. Semiotica" 158: 35–69.

Klein, Melanie. 1952. "Some Theoretical Conclusions Regarding the Emotional Life of the Infant," in *Developments in Psycho-Analysis* with Heimann, Isaacs and Rivière. London: Hogarth.

LeMahieu, Dan L. 1990. "The History of British and American Sport." *Comparative Studies in Society and History* 32(4): 838–844.

Loeffler, Philipp. 2014. "'Longing on a Large Scale Is What Makes History': The Uses of Baseball and the Problem of Storytelling in Don DeLillo's *Underworld.*" *NINE: A Journal of Baseball History and Culture* 23 (1): 91–109.

Maroudas, Celine, Wiseman, Hadas & Harel, Judith. 2023. "The 'Wave-Particle' Child: Reconnecting the Disconnect in the Context of Latency." *Journal of Child Psychotherapy* 49(3): 412–431.

McDougall, Joyce. 1989. *Theatres of the Body: A Psychoanalytic Approach to Psychosomatic Illness*. Free Association Books.

Meissner, William. 1997. "The Self and the Body: The Body Self and the Body Image." *Psychoanalysis and Contemporary thought* 20: 419–448.

Milner, Marion. 1987. *The Suppressed Madness of Sane Men*. London: Routledge.

Nagera, Humberto. 1968. "The Concept of Ego Apparatus in Psychoanalysis: Including Considerations Concerning the Somatic Roots of the Ego." *The Psychoanalytic Study of the child* 23: 224–244.

Ogden, Thomas. 2001. "Re-minding the Body." *American Journal of Psychotherapy* 55(1): 92–104.

Schrödinger, Erwin. 1935. "Die gegenwärtige Situation in der Quantenmechanik (The present situation in quantum mechanics)." *Naturwissenschaften,* 23 (48): 807–812.

Sherick, Ivan. 2012. "The Emergence of Athleticism and Participation in Athletics: A Proposed Line of Development." *Psychoanalytic Review* 99(5): 697–715.

Spitz, Rene A. 1953. "Aggression: Its Role in the Establishment of Object Relations." In R.M. Loewenstein (Ed.), *Drives, Affects, Behavior.* New York: International Universities Press, pp. 126–138.

Tustin, Frances. 1992. *Autistic States in Children*. London: Routledge.

Winnicott, Donald W. 1952. "Psychoses and Child Care." In *Through Pediatrics to Psychoanalysis*. London: Routledge (1984).

Winnicott, Donald W. 1954. "Mind and Its Relation to the Psyche-Soma." *The British Journal of Medical Psychology* (27): 201–209.

Winnicott, Donald W. 1971. *Playing and Reality*. London: Tavistock

Zehavi, Ohad. 2018. "Becoming-Woman, Becoming-Child: A Joint Political Programme." In R. Rosen & K. Twamley (Eds.), *Feminism and the Politics of Childhood: Friends or Foes?* London: UCL Press.

Zehavi, Ohad. 2019. "Undoing the Parent-Function: The Metaphysics and Politics of the Deleuzian Child." In M.P.J. Bohlmann & A. Hickey-Moody (Eds.), *Deleuze and Children*. Edinburgh: Edinburgh University Press.

Chapter 12

Play, Sport, and the Creativity of Sublimation

Understanding the Importance of Unimportant Activities

Jack Black

To what extent can we make sense of the phenomenon of play? We have all, to a greater or lesser degree, partaken in "play," either as children or, perhaps, as adults. Play is something that we make time for, both with ourselves and with others. There are subsequently many ways in which play has been defined and understood.[1] Whether it be conceived as spontaneous action, done for no other purpose than its own completion; a practiced form of physical activity, conducted in order to "let off steam"; or a desire for some relaxation, separate to the world of "work" . . . understandings of play are frequently tied to a sense of instinctual gratification—a something that must be completed, that all humans, young or old, should or need to partake in.

Though it is possible to imbue play with a sense of spontaneity, it is also apparent that its use has been applied to more functional contexts, with it frequently being referred to as a source of education. This goes beyond the idea that education can be playful—in short, that education should be fun—towards the assertion that it is through the act of play that we can be educated. Forming part of a child's learning process, it is through play that the child learns the importance of "role-playing," which, across a variety of social relations, allows them to identify appropriate social restrictions. In effect, "Play prepares children for the experience of playacting by teaching them to treat conventions of behavior as believable" (Sennett 2002, 266). In either case, whether we prescribe play an innate function or endow it an educational or social importance, what is clear is that understanding the inherent purpose of play, beyond its biological or social application, requires us to appreciate that play may hold no inherent purpose or value.

Such thinking underscores Bernard Suits widely cited claim that playing is "a voluntary attempt to overcome unnecessary obstacles" (2005, 10). Specifically, it is these obstacles which constitute the game of play, for which Suits draws a distinction between a game completed for some instrumental purpose, and, the alternative, intrinsic value that a game avers when completed, unnecessarily, for its own sake. From this distinction, it is the latter that Suits prefers, embedding it in his conception of utopia: a utopia in which the only activity that would be possible would be the playing of games that hold no instrumental purpose. In Suits's utopia, games and playing would be subject to their own inherent value.

Despite Suits's assertions, it is difficult to fully follow his distinction, if only for the reason that overcoming some unnecessary obstacle would in and of itself provide some instrumental purpose beyond the simple performance of some ordinary activity. If anything, Suits confirms the separation between the value of play as a unique form of activity and the lesser, more ordinary, activities that constitute our day-to-day lives; it reasserts the assumption that play pertains to some type of haven, one marked by a lack of seriousness when compared to our "normal" lives (Caillois 2001). Though such separation is unhelpful, it nonetheless maintains a certain importance in how play is conceived: for many, play is characterised as a unique activity that stands apart from the ordinary and everyday.

Indeed, such assessments prefigure a clear demarcation between the fun of play and the more laborious aspects of profane life. Yet, what this distinction alludes to is a greater sense of the creativity that underlies play. Play's uniqueness does not stand separate to the boredom and mundanity of our of day-to-day existence, but remains intricately related to it: "Boredom opens up the space, for new engagements," from which "Without boredom [. . . there is] no creativity" (Žižek 2014). This points to the creativity that is enveloped in our understandings of and relations to play. For Freud (1908), it is this sense of creativity that resembles "the child at play." Through play, "a world of phantasy" is established (Freud 1908).[2]

Jacques Lacan undertakes a slightly different approach; distinguishing his understanding of creativity from any romanticised notion of inherent human endeavour and instead locating it in the signifiers we employ (Lacan 1997a; 1997b).[3] Importantly, the extent to which the subject has the ability to creatively define their world through the act of signification is not one of mere functionality. On the contrary, "Lacan envisions creativity in terms of the subject's capacity to take a poetic approach to the world—an approach that is content to play with meaning without attempting to arrest it in unequivocal or transparent definitions" (Ruti 2008, 492).

In such a poetic approach there remains a certain understanding of play that steers clear of romanticising its transgressive capacity to create something outside the confines of the symbolic field, and a more functional application that sees our creativity as fulfilling some preordained objective—a creativity that fails to ever achieve the new. Against these two contentions, we can consider how the act of creativity is intricately tied to the very lack that constitutes the Lacanian subject. Ultimately:

> it is because we lack that we are prompted to create, and it is through our creative activity that we manage, in an always necessarily precarious manner, to withstand our lack. On this view, the signifier is not merely what mortifies the body, but also what empowers the subject to move to an existential space beyond mortification by granting her the gift of creativity. (Ruti 2008, 491)

This gift stems from the subject's "symbolic castration," a castration which not only constitutes the subject with an unabating sense of loss, but which also provides the basis for a generative and creative process of continually propelling the subject to overcome their lack; a nonetheless futile endeavour that proves fundamental to the subject's capacity to create.[4] Drawing from a Lacanian perspective, the following chapter will determine that an essential aspect of play and sport is the creativity it provides.

PLAY, SPORT, AND CREATIVITY

It is with regards to such creative activity that a more significant contention in our understandings of play can be identified: specifically, to what extent does play require a function or some attributable result? This underscores Richard Sennett's account of play, where he notes, "One has to see play activities preparing for creative activities, in order to maintain a sense of the differences about the quality of the results" (2002, 317). Such quality undergoes a sociological priority in Norbert Elias and Eric Dunning's account of the lack of excitement that characterises our everyday lives (Elias and Dunning 2008). Over time, greater levels of social interdependency have resulted in greater levels of self-control, for which a decrease in opportunities for excitement has led to a corresponding rise in "mimetic" activities (Elias and Dunning 2008). Where such activities provide a "make believe" setting, bounded by an "Excitement . . . elicited by the creation of tensions," it is through a controlled decontrolling of emotional restraint that a range of leisure activities provide the opportunity for "imaginary or controlled 'real' danger, mimetic fear and/

or pleasure, sadness and/or joy" to be performed, enacted, and embodied by its participants (Maguire 1991, 28).

This is continued somewhat in the distinction Todd McGowan draws between play and sport. For McGowan, "Although animals of all stripes spend time playing, none invest themselves in sport the way in which speaking subjects do" (2018, 186). He elaborates:

> A lack of seriousness defines play: While at play, animals and humans engage in activities that could be serious without treating them seriously. A cat playing at trying to seize a piece of string from its human partner does not really want to have the string but merely wants to play at having it. Two dogs playing with each other act as if they are fighting but do not try to injure the other. While just playing, humans hit the tennis ball to each other without starting a game or keeping score. These cases all exemplify play rather than sport. Play becomes sport at the moment it becomes serious. Sport is play taken seriously—for example, when a tennis match begins after two friends stop just hitting the ball back and forth. (McGowan 2018, 186–187)

Importantly, what underlies McGowan's distinction between play and sport is that "sport engenders an excessive investment because of its seriousness" (2018, 187). As he describes, it is this sense of seriousness which results in the subject making decisions that may in fact threaten their social relationships (such as, missing a family occasion in order to watch "the game"), or, in the case of the athlete, their own personal health (such as, when an athlete continues to play through injury). Consequently, if sport is performed for the sake of releasing tension via an outlet that is separate to our profane, everyday existence (Elias and Dunning 2008; Maguire 1991), and, if these tensions serve to underwrite the excessive seriousness that is attributed to sport, thus separating it from mere play (McGowan 2018), what remains central to this distinction is that "sports fans *avoid* confronting the fact of this excessiveness" (McGowan 2018, 187, italics added).

Indeed, if our relation to sport's excessiveness remains predicated on a clear sense of avoidance, then it becomes apparent that our very passion for sport does not follow a path of rational judgement. Equally, though sport may provide an opportunity for risk, aggression, and wild moments of physical excursion to be performed, the extent to which these opportunities become "second nature" rests upon the opportunities that sport makes available for moments of unrestrained creativity. Accordingly, it may not necessarily be the case that the distinction between play and sport occurs from the fact that "play" is evacuated at the point at which sport becomes serious. Instead, while we can think of numerous sporting examples where a proffessionalr athlete has suddenly, almost spontaneously, displayed a moment of unbridled brilliance—a performance that exhibits the creativity that play endows—we can also think of those incidences where an excessive seriousness and tactical proficiency has in fact hindered creativity; where the capacity to play "freely" is expelled from the sporting spectacle. We can consider the various occasions where an athlete or team has become so frustrated that it is their creativity that is being hampered by the opponent; or, how a particular manager, coaching regime, or performance style can hinder the creative talent of a particular player.[5] Though, competitively, such frustrations remain an important part of sport, and the seriousness in which it is endowed, it remains apparent that one's very competitiveness emerges from the codified restrictions that both limit and constrain the opportunity for play, and, specifically, the creativity it prescribes.

For this very reason, rather than stand opposed, the relation between play and sport is one that remains in continuous tension, so much so, that what makes a sporting endeavour exciting, or what endows it the seriousness it requires, is itself forged through the creativity that play provides. It is in the context of our capacity for creativity that our understandings of play and sport, and, in particular, the relation *between* play and sport, can be reconsidered. Importantly, this creativity does not need to be applied to some instrumental purpose or prescribed achievement, both of which remain essential characterizations of sport (McGowan 2018), but can instead be perceived as working in accordant with the subject's inherent lack and the subsequent excesses and opportunities for creativity that this lack produces.

Bound together, it is in the interlinkages between lack and excess that "Sports, games, and intense bodily pursuits, as well as other activities, such as gardening, stargazing, and caring for and playing with pets, enable us to rediscover and retain our connection to an essential source of creativity and vitality" (Greif 2010, 560; see also Reynoso 2021). In fact, while, for McGowan, "The naturalization of sport enables subjects to disavow their excessive investment in an inherently insignificant activity" (2018, 187),[6] this can overlook how such an investment in insignificance provides the opportunity for the intersection of lack and excess in play. Indeed, while the very purpose of play is that it remains an activity done purely for its own sake, it nonetheless remains an important site for the intersection of lack and excess to be revealed. By way of elaborating on this intersection, the following discussion will extend McGowan's contention that "More than any other activity, sport is the site for sublimation" (2018, 187). In doing so, it will consider how it is through the act of sublimation that our creativity is related to examples of play and sport.

SUBLIMATION IN PLAY AND SPORT: THE IRRATIONAL, THE RIDICULOUS, AND THE MUNDANE

Lacan's well-known definition of sublimation describes it as an act which raises an object "to the dignity of the Thing" (1997b, 112). Attached to the subject's lack—the very loss that characterizes the subject's entry into language—"the Thing is merely a retroactive fantasy of everything good, whole, and plentiful" (Ruti 2023). It is thus in the act of dignifying this Thing that a certain object or objective—and this can include a goal, ideal, or belief—is creatively elevated beyond the mundanity of everyday life. In effect, the object elevated to the Thing remains a substitution. The crux of this substitution lies upon the fact that, while, in and of itself, the Thing can never be obtained—its essence forever unobtainable to the subject—it is the subject's sublimation of the object that nonetheless "comes closer to the Thing than other objects" (Ruti 2023).[7] For this reason, it is not necessarily the object which is important, but the desire towards this object that remains significant. Indeed, while so much of sport remains directed towards a particular goal or objective (the success that is attributable to the win that sport requires), what may be lost is the sense of play and creativity that characterizes sublimation.

This is brought to bear when we consider the levels of training that is required to become a competent competitor in a certain sport. Drawing upon the work of Dervin (1985), Sykes proposes that "we can think of athletic training as [a] culturally validated sublimation of aggression into determination to train and succeed" (2007: 137).[8] While this "determination to train and succeed" may stand apart from the characterization of play, we must "also be alerted to the ambivalent aspects of such determination, or the aggression driving athletic mastery" (Sykes 2007, 137); in other words, to the fact that such training can very easily become a monotonous activity, for which sport carries the threat of desublimating one's desire to participate. This reveals how "The overanimation or overagitation that can accompany our creative endeavors" follows closely the mundanity of repetition that sport relies upon (Ruti 2023). When so much of sport requires repetition—repeated drills in training sessions; repeated tactical arrangements; the repeated tournaments and seasons—it is through this process of repetition that the opportunity to play, as well as the creativity that sport requires, can be obscured or even lost.

With this in mind, we can recall the assumption that, today, sport has become too serious. Advancements in sport science, an over-reliance on statistical analysis, technological improvements in the use of equipment, and tactical innovations have all resulted in the over-professionalization of sport. We can assert that, following the Frankfurt School philosopher and sociologist, Herbert Marcuse, sport has suffered from a process of "repressive desublimation" (Marcuse 2002). Such repression is apparent in the disciplinary and restrictive practices that sport enacts upon the body (Brohm 1978). Needless to say, while such frustrations are routinely expelled, the popularity of sport has not abated.

Instead, what we must return to is "the arbitrary nature of sublimation" (Žižek 2019); or, as Ruti notes, "the irrational manner in which we at times remain devoted to objects that we know are likely to make us miserable, sometimes because they are unavailable (already lost) and sometimes because they are obviously injurious (such as hurtful lovers)" (2023). Such remarks speak directly to the sport enthusiast. Too often, sport is "likely to make us miserable," when the opportunity for success seems unobtainable, or "obviously injurious," such as the inevitable sporting injury. For many, we attach ourselves to sport in full view of the fact that it may not make us happy.

By "explain[ing] why we attach ourselves to objects that do not even bother to promise happiness, that are frank about the fact that they will never make us happy" (Ruti 2023) is to appreciate that the arbitrariness of sublimation is itself closely related to the irrationality of a necessary failure that characterises the sublimated object. McGowan explains:

> The act of sublimation occurs when the subject creates an object that is out of reach, but it is precisely the status of being out of reach that serves to animate the subject. If we did not have an object that we could not obtain, we would cease to be active subjects because we would find ourselves with no incentive to act. Everything would be attainable, and nothing would be worth attaining. Sublimation provides a way for the subject to fail, and the subject satisfies itself by repeating a necessary failure. It produces satisfaction for the subject, but this satisfaction is never that of obtaining the object. (2016, 215)

Notably, it is the necessity of failure that closely characterizes both play and sport. Given that so much of sport is steeped in failure and the inevitability of loss (even when one "wins," there is, almost immediately, a new season, a new tournament), what characterises play is the sublimation of this very failure—the fact that play remains an unnecessity activity, where, in its most general capacity, the failure to achieve anything substantial, beyond its own completion, is characteristically what makes it play (Black 2023).

Therefore, in the same way that Russell Sbriglia highlights how "Žižek frequently sees works of literature as animated by and grappling with miserable/ridiculous sublime objects" (2017, 7), we can turn to Alenka Zupančič's contention that, "To raise an object to the dignity of the Thing is not to idealize it, but, rather, to 'realize' it" (2003, 77). This underscores the paradox at play when considering sublimation and one's relation to the Thing, as exhibited in Žižek's account of Kafka:

> The Kafkan Thing is either transcendent, forever eluding our grasp (the Law, the Castle), or a ridiculous object into which the subject is metamorphosed and which we cannot ever get rid of (like Gregor Samsa, who changes into an insect). The point is to read these two features together: jouissance is that which we cannot ever attain *and* that which we cannot ever get rid of. (Žižek 2005, 164, italics in original)

It is on this basis that we can conceive of what Lacan meant when he referred to the "problem of sublimation" (Lacan 1997): a problem enacted by the fact that in view of the transcendent Thing, which can never be represented or grasped, we are nonetheless left with the elevation of a "ridiculous object."

This is apparent when "Individuals give outsized importance to an activity that has nothing to do with human survival, self-interest, or sexual satisfaction" (McGowan 2018, 187). In fact, when McGowan asserts that "Looking at what fans do without the lens of sublimation renders everything completely ridiculous—the costumes, the painted faces, the dyed hair, the wasted money" (2018, 186), it is this very ridiculousness that underscores the sublimation of such unimportant endeavours to the dignity that is characteristic of sublimation. While one's devotion to a particular team may be explained by geographical location, family allegiance, or a particular liking for a player, coach, or playing style, it is the *irrationality* of the sport's fan that characterizes their fandom. This acknowledges that what sport and play provide is an opportunity to creatively partake in activities that inherently bear no significance or importance (the hours spent training or years spent watching one's favourite team), so much so that, in the case of sublimation, the subject "derive[s] all their satisfaction from an otherwise mundane process" (McGowan 2018, 183).

This is best expressed when we consider that, in the case of "true love," "while the beloved remains a Thing, it is simultaneously 'desublimated,' accepted in all her ridiculous bodily imperfections" (Žižek 2020, 162). In this sense, the sublimation of the object (that ordinary Thing which constitutes the beloved), is itself countered by, or read alongside, it's mundanity (Black 2021c). Importantly, this conceives of the inherent paradox that underscores sublimation as occurring not when a sublimated object is simply made mundane, but when a desublimation functions to accentuate the ridiculous triviality of the sublimated object; thus, revealing the very "problem" at its core (Lacan 1997), or the lack that constitutes it. What is more, while "true love doesn't idealize," we can nonetheless consider how "A true miracle is thus achieved: I can hold the Thing-*jouissance* in my hands, making fun of it and playing games with it, enjoying it without restraint" (Žižek 2020, 162). In the act of sublimation, it is the capacity to "make fun of" and "play games" that constitutes the creativity inherent to both play and sport. Though, practically, there are clear differences in the extent to which play and sport may be organised, when considered together, what characterizes their inherent unimportance is the fact that it is the very unimportance of a ridiculous, mundane activity that is creatively affirmed through the act of sublimation.

THE CREATIVE INTENSITY OF PLAY

It is this devotion which becomes clear when we consider how it is through play that sport is endowed with "an inherent intensity that seizes players even more strongly than everyday life, and even leads them to disregard all considerations of that life" (Pfaller 2014, 87). Such intensity, such seizure, bears a resemblance to Lacan's account of *jouissance*, which, for Ruti, remains "both an animating and destructive force" (2023). While this force can be "derailing, dislocating, and disorienting," the creativity it can unleash is one that proffers "an enormous creative energy" (Ruti 2023).[9] Here, "the rigor of Lacan's notion of sublimation[,] as a mode of welcoming jouissance without letting it engulf us" (Ruti 2012, 163), is encapsulated through an act of creativity that immerses the subject in the "inherent intensity" of play (Pfaller 2014, 87).[10]

To better understand how sublimation requires a certain level of *jouissance*, we can return to the assertion that for the subject lack is always dialectic to excess (Black 2023; Reynoso 2021). It is the noncoincidence between lack and excess that defines the Lacanian subject, from which "The subject's [excessive] attempts to name her lack are transient at best, giving her access to no permanent meaning, no solid identity, no unitary narrative of selfactualization" (Ruti 2023). This provides a unique perspective on the assertion that one's involvement in sport can form an important part of one's "identity formation" or as a "quest for self-realization and the presentation of self" (Maguire 1991, 30). While "mimetic" activities "provide a 'make believe' setting which allows emotions to flow more easily, and which elicits excitement of some kind imitating that produced by real-life situations, yet without its real dangers or risks," the extent to which such activities can delimit a "socially permitted self-centredness" may in fact stand opposed to those excessive forms of behaviour that in the case of sport are generated from, but also fail to elide, one's inherent lack (Maguire 1991, 28). In sum, it is not that sport provides the subject its identity, but, rather, an unending level of creativity that fundamentally fails to confer any form of self-actualization or self-centredness. Indeed, "far from being a hindrance to existential vitality, this intrinsic impossibility—the fact that every attempt to redeem lack unavoidably falls short of its mark—is what allows us, over and again, to take up the endless process of signifying beauty" (Ruti 2008, 491).

In sport, such an "endless process" is brought to bear by the fact that sport requires one to try and try again. Whether participating in a regular training session, or, in attempting, once again, to break a certain record, or win a particular tournament, sport requires one to get back up and try again. For, as the former Liverpool midfielder, Steven Gerrard, proclaimed, "We go again!"[11]

KNOWING BETTER AND THE CREATIVITY OF ILLUSION

To help supplement our understanding of the creativity endowed in sublimation we can turn our attention to the Dutch historian, Johan Huizinga, and his study of play in human culture (Huizinga 1980). According to Huizinga, play displays a number of important characteristics: play is a voluntary activity, that allows one to enact their freedom, within certain rules; play is separated from what can be considered to be "ordinary life," occurring in its own designated spaces and providing opportunities for imaginative creativity and experimentation; and, finally, play creates and requires a certain level of regulation, not some preordained order, but what Sennett refers to as "disinterested activity" (2002, 317). Here, Sennett explains, "Disinterested does not mean uninterested. Children at sport could hardly be called bored. Huizinga means disinterested in the sense of stepping away from immediate desire or instant gratification. That stepping away permits people to play together" (2002, 317).

On the face of it, Huizinga's thesis echoes those that would see a distinction between play and sport, with Huizinga privileging the former over the latter. In fact, for Huizinga the disappearance of play from culture is attributable to the professionalization of sport (similar to the repressive desublimation of play that sport encourages). Indeed, what is lost within sport is what Huizinga refers to as its "ludic quality." This refers to the playful, game-like elements that are present in various aspects of human culture, including language, art, and religion, as well as in how societies are structured and organized. Yet, on this point, Robert Pfaller observes:

> even professional athletes, in spite of high material stakes, are occasionally utterly and completely absorbed in the ludic sphere—football players and ice hockey players become "intoxicated by play" in the best cases, and in the worst start violently attacking their opponents; highly paid boxers bite their adversaries' ears even though this might lead to a suspension or ban from the sport, severely damaging or even ending their careers. (2014, 108)

For this reason, Pfaller goes further, emphasising that in order for play to emerge, the distinction between play and sport doesn't really matter. Essentially, "what is decisive is that those carrying it out treat it as play, regardless of what it might actually be" (Pfaller 2014, 108).[12] Here, Pfaller extends Huizinga's account of play in order to identify how "Huizinga's theory makes plausible a new type of conviction: the type of illusion that is kept suspended by knowing better, yet thereby adhered to with even greater devotion" (Pfaller 2014, 95).

We can elaborate upon the effects of this devotion via the "suspended fiction" that play requires (Pfaller 2014, 113; see also Huizinga 1980). This "suspended fiction" forms an important part of Huizinga's account of play, later drawn upon by Pfaller, who asserts: "all play operates with illusion, and requires a moment in which this illusion is seen through" (2014: 94). What this reveals is that our involvement in play posits a unique relation to one's knowledge. For example, according to Pfaller, "All play acts as if it were real and, in order to play, all players must know that this is not so. When players know (or at least believe) that it is notreal, but rather just play, then they succumb to sacred seriousness" (2014, 94).[13] By following closely Huizinga's thesis, Pfaller asserts that the "fascination of play depends upon the knowledge that it is 'just' play," and, more importantly, "This knowledge essential for play consists in 'knowing better' about an illusion" (2014, 91).

The significance of this illusion is that we can now begin to assert that what characterizes play, and what seems to underlie play's capacity for creativity, is a unique illusion, which is not simply "accepted" by the subject, but which is simultaneously acknowledged *and* unacknowledged by the subject. Whereas one would usually interpret knowledge as working against illusion, in the case of play, *one's very knowledge functions to maintain the illusion* (Black 2021b). As a result:

> The astonishing part of Huizinga's discovery is this dependence of the affective moment on the intellectual one: *we will be absorbed by the illusion of play only if and when we see through it*. Knowledge does not help us gain emotional distance—on the contrary: our intellectual distancing from play pushes us into the throes of the affective captivity of play. (Pfaller 2014, 93, italics in original)

We can reinterpret this final sentence as describing play's affective creativity; a creativity which is predicated on a certain self-sacrifice or "intellectual distancing" from the act of play itself; it is by sacrificing our own knowledge that the "creative power of sacrifice" can be achieved (McGowan 2016, 110).

Further still, in the case of sublimation, we can now begin to determine how the elevation of the mundane object is not ignored by the subject, but, rather, forms a constitutive part of the creativity it is prescribed. That is, rather than the subject being unaware of the object's inherent ordinariness, it is its very ridiculousness, it's desublimation as a mundane object, which nonetheless holds the power for creative agency. It is this same process that "Huizinga detected as the 'sacred seriousness' of the [football] game" (Pfaller 2014, 104). Ultimately, while "the crowd is roused to a frenzy when a goal is scored precisely because they have not forgotten where they are, they know they are dealing with 'merely' a 'foolish' game in a football stadium" (Pfaller 2014, 104), it is, nonetheless, the unimportance of the "'foolish' game" that sustains the act of sublimation on behalf of the fan.

What this reveals is a unique form of self-decentrement inherent to the performance of play and the creativity it endows.[14] Importantly, what is unique to this self-decentrement is the fact that one's acknowledgement of play requires that one adheres to an illusion that would, at first, contradict one's very knowledge (one is, in a way, "decentred" from one's knowledge).[15] Such self-decentrement is confirmed when we consider that "play . . . is a practice that is based on the *illusion of others*" (Pfaller 2014, 90, italics in original). While the subject remains in full knowledge that play is merely play—a "knowing better" that endows them the capacity to play by seeing through its illusion—this nonetheless requires that the very fiction that play relies upon demands an Other who *does* believe in play's illusion. It is here that the Other occupies an important role in the process of sublimation and the creativity it provides. Indeed, "it is through the Other that we come to constitute ourselves as creatures of sublimation, that is, creatures who possess the capacity to resculpt the world" (Ruti 2012, 159).[16] Moreover, it is through the Other that play can be referred to as an "illusion of the Other"; an Other for whom the playing subject remains interdependent to (Black 2021b). It is through this illusion that one is afforded the opportunity for creativity. That is, in the case of play, our reliance on the Other is displayed through the illusion *it* upholds.

For this reason, we can begin to determine how this reliance is related to the rules and regulations that govern a particular sport, but which all the while function as "an accepted illusion that allows one to fully participate in the game" (Black 2021b, 100). Rather than inhibit one's enjoyment, and, thus, one's capacity to play, it is in relation to sport's "accepted illusion" that its rules allow for the creativity that can occur. Here, sport's unimportance is acknowledged via a variety of contrived rules and regulations that paradoxically bestow it a certain level of importance, perhaps best reflected in debates on "fair play" (the fairness of which should not matter if sport was simply considered to be "unimportant"). Again, "It is in this way that our involvement in sport presents a form of 'self-decentrement': indeed, a space between sport's objective adherence (i.e., following its rules) and our subjective divestment from the demands of its illusion (an illusion of the Other)" (Black 2021b, 100).

What the illusion of the Other provides, therefore, is a form of self-decentrement that functions to provide the very space in which one's creative sublimation occurs in play. Indeed, while the Other remains essential to the work of sublimation and the creative act, in the case of play, this is observed in the extent to which the Other's ignorance—let's say, the Other's stupidity (its inherent *lack* [of knowledge])—is required to maintain the subject's relation to play. Where such ignorance resides is in the illusion it adheres to—the illusion of the Other. Without the Other shouldering this illusion there would not be the creative space available for the subject to play. Note, how a similar process is outlined in McNulty's account of the Jewish law and the role of the "absent Other":

> Moses founds an institution (the Jewish law), and this institution is the legacy of his desire. It provides a structure or a space in which the subject can encounter and explore the lack in the Other in a creative manner, without being so consumed by his anxiety that he violently rejects and represses it. This is what we see in the practice of the oral law or Talmud, where the collectivity engages in the exploration of God's absence as the creative foundation of the rabbinic community. The law is a structure that allows for a work on the absent Other, and in this respect functions as a sublimation for the age (and indeed for subsequent ages, as Kant attests: the sublimation functions not only for members of the Mosaic religion but potentially for anyone who takes up this object). (2014, 105)

Much like the law, it is the illusion of the Other—an Other absented from the knowledge of the illusion—that provides the very structure for play and for the creative work to occur.

This points to an important characteristic in our understanding of play and sport, one that is perhaps best expressed in considerations of sport. Indeed, in accordance with the sublimation of sport, there resides the undeniable love-hate relationship: in the act of following a particular team, there is the frustration and anguish that undoubtedly, and more commonly, follows a team's potential decline or repeated lack of success. Yet, as emphasized by Geal, "does even the fan of a club who has never won a major trophy shirk from singing that they support 'by far the greatest team the world has ever seen'" (2023, 7). While so much of this love-hate relation can be observed in the sacrifices sport requires, we can also consider how such "hate" nonetheless provides an important part of the "love" one has for the beleaguered team. Whereas this can be observed in the playful manner in which one may approach their team's prospects,[17] it is also apparent in those incidences where one's performance and success is tied to a team that may not necessarily be very good. Though the athletically gifted amongst us may have the ability, and sense, to join a better team, for many, playing in a losing side is not something that one can simply give up on, despite the aggravation it can cause. Rather, as Pfaller asserts, what play prescribes is a principle of: "I love it so much because I hate it" (2014, 105). Pfaller adds, "This explains why a person's better knowledge not only creates a possible opportunity, but even becomes a necessary requirement for a greater amount of passion, . . . since without the knowledge that the matter is nonsense, there would be no contempt felt for it" (2014, 105).

The venture to be made here is that such ambivalence does not serve as a hindrance to creativity. In fact, it is this same, "I love it so much because I hate it," which underlies how the very act of sublimation requires the elevation of a desublimated, mundane object: a nonsense object that is *unacknowledged* by the unknowing Other, while, at the same time, *acknowledged* by the subject who is left free to enthuse their passion for the object itself. Despite a run of bad luck, despite the failure to achieve any sporting success, for many, such nonsense does not negate or put a stop to one's sporting participation or fandom. Analogous to the very way in which sublimation can bring to light both the positive and negative aspects of a particular object, this same contradiction is brought to bear in the sporting performance. Instead, "precisely because the game is 'nonsense' in their eyes, a mere game, and because they therefore disdain and hate the game (while simultaneously loving it, whether for the suspended illusion that is presented in it or for the suspension of that illusion), they ['we'] fall under its spell" (Pfaller 2014, 104).

CREATIVITY AND THE LIMIT

It is in accordance with this love-hate paradox that we can begin to reflect on one final significance in the relationship between play and sport. As has been discussed throughout this chapter, one widely recited characteristic of play is the opportunity it provides for creative expression. While sport provides an avenue for such expression to be displayed, the tension between play's capacity for spontaneity and innovation, and its subjection to regulation and order, remains an important point of contention (Gruneau 1980). Indeed, as Gruneau asserts, "The real subject in question here is the relationship of play, games and sports to the broader problems of freedom and constraint, liberation and domination in human existence" (1980, 69). To the extent that "Play allows us to be totally frivolous about important things in our work-centered lives or else completely serious about things that are trivial" it is "because we so deeply enjoy such freedom, [that] we are frequently prone to celebrate play's expressive spirit and creative autonomy" (Gruneau 1980, 68).

Yet, as the preceding discussion has sought to elaborate, what comes to underscore our very act of creativity is the sacrifice it requires. Though play may provide opportunities for what seems like an open field for free agency and unbridled expression, it is in the act of sublimation that our ability to endow play and sport with a sense of creativity is itself concurrent to the elevation of one's lost object (or, one's inherent lack). Notably, sublimation does not provide the subject with this lost object, but instead remains creatively enveloped along a path of continually aiming for this very object. On this basis, what proves so alluring about play, and what comes to characterise the excessiveness of our sporting endeavours, is the sacrifice they require and the self-decentrement they enact (Black 2021b).

This does not act as a hindrance to the subject, but can instead be conceived "as the quest for an impossible" (McNulty 2014, 89)—be it the impossible sporting achievement or the unencumbered capacity to play "freely." In so doing, sacrifice reveals a fidelity to creativity. Whether it be in sacrificing one's knowledge of the illusion that play requires, or in sacrificing the knowledge that one's acquirement of the lost object can never be achieved, what comes to characterise our relation to both play and sport is how one's very creativity and freedom relies upon the space in which this sacrifice can be averred and expressed (what is more, whether it be the performance of a live sporting event, a theatre production, or the act of writing for some imagined reader, these spaces are inherently social).

The importance of this space is helpfully revealed in the "fundamental paradox" that Gruneau conceives in play:

> When people organize their play in order to play with or against others they create rules whose expressed purpose is to define standards for playing that are binding on all the players and insulate the activity from the society at large. These rules are not spontaneous individual creations, rather they are cultural products that stem from the collective social experiences of the participants. Thus, while one of the purposes of rules is to separate play from reality, the very act of rule construction has the effect of embedding play deeply in the prevailing logic of social relations and thereby diminishes its autonomy. For this reason, the study of play is haunted by a fundamental paradox. Play gives the impression of being at once both an independent and spontaneous aspect of human action or agency and a dependent and regulated aspect of it. (1980, 68)

In effect, whether revering the freedom of expression that play can provide or in critiquing the codified rules and regulations that sport both asserts and requires, what is ignored is the importance of the limit. Rather than conceiving of this limit as a barrier to creativity, what is revealed in sublimation is how this limit proves constitutive of our very creativity. That is, the ability to sublimate—to creatively perform unique displays of physical or artistic expression—lies in the mundanity and the utter importance of the playful and sporting activity and, more importantly, in the inherent restrictions and constraints these activities impose. While such restrictions are easily recognised in the case of sport—it's there in the very rules and regulations that codify any sporting practice—in the case of play, it is the enjoyment that is required in the act of self-sacrifice that provides one with the capacity to creatively endure one's freedom. It is in accordance with the limit that one's creativity can expose an emancipatory potential in the context of play and sport.

This is perhaps best expressed in the sporting failure; failures which, however common, in no way inhibit or restrict the act of play itself. Instead, what underscores the desire that sport evokes is the very way in which it encounters the drive: the enjoyment obtained not when one obtains one's desired object—the sporting achievement, in whatever form—but the unconscious satisfaction derived from loss itself (Black 2023). Here, "Creativity manifests itself in the act of repetition that enjoys the postponement of the solution, of fulfilment" (Finkelde and McGowan 2023, 9). Thus, it is in the creative act of repetition that "the pursuit of subjective freedom may be enabled—and not impeded—by the struggle with limits, obstacles, and constraints" (McNulty 2014, 1). Where these obstacles are integral to the arbitrary rules, regulations, and codification that constitute both play and sport, it is "the enabling function of constraints" as fundamental to creativity, which sustains our acts of sublimation (McNulty 2014, 13). In the context of play and sport, what sublimation reveals is "the fecundity of the limit" (Engley 2023, 3)—both as a restriction and a source of our creativity.

NOTES

1. The theoretical intervention undertaken in this chapter will be a decidedly Lacanian one and will, therefore, stand separate to the object relations theorist, Donald Winnicott. Winnicott's distinctive perspective on play and its importance in child development is well-known within psychoanalytic theory. For Winnicott, play is not just a leisure activity but a fundamental process through which children explore and integrate their internal and external worlds. For more on the relationship between play and sport, see Steve Tuber and Karen Tocatly's, "Why do we act like fans? What would Winnicott say bout it?" (2023).

2. In the case of Leonardo da Vinci, what characterizes his creativity, and, for later purposes, what characterises his art as an object of sublimation, is his capacity to render his own fantasy, his own psyche, visible in the context of the collective field (Freud 1910).

3. Importantly, "sporting activities . . . operate within [a] symbolic and linguistic milieu" (Geal 2023, 2).

4. This is taken-up by Slavoj Žižek, for whom, the capacity to be human is marked by an inherent alienation that both constitutes the human, while, at the same time, establishing the very process that encourages human creativity (Žižek 2016; 2020).

5. This criticism is often levelled at football managers, where, in the case of the highly successful, Pep Guardiola, criticisms often refer to his tendency to "tinker too much" with team formations and tactical ambitions that end-up inhibiting the creativity of notable players (at the same time, there is the counter-claim that Guardiola's coaching talent rests upon identifying and encouraging the unrealised creativity of certain players (Onuoha 2023; Ronay 2021)). In most cases, however, criticisms of poor performance are, in the case of football especially, levelled at the team's lack of creativity and the manager's decisions (Olley 2021).

6. Such disavowal can be perceived as perpetuating the separation between lack and excess (Reynoso 2021).

7. Importantly, the relation to the Thing is not beholden to the individual subject, but can take on a symbolic significance, such as the symbolic identification that occurs when supporting one's national team (in addition to the fact that supporting a domestic team is itself a collective endeavour). Here, the national team comes to imbue a shared relationship amongst a particular population, for which the national Thing encapsulates the apparent essence of the nation through various forms of substitution (such as, national chants and attire) (Black 2021a).

8. Sykes adds, "The training involved in playing a sport is immense. Training is an explicit acknowledgment of athletic embodiment as an achievement. Training is what sets apart athletic embodiment from mundane, infantile or geriatric embodiment" (2007, 137).

9. As Ruti (2012; 2023) considers with regards to Lacan's account of the Irish novelist, James Joyce.

10. Certainly, the capacity to welcome *jouissance* is acknowledged by Ruti when she asserts that "No doubt there are times when this mechanism fails, when the anxiety generated by jouissance gets the better of us. But it may also succeed more often than we realize. After all, it succeeds every time we manage to deal with multiple tensions, multiple stimuli, in a manner that grants us a sense of aliveness. And during our most creative moments, we may even be able to draw productive connections between the various stimuli that threaten to overpower us, thereby turning their pressure into a resource for originality" (2012, 163–64).

11. After beating their title rivals, Manchester City, during the 2013/14 English Premier League season, Liverpool captain, Steven Gerrard, rallied his teammates with a post-match speech that was, thankfully, caught on camera. Gerrard can be heard saying to his teammates, "This does not fucking slip now! This does not fucking slip! Listen: we go to Norwich, exactly the same! We go again!." Following their win over Norwich, Liverpool then played Chelsea. During the game, an unchallenged Gerrard slipped while in possession, giving the ball to Chelsea striker, Demba Ba, who subsequently scored. Liverpool went on to lose the game, with City eventually winning the league.

12. Furthermore, Pfaller highlights how one's "'knowledge' in this case even seems to be reversed idiosyncratically. Rather than representing the attitude *I know perfectly well that it is only a game, but still I attempt to make it seem as serious as possible (for the benefit of the paying audience)*, these professional athletes assume exactly the opposite, paradoxical attitude: *I know that it is only my secular profession, but*

nonetheless I am caught in the spell of the ludic sphere and have to do something monstrous" (2014, 108).

13. With regard to such "sacred seriousness," it is the "excessive happiness, which is the 'sacred seriousness' of play, [. . . and] is bound to the condition that the practising persons are initiates who see through the illusion of the game" (Pfaller, 2014, 90).

14. Here, "*Decentrement* indicates that a position of nonidentity of a nonsubstancial concept of subject always will support it in the presence of representational spaces, of reflexive auto-apprehension and social identification" (Safatle 2016, 71, italics in original).

15. This echoes our discussion on sublimation where the object's ordinariness is acknowledged, yet also unacknowledged, as part of its sublimation.

16. Ruti adds: "While it is true that a specific subject can be defiled in specific ways by its relationship to the Other/others, the belief that this relationship is intrinsically defiling overlooks the fact that it is this very Other/other that gives us access to the meaning making capacities of language—that, more broadly, gives us the gift of sublimation" (2012, 159).

17. After losing their first three games of the 2021/22 English Premier League season, I remember seeing an Arsenal fan with a shirt that read, "Keep Calm, I'm a Gooner," a playful reworking of the (rarely used) 1939 U.K. government "motivational" poster, "Keep Calm and Carry On."

BIBLIOGRAPHY

Black, Jack. 2021a. "Sport and the 'national Thing': exploring sport's emotive significance." *Sport in Society* 24, no. 11, 1956–1970.

Black, Jack. 2021b. "Football is 'the most important of the least important things': The Illusion of Sport and COVID-19." *Leisure Sciences* 43, no. 1–2: 97–103.

Black, Jack. 2021c. "'A form of socially acceptable insanity': Love, comedy and the digital in Her." *Psychoanalysis, Culture & Society* 26: 25–45.

Black, Jack. 2023. "Desire, Drive and the Melancholy of English Football: 'It's (not) Coming Home.'" In *Critical Issues in Football*, edited by Will Roberts, Stuart Whigham, Alex Culvin, and Daniel Parnell, 53–65. Abingdon, UK: Routledge.

Brohm, Jean-Marie. 1978. *Sport: A Prison of Measured Time*. London, UK: Ink Links.

Caillos, Roger. 2001. *Man, Play and Games*. Translated by Meyer Barash. Urbana, Ill: University of Illinois Press.

Dervin, Daniel. 1985. "A psychoanalysis of sports." *Psychoanalytic Review* 72, no. 2: 277–299.

Elias, Norbert, and Eric Dunning. 2008. *The Collected Works of Norbert Elias, Volume 7: Quest for Excitement: Sport and Leisure in the Civilising Process*, edited by Eric Dunning. Dublin, IE: University College Dublin Press.

Engley, Ryan. 2023. "The limitation of the bottle episode: Hegel in Community." *New Review of Film and Television Studies*. DOI: 10.1080/17400309.2023.2246348

Finkelde, Dominik, and Todd McGowan. 2023. "Introduction." In *Žižek Responds!*, edited by Dominik Finkelde and Todd McGowan, 1–24. London, UK: Bloomsbury.

Freud, Sigmund. 1908. "Creative Writers and Day-Dreaming." In *The Standard Edition of the Complete Psychological Works of Sigmund Freud, Volume IX (1906–1908)*, edited by James Strachey, 141–154. London, UK: The Hogarth Press.

Freud, Sigmund. 1910. "Leonardo da Vinci and a Memory of His Childhood." In The Standard Edition of the Complete Psychological Works of Sigmund Freud, Volume XI (1910), edited by James Strachey, 63–137. London, UK: The Hogarth Press.

Geal, Robert. 2023. "Football and fetishism." *Psychoanalysis, Culture & Society*. DOI: https://doi.org/10.1057/s41282-023-00387-4

Greif, Don. 2010. "Revaluing Sports." *Contemporary Psychoanalysis* 46, no. 4: 550–561.

Gruneau, Richard S. 1989. "Freedom and Constraint: The Paradoxes of Play, Games, and Sports." *Journal of Sport History* 7, no. 3: 68–86.

Huizinga, Johan. 1980. *Homo Ludens: A Study of the Play Element in Culture*. London, UK: Routledge & Kegan Paul.

Lacan, Jacques. 1997a. *The Seminar of Jacques Lacan, Book III: The Psychoses, 1955–1956*, edited by Jacques-Alain Miller, translated by Russell Grigg. New York, NY: W.W. Norton & Company.

Lacan, Jacques. 1997b. *The Seminar of Jacques Lacan, Book VII: The Ethics of Psychoanalysis, 1959–1960*, edited by Jacques-Alain Miller, translated by Dennis Porter. New York, NY: W.W. Norton & Company.

MacCannell, Juliet Flower. 2002. "Death Drive in Venice." *(a): The Journal of Culture and the Unconscious* 11, no. 1: 71.

Maguire, Joseph. 1991. "Towards a sociological Theory of Sport and the Emotions: A Figurational Perspective." *International Review for the Sociology of Sport* 26, no. 1: 25–35.

Marcuse, Herbert. 2002. *One-Dimensional Man*. London, UK: Routledge.

McGowan, Todd. 2013. *Enjoying What We Don't Have*. Lincoln, NE: University of Nebraska Press.

McGowan, Todd. 2016. *Capitalism and Desire*. New York, NY: Columbia University Press.

McGowan, Todd. 2018. "Like an Animal: A Simile Instead of a Subject." In *Lacan and the Nonhuman*, edited by Gautam Basu Thakur and Jonathan Michael Dickstein, 177–198. Champagne, CH: Palgrave Macmillan.

McNulty, Tracy. 2014. *Wrestling with the Angel*. New York, NY: Columbia University Press.

Olley, James. 2021. "Arsenal's bad habits like defensive errors, lack of creativity lead to deserved defeat at Aston Villa." *ESPN*, February 6, 2021. https://www.espn.co.uk/football/story/_/id/37613758/arsenal-bad-habits-defensive-errors-lack-creativity-lead-deserved-defeat-aston-villa

Onuoha, Nedum. 2023. "Tottenham 1–0 Man City: Pep Guardiola's side lacked creativity." *BBC Sport*, February 5, 2023. https://www.bbc.co.uk/sport/football/64531009

Pfaller, Robert. 2014. *On the Pleasure Principle in Culture*. London, UK: Verso.

Reynoso, Joseph. S. 2021. "Boston sucks! A psychoanalysis of sports." *Psychoanalysis, Culture & Society* 26: 591–607.

Ronay, Barney. 2021. "Pep Guardiola dons de-thinking cap to turn game around with De Bruyne." *The Guardian*, April 28, 2021. https://www.theguardian.com/football/2021/apr/28/pep-guardiola-dons-de-thinking-cap-to-turn-game-around-with-de-bruyne

Ruti, Mari. 2008. "The Fall of Fantasies: A Lacanian Reading of Lack." *Journal of the American Psychoanalytic Association* 56, no. 2: 483–508.

Ruti, Mari. 2012. *The Singularity of Being*. New York, NY: Fordham University Press.

Ruti, Mari. 2023. "Creativity Between Anxiety and Aliveness." *Sublation Magazine*, June 17, 2023. https://www.sublationmag.com/post/creativity-between-anxiety-and-aliveness

Safatle, Vladimir. 2016. "Politics of Negativity in Slavoj Žižek: Actualizing Some Hegelian Themes." In *Slavoj Žižek and Dialectical Materialism*, edited by Agon Hamza and Frank Ruda, 69–84. Basingstoke, UK: Palgrave Macmillan.

Sbriglia, Russell. 2017. "Introduction: Did Somebody Say Žižek and Literature." In *Everything You Always Wanted to Know about Literature but Were Afraid to Ask Žižek*, edited by Russell Sbriglia, 1–34. Durham, NC: Duke University Press.

Sennett, Richard. 2002. *The Fall of Public Man*. London, UK: Penguin.

Suits, Bernard. 2005. *The Grasshopper*. Plymouth, UK: Broadview Press.

Sykes, Heather. 2007. "Anxious identification in 'The Sopranos' and sport: psychoanalytic and queer theories of embodiment." *Sport, Education and Society* 12, no. 2: 127–139.

Tuber, Steve, and Karen Tocatly. 2023. "Why do we act like fans? What would Winnicott say about it?" *Psychoanalysis, Culture & Society*. DOI: https://doi.org/10.1057/s41282-023-00390-9

Žižek, Slavoj. 2005. "Neighbors and Other Monsters: A Plea for Ethical Violence." In *The Neighbor*, by Slavoj Žižek, Eric L. Santner, and Kenneth Reinhard, 134–190. Chicago, IL: The University of Chicago Press.

Žižek, Slavoj. 2014. "Slavoj Žižek webchat—as it happened." *The Guardian*, October 8, 2014. https://www.theguardian.com/books/live/2014/oct/06/slavoj-Žižek-webchat-absolute-recoil?page=with:block-54353ab2e4b055589a2e7d6e

Žižek, Slavoj. 2016. *Disparities*. London, UK: Bloomsbury.

Žižek, Slavoj. 2019. "Let's not demystify the vagina, please." *The Spectator*, February 15, 2019. https://thespectator.com/book-and-art/please-lets-not-demystify-vagina/

Žižek, Slavoj. 2020. *Hegel in a Wired Brain*. London, UK: Bloomsbury.

Zupančič, Alenka. 2003. *The Shortest Shadow*. Cambridge, MA: The MIT Press.

Index

About the Editors and Contributors

Jack Black is Associate Professor of Culture, Media, and Sport at Sheffield Hallam University, UK. He is an interdisciplinary researcher with research interests in psychoanalysis, media and cultural studies, and sport. With numerous publications in various international journals, Jack is the author of *The Psychosis of Race: A Lacanian Approach to Racism and Racialization* (Routledge, 2023), *Race, Racism and Political Correctness in Comedy—A Psychoanalytic Exploration* (Routledge, 2021), and co-editor of *Sport and Physical Activity in Catastrophic Environments* (Routledge, 2022). Jack is currently Associate Editor for *Psychoanalysis, Culture & Society* and the *International Journal for the Sociology of Leisure*.

Joseph S. Reynoso is a psychoanalytic clinical psychologist in New York City, where he treats children and adults in private practice. He is also provider for the National Basketball Players Association's mental health and wellness program. Dr. Reynoso previously held positions at Barnard College, Columbia University and Kings County Hospital and is the former Book Review Editor for the American Psychological Association's *Psychoanalytic Psychology* journal, and currently serves on the editorial boards of *Psychoanalysis, Culture and Society* and the *Journal of the American Psychoanalytic Association*. He research and theoretical interests have been in the areas of ADHD's effect on children's relationships, the psychological functions of reading and writing fiction, identificatory processes with celebrity figures, psychoanalytic teaching, the unconscious investments in sports fandom, and the history and treatment of narcissistic and borderline pathology. His 2021 paper, "The Racist Within," published in the *Psychoanalytic Quarterly*, was a finalist for the Gradiva Award.

* * *

Benjamin Bernstein is a clinical psychologist at Silver Hill Hospital in Connecticut, where he also maintains a private practice. Additionally, he serves as a supervisor for the City College of New York doctoral psychology program. His academic work has been published by the American Psychological Association and his creative writing has appeared in The New Yorker and The New York Times. He is currently writing a book on "feeling real."

Monique S. Bowen is professor in the department of clinical psychology and core faculty in the PsyD Program at Antioch University's School of Counseling, Psychology and Therapy. She is clinical faculty in the Couples Therapy Training and Education Program at the William Alanson White Institute. In 2019, she was named research fellow (inaugural cohort) to the College of Research Fellows of the American Psychoanalytic Association. Dr, Bowen is a 2016 graduate of the Columbia University Center for Psychoanalytic Training and Research (Child and Adolescent Division) certificate program in school consultation. She serves as chair of the awards committee for the Society for Psychoanalysis and Psychoanalytic Psychology (APA Division 39), a reviewer for the APA journal *Professional Psychology: Research and Practice*, and book series associate editor for the Association of Psychology-Law Society (APA Division 41).

David G. Cushman is a licensed clinical psychologist. He is a core faculty member of the Clinical Psychology (PsyD) Department at the California Institute of Integral Studies. He came into the field of psychology with an interest in thinking about both individuals and systems, and locating the individual within larger socio-cultural-political structures that produce marginalization, trauma, and widespread disenfranchisement. He has written and published on community mental health from a psychoanalytic perspective and on whiteness within the clinical encounter. His involvement in psychoanalytic organizations has centered on integrating psychoanalytic thinking with community mental health. Dr. Cushman trained and worked for several years at RAMS Inc., a community mental health clinic in San Francisco, where he was a clinician, supervisor, and program manager. He has a private practice in Oakland, California, where he works with children, teens, adults, and couples from a relational psychoanalytic perspective.

Rayyan Dabbous is a novelist, journalist, and PhD student at the University of Toronto's Centre for Comparative Literature. His research project investigates George Sand's and Lou Andreas-Salomé's response to faith in predictive scientific models in human affairs. His books include *DIY Creative Activism: A Handbook* (2019) and *Psychoanalysis of a Teenage Novelist*(2020). His novels include *Bad Men* (2015), *Syrians for Sale, Lebanese Style* (2018) and *Torontino* (2022). His articles have appeared on

Football Talk (UK), the LA Review of Books, the Brussels Times, and The Conversation Canada.

David W. McIvor is Associate Professor of Political Science at Colorado State University. He is the author of *Mourning in America: Race and the Politics of Loss* (Cornell University Press, 2016) and the co-author, along with Ali Aslam and Joel Schlosser, of *Earthborn(e) Democracy: A Political Theory of Entangled Life* (Columbia University Press, 2024). He is also the co-editor, along with Matthew Bowker, of the Psychoanalytic Political Theory book series at Routledge.

Shani Samai-Moskovich is a clinical psychologist and supervisor, a lecturer at the drama therapy graduate program at Tel-Hai Academic College, researcher of psychoanalysis, literature and culture. Her Ph.D. dissertation "Look for Becomings: Realizations of Schizoanalysis in Literature and Clinic" explores the contribution of Deleuze and Guattari's theory to psychoanalytic theory and practice, as well as to culture and society. Her research focuses on the relations between the mental and the socio-political, and the contribution of literature to psychoanalytic thought.

Robert Samuels has Doctorates in Psychoanalysis and English. He teaches at UCSB, and is the author of fifteen books, including *Between Philosophy and Psychoanalysis, Freud for the Twenty-First Century,* and *Gen X and the Rise of the Entertainment Subject.*

Patrick Scanlon focuses his writing, performance, and film on the composition of attention—that catalog of shapes and movements through which it gathers, disperses and sustains. This research is concentrated in the book proposal *Fastened from the Start: Inquiry and the Poetics of Attention*, and based off his phd work at Columbia University, and his mfa studies at Naropa's Jack Kerouac School. Currently, he teaches writing in the University Writing Program at the University of Florida, emphasizing epistolary, autotheory and poetics as the methods of note. He played middle infield for Springfield College, and has coached baseball at a variety of levels and institutions.

Bradley A. Thomas is the CEO and founder of Dr. Brad Therapy—a private practice in Manhattan specializing in adults and couples. As a licensed clinical psychologist, he has presented insights on implicit racial bias to Fortune 500 companies and has been featured on *Your Best Self* (CBS-TV). Dr. Brad is also a regular contributing writer for *Psychology Today*. Before practicing psychology, Dr. Brad received a full football scholarship to Boston College before graduating with honors from Hampton University. He later worked as a celebrity fitness trainer—a practice he still continues more than 20 years later. Dr. Brad obtained an MA in Psychology and an MFA in Creative Nonfiction from The New School before earning a Ph.D. in Clinical Psychology from The Graduate Center, CUNY. His doctoral dissertation is titled *The Effects of Two Kinds of Stereotype Threat on Implicit Racial Bias in African Americans*.

Hub Zwart is professor of philosophy and Dean of *Erasmus School of Philosophy* (Erasmus University Rotterdam). His research develops a philosophical perspective on contemporary science against the backdrop of global societal challenges, using dialectics (e.g., Hegel) and psychoanalysis (e.g., Lacan) as his conceptual framework. Special attention is devoted to the interaction between science and genres of the imagination (drama, poetry, cinema, novels, music). He is editor-in-chief of the *Library for Ethics and Applied Philosophy* (Springer) and has recently published *Continental Philosophy of Technoscience* (Springer 2022).

www.ingramcontent.com/pod-product-compliance
Ingram Content Group UK Ltd.
Pitfield, Milton Keynes, MK11 3LW, UK
UKHW041834031026
15587UKWH00002B/760

9 781666 938425